Important Bird Areas
in the Czech Republic

Editors:
Petra Málková, David Lacina

Czech Society for Ornithology
Prague, Czech Republic, 2002

Foreword:
Zoltán Waliczky, Petr Roth

Introductory chapters:
Vladimír Bejček, Jan Hora, David Lacina, Petra Málková, Pavel Marhoul, Jan Plesník,
Karel Šťastný

Area chapters:
Peter Baláž, Jiří Bureš, Josef Chytil, Jiří Flousek, Petr Horák, David Horal, Bohuslav Kloubec,
Petr Macháček, Eva Nedozrálová, Jan Pavelka, Karel Pavelka, Karel Pecl, Šárka Pochová,
Zdeněk Polášek, Jiří Pykal, Jan Ševčík, Vít Tejrovský, Milan Tichai, Lubor Urbánek

Photographs:
Peter Baláž, Dušan Boucný, Luděk Boucný, Jaroslav Červený, Jiří Formánek, Josef Hlásek,
Karel Hník, Petr Horák, Bohuslav Kloubec, Petr Macháček, Jan Pavelka, Karel Pavelka, Karel
Pecl, Šárka Pochová, Jan Ševčík, Vít Tejrovský, Lubor Urbánek

Cover:
Jan Ševčík

Translation:
David Lacina, Jennifer Koenig

The original Czech version of this book was published in cooperation with the Agency for Nature Conservation and Landscape Protection of the Czech Republic and was sponsored by BirdLife/Vogelbecscherming Nederland with support from the Dutch Ministry of Agriculture, Nature Conservation and Fisheries and from the Dutch Ministry of Foreign Affairs (MATRA Management/Programme International Nature Management).

The editors would like to thank (in alphabetical order) Jan Hora, Pavel Marhoul, Petr Roth, Karel Šťastný, Tomáš Tichý, Zoltan Waliczky, Johanna Winkelman, and Jan Zárybnický without whose considerable help this book could never have been achieved. We are especially grateful to Vladimír Vyskočil and his wife Věra for the endless hours that they spent on design and preparation of the manuscript for printing. Many thanks also go to the authors of texts and photographs.

P. Málková a D. Lacina

Contents

Czech Society for Ornithology (CSO) is a non-governmental organisation uniting birdwatchers, nature lovers, amateurs and professionals interested in the research and protection of birds. It is the Czech national partner of *BirdLife International.*

CSO runs its own projects and cooperates on international projects aimed at conservation of birds and their habitats, focusing on education, popularisation and promotion of bird protection. One of the international programmes that the CSO takes part in is the Important Bird Areas Programme; other projects include rescue programmes for globally threatened species in Europe, management plans for key European bird habitats and International Waterbird Census. Examples of CSO's own projects include the mapping of breeding distribution (1973–1977, 1985–1989) and wintering distribution (1982–1985) of birds in the Czech Republic, surveys of bird populations in small areas and large cities, inventory of localities of local, regional and national importance for birds, monitoring breeding water bird populations, ornithological surveys and research using radio transmitters and bird-ringing. There are working groups within the CSO concentrating their activities in research and conservation of a particular species or group (White Stork, Black Stork, Mute Swan, Birds of Prey and Owls, Fowllike Birds, Corncrake, Waders, Shrikes), and these working groups also participate in various international programmes.

CSO participates in preparing and ammending national laws and public notices and proposing the establishment of Special Protection Areas. The organisation is represented in national committees for international agreements and actively participates in the preparation of the Czech Republic and its legal system for EU entry.

CSO members help the birds by providing nestboxes and artificial nest platforms for storks, raptors, and water birds and by feeding in the winter. Educational work of the CSO is based on popular activities for the public such as the *International Dawn Chorus Day* and *World/European Birdwatch* and other various actions aimed at popular and well-known species – spring return of a selected species, Bird of the Year campaign, Mute Swan and White Stork census and others. Various lectures and exhibitions are organised and the media is increasingly involved in the promotion of bird protection.

The publishing activities of the CSO include a wide range of materials: scientific journals *Sylvia* (biannually) and *Buteo*, an internal magazine *CSO News* (biannually), a popular newsletter *The World of Birds* (quarterly), a *Bird of the Year* brochure and other various scientific, educational and promotional materials.

CSO welcomes all individuals interested in the protection of birds and their habitats, and everybody with an interest in birdwatching and nature as a whole. CSO members can choose from a long and rich list of activities and programmes according to their individual interests. CSO members are welcome to use the organisation's extensive library, and they can participate in various excursions, lectures, seminars and workshops. The organisation also maintains several cabins at attractive localities that can be visited by CSO members throughout the year. There is a network of regional branches of CSO (in southern, western, northern and eastern Bohemia as well as in northern and southern Moravia) and local CSO clubs, that offer further activities and programmes for members and the wider public in their respective regions. Anyone who is interested is encouraged to join.

Czech Society for Ornithology
Hornoměcholupská 34
102 00 Praha 10 – Hostivař
Czech Republic

www.birdlife.cz

BirdLife International, established in 1922 under the name *International Council for Bird Preservation* (ICBP), is a global partnership of national organisations focused on the protection of birds and their habitats. It has Partner organisations in almost a hundred states (each country is represented by one organisation). The BirdLife International Partnership strives to conserve birds, their habitats and global biodiversity, working with people towards sustainability in the use of natural resources.

Birds are beautiful, inspirational and international. Birds are excellent flagships and vital environmental indicators. By focusing on birds, and the sites and habitats on which they depend, the BirdLife International Partnership is working to improve the quality of life for birds, for other wildlife (biodiversity) and for people.

BirdLife's long-term aims are to:
• prevent the extinction of any bird species
• maintain and where possible improve the conservation status of all bird species
• conserve and where appropriate improve and enlarge sites and habitats important for birds
• help, through birds, to conserve biodiversity and to improve the quality of people's lives
• integrate bird conservation into sustaining people's livelihoods.

BirdLife International promotes sustainable living as a means of conserving birds and all other forms of life.

International programmes, such as the IBA programme, lead to conservation initiatives which address local issues and are directed by local people as part of nationally agreed upon programmes. These in turn form part of regional, continental and global conservation initiatives

International festivals, various campaigns and other events are organised at the national and international level. For example, World Birdwatch when over 180,000 people in more than 90 countries go birdwatching over one weekend, and the NTT-ME World Bird Count event during October when birdwatchers all over the world observe more than 6,000 bird species. These events raise the profile of bird conservation and build an understanding of its impact towards the protection of the world's biodiversity. The benefits of this are enormous as greater interest from the general public translates into pressure for action on decision-makers at a local, national and international level.

BirdLife International strives to make the world a better place for birds and in so doing aims to improve the quality of life for people. The needs of birds and people are basically the same – a healthy environment in which the use of natural resources is sustainable.

BirdLife International works with all like-minded organisations, national and local governments, decision-makers, landowners and managers, in pursuing bird and biodiversity conservation. The global work of the BirdLife Partnership is funded entirely by voluntary donations. To find out more about how you could support this work please contact the BirdLife International Secretariat, Wellbrook Court, Girton Road, Cambridge, CB3 0NA, United Kingdom.

Tel: +44 1223 277318
Fax: +44 1223 277200
Email: birdlife@birdlife.org.uk
Internet: www.birdlife.net

Foreword

The Important Bird Areas (IBA) programme of BirdLife International aims to safeguard the most valuable sites for the conservation of Europe's threatened birds. The programme started in 1990, immediately after the publication of the landmark book *Important Bird Areas in Europe* (Grimmett and Jones 1989). The Czech Society for Ornithology (CSO), the BirdLife Partner in the Czech Republic, was among the first organisations to start implementing the IBA programme to protect these key sites. In 1992 they published the first national IBA inventory for the whole territory of the then Czechoslovakia, one of the first such national publications in Europe. Eleven years on, CSO's conservation work is going stronger than ever. This new, up-dated and revised national IBA inventory is excellent proof of this.

Important Bird Areas are an international currency in bird conservation. They are identified by using standard criteria applicable anywhere on Earth. Sites are identified at the global, European and European Union levels. IBAs of European Union importance are those sites that satisfy the requirements of the EU Birds Directive (a very important supra-national law that came in force in 1979) to select candidate Special Protection Areas (SPAs). In a very important judgement against the Netherlands in 1996 the European Court of Justice declared that IBA inventories are the best scientific evidence to establish whether a country has fulfilled its obligations under the Directive, to set up a network of SPAs in the respective country. This judgement has provided support to our long-held conviction that IBAs should all be protected as SPAs in the European Union and eventually to form part of the Natura 2000 network of protected areas.

The Czech Republic is one of the Candidate Countries to join the European Union in the near future. EU membership carries with it a number of obligations, including the adoption and implementation of EU environmental legislation and standards. Amongst other tasks, the Czech Republic has to identify and designate SPAs by the time of its accession to the EU. At the same time, its government and people need to ensure that the development and implementation of other sectoral programmes and policies, some of which are co-funded by the EU under such pre-accession instruments as ISPA and SAPARD, do not inflict lethal damage to these important habitats. With the publication of the current new IBA inventory this job is made easy. Developers, politicians, land-use planners and interested members of the public will find all the important information here to make sensible, informed decisions about the future of the Czech countryside.

Volunteers and staff of the Czech Society for Ornithology must be congratulated for painstakingly collecting and analysing this enormously valuable data on IBAs, and to present it in such an attractive package. This book is a hugely important contribution from a relatively small number of dedicated professionals and amateurs to the cause of nature conservation and sustainable development in their country. I invite everyone reading this book to use the information presented in it to help CSO safeguard the unique natural heritage of the Czech Republic for many generations to come.

Zoltán Waliczky
EU Accession Officer
Royal Society for the Protection of Birds

Foreword II

In 1979 the Member States of the European Union adopted the first legal document concerning nature protection – the Council Directive on the conservation of wild birds 79/409/EEC. This directive introduced two new obligations for all Member States – to ensure the protection of all bird species and to designate Special Protection Areas for selected taxa. The directive provides a very good guideline for the first obligation. The second task, however, has shown to be much more difficult to fulfil, as a good guide was not available. The IBA programme of *BirdLife International* became an important starting point for independent designation of Important Bird Areas *(IBAs)* from the ornithological viewpoint. It also, as Zoltán Waliczky fittingly describes, forces the Member States of the European Union to fulfil the obligations of the directive based on the programme.

Without knowing whether the Central and Eastern European Countries would ever become members of the EU, the IBA Programme started even in the former Czechoslovakia. The results of the Programme were very useful both at the beginning of the screening process and for the first proposal of protected areas for selected bird species mentioned by the directive. Through the existence of the IBA Programme in the Czech Republic some initial shortcomings were eliminated and the criteria were revised so that they truly reflect the importance of sites selected based on them for the protection of birds. The Ministry of Environment welcomed the effort to refine the selection of IBAs according to the new criteria. The Ministry also appreciated that this task is done by a non-governmental organisation – the Czech Society for Ornithology. This book is proof of their successful work. It also signifies that the Czech Republic may reach a state common in Western countries, where the non-governmental organisations are equivalent, and sometimes the only reliable, partners of the state administration.

Parallel to the process of IBA revision, the CSO works on another important task – the designation of protected areas according to the Birds Directive. The result of both activities, which are difficult to separate, is a list of 50 Special Protection Areas (SPAs) on the territory of the Czech Republic. This proposal is useful background for establishing SPAs, which is a duty the Czech Republic's government obliged to fulfil when closing the chapter 'Environment' in June 2001. Even though it is still preliminary to say that the fulfilment of the duty is within grasp, it is obvious that we are going in a good direction thanks to the cooperation with the CSO. This book is also good proof of that. I believe that this book will be a useful tool both for ornithologists and for those responsible for fulfilling our "European" duties in nature conservancy.

Petr Roth, Ph.D.
responsible for approximation of the Czech law to that of EC
Ministry of Environment of the Czech Republic

Introduction

David Lacina

The pan-European programme Important Bird Areas (IBAs) began in 1989 at the European conference of the International Council for Bird Preservation (ICBP, now BirdLife International). This programme is aimed at the identification and protection of a network of sites that are important for bird conservation, such as breeding and wintering sites and migration stopovers. The selection of such localities is based on criteria that ensures the survival of populations of wild birds (for which site-based conservation is possible and appropriate) should remaining habitat elsewhere be lost or damaged. The goal of the program is to monitor and research the localities and ensure their adequate management and conservation measures according to national and international agreements and legislature. Other tasks include the education and promotion of the sites.

Twelve years ago, the book *Important Bird Areas in Europe* (Grimmett, Jones 1989) published by the ICBP in cooperation with the *International Waterfowl and Wetlands Research Bureau* became the foundation of the IBA programme in Europe. The book describes 2,400 Important Bird Areas of 32 European countries. Many national inventories followed this publication and these were often more detailed and representative, such as the book *Important Bird Areas in Europe, Czechoslovakia* (Hora, Kaňuch et al. 1992) which was a result of the Czechoslovakian IBA programme.

In 1989, national IBA programmes started in more than 30 European countries and since then new data has been collected, the criteria revised and many new IBAs identified. One of the results of this process is the book *Important bird areas in Europe: Priority sites for conservation* (Heath, Evans 2000), published two years ago. It describes 3,619 Important Bird Areas in 51 countries or autonomous regions of Europe in two comprehensive volumes.

A national follow-up to the above mentioned book is this inventory for the Czech Republic, which you are holding in your hands. It describes 16 Important Bird Areas and provides up-dated information about the situation at these sites. This book is a result of the volunteer work of the members of caretaker groups working under the auspices of the Czech Society for Ornithology's (CSO) IBA programme. The publication of the Czech version of this book was possible thanks to CSO's project Conservation of Forest and Wetland Important Bird Areas in the Czech Republic 2001–2003, sponsored by BirdLife/Vogelbescherming Nederland, with support from the Dutch Ministry of Agriculture, Nature Conservation and Fisheries and from the Dutch Ministry of Foreign Affairs (MATRA Management/Programme International Nature Management).

IBA Programme and its Objectives

Birds are one of the best-researched and most reliable indicators of biodiversity loss in Europe (Tucker, Heath 1994, Tucker, Evans 1997). Nearly 40% of bird species in Europe currently have an unfavourable conservation status. Of these 195 species, 20 are globally threatened with extinction (Collar et al. 1994). The European programme of *BirdLife International* is thus aimed at the following tasks:
- preventing the extinction of any bird species.
- reduceing the number of bird species that are globally threatened.
- maintaining and where possible enhancing the conservation status of all bird species.
- conserveing sites and habitats important for birds.

BirdLife International approaches the conservation of birds, in Europe as elsewhere, in three different ways: conservation of species, sites and habitats. Each approach is essential for the effective conservation of a large number of species, while different, each is complementary and interdependent.

The BirdLife International Important Bird Area Programme is aimed at the site conservation approach. Important Bird Areas are priority sites for bird conservation in Europe that are selected based on standard scientific criteria. Their network is important for maintaining wild bird populations across their ranges. The IBA Programme's goal is to identify these sites and ensure adequate protection and management.

The target audience of an IBA inventory is wide: from land-use planners, developers and politicians, to nature conservationists, birdwatchers, ornithologists and scientists.

The principle objectives of an IBA inventory are:
- to identify and promote awareness of the most important sites in Europe for the conservation of birds.
- to help direct conservation activity and available funding towards these sites.
- to present the ornithological value of each site in a standardised but also reliable way, using numerical criteria.
- to provide a tool for planning and management, at practical and political levels, through the presentation of key information on birds, habitats, land-uses, threats, legal protection, and conservation status.
- to develop networks of local experts, fieldworkers and volunteers, and motivate them to monitor and protect IBAs.
- to stimulate national and international cooperation and coordination in conserving Europe's most important sites for birds.
- to establish a more rigorous baseline for measuring Europe's success or failure in conserving it's most important sites for birds.
- to facilitate the comparison of information at local, national and international scales.
- to promote awareness of the value of a site-based approach for the conservation of birds and biodiversity.

Abridged from Heath and Evans (2000)

History of the Important Bird Areas Programme in the Czech Republic

Petra Málková, Jan Hora, David Lacina

The Important Bird Areas international programme, which aims to protect birds and their habitats on a global scale, started in 1987 when the International Council for Bird Preservation (ICBP) asked representatives in European countries to work on a list of localities important for birds. Two years later the ICBP in cooperation with the International Waterfowl and Wetlands Research Bureau (IWRB) published the book Important Bird Areas in Europe (Grimmett, Jones 1989) describing 2,444 Important Bird Areas in 32 European countries. The book included 29 areas from the former Czechoslovakia (13 sites in today's Czech Republic and 16 sites in today's Slovakia). The main coordinators of the original Czechoslovak programme were Z. Veselovský and J. Hora. Data in the form of questionnaires was submitted by other collaborators from individual areas: J. Flousek and P. Miles – Krkonoše mountains, P. Bürger – Šumava mountains, J. Janda – Třeboňsko, B. Kloubec – Dehtář pond, K. Pecl – Řežabinec pond, M. Honců – Novozámecký rybník pond, L. Urbánek – Žehuňský rybník pond, J. Chytil and P. Macháček – Pálava, Confluence of the Morava and Dyje rivers, Lednické rybníky ponds, Nové Mlýny middle reservoir, K. Hudec – Pohořelické rybníky ponds, Znojemsko (Table 1), data from Slovakia was submitted by V. Randík.

The subsequent years brought changes. In 1992, the law nr. 114/1992 Sb. on the protection of nature and landscape followed by the public notice nr. 395/1992 Sb. came into force, and these legal measures allowed for improvement in the conservation of protected and unprotected areas.

Following the European inventory of 1989, a national inventiory of Czechoslovak IBAs *Important Bird Areas in Europe, Czechoslovakia* (Hora, Kaňuch et al. 1992) was published in 1992 in cooperation with the Slovak section of ICBP. The book presented more in-depth and up-to-date information on the areas than the previous European inventory and the number of sites covered rose to 36 (18 in the Czech Republic and 18 in Slovakia). New areas in the Czech Republic included Břehyňský rybník pond, Skařiny, Poodří, the Beskydy mountains and the Jeseníky mountains.

When Czechoslovakia became two separate countries in 1993, the Czechoslovak section of ICPB broke into two separate sections as well. After the reorganisation of ICBP into BirdLife International the national ICBP sections closed. In comparison to the concept of the ICBP, which had its national sections in every country composed of various governmental and non-governmental organisations aimed at bird protection, *BirdLife* is represented by one non-governmental organisation, a BirdLife Partner in every country. The Czech Society for Ornithology became such a partner in 1994 and since then the organisation has continued the work of the previous Czech ICBP section. In 1994 the IBA project was included in a broader programme called *"Strategy of birds and their habitats in the Czech Republic,"* which was supported by the Ministry of Environment of the Czech Republic.

The European project has gone through many changes and 500 new areas were added to those 2,444 identified in 1989. New data on the numbers and threats to European bird species was collected (Rose, Scott 1994, Tucker, Heath 1994). When the International Union for Conservation of Nature and Natural Resources (IUCN) published new criteria for evaluation of threatened animal species *BirdLife* based its World Bird Red Data Book (Collar et al. 1994) on these criteria. In August 1994, at the *BirdLife* world conference, the revision of the European list of Important Bird areas was started. The work in the Czech Republic began with a seminar in October 1995 in Prague with the European coordinator of the project, Melanie Heath, participating. After a major revision, five sites (Novozámecký rybník pond, Břehyňský rybník pond, Skařiny, Pohořelické rybníky ponds and Znojemsko) were excluded from the list of IBAs.

With the revision, work on the new European IBA inventory could begin, resulting in two comprehensive volumes published in 2000 under the name *Important Bird Areas in Europe: Priority Sites for Conservation* (Heath, Evans 2000). The new inventory includes the description of 3,619 Important Bird Areas from 51 European countries. The Czech Republic is represented by 16 areas (Tables 1, 2 and 3). After the reduction in 1994, three more IBAs (Křivoklátsko, Doupov hills and Heřmanský stav pond-Stružka wetlands were added to the Czech list. The European inventory was meant to be followed by up-dated national inventories for each European country and this book is one such inventory.

There were also some personnel changes. After eleven years of the programme being coordinated by Jan Hora, Petra Málková took over the reins in 1999. In 2000, David Lacina joined the CSO staff as an additional national coordinator.

A detailed overview of the Important Bird Areas project in the Czech Republic is given in three extensive reports (Hora 1992a, 1995a, Hora, Málková 2000).

Funding of the IBA Programme

- The IBA Project, submitted by the Czech section of ICBP, was awarded a grant of 18,000 CZK from the Ministry of Environment of the Czech Republic.
- Between 1994 and 1997, the IBA Project was included under a broader programme run by the CSO - *"Strategy of birds and their habitats in the Czech Republic,"* which was supported by the Ministry of Environment of the Czech Republic within the framework of the Landscape Management Programme.
- The Royal Society for the Protection of Birds (RSPB, BirdLife Partner in Great Britain) supported the programme in 1995–1996.
- In 1999 and 2000 the programme was supported by *Vogelbescherming Nederland* (BirdLife Partner in the Netherlands) within a two-year project *"IBA Programme in the Czech Republic."*
- Since November 2000 the IBA Programme in the Czech Republic has been funded within the project *"Conservation of Forest and Wetland IBAs in the Czech Republic,"* sponsored by *BirdLife/Vogelbescherming Nederland* with support from the Dutch Ministry of Agriculture, Nature Conservation and Fisheries and from the Dutch Ministry of Foreign Affairs (MATRA Management/Programme International Management).

Protection status of the Important Bird Areas in the Czech Republic

One of the most important goals of the European IBA Programme is to ensure the legal protection of the greatest possible number of IBAs. In the Czech Republic law nr. 114/1992 Sb. on the protection of nature and landscape and the following public notice nr. 395/1992 Sb. changed the categories of protected areas. State Nature Reserves became National Nature Reserves, which affected four sites - Řežabinec pond, Žehuňský rybník pond, Žehuňská obora game preserve and the Lednické rybníky ponds. The Nature Reserve Nové Mlýny middle reservoir was established in 1994. Currently, eleven Important Bird Areas are protected by national legisation as a whole (Table 4): two National Parks –Krkonoše mountains and Šumava mountains; six Protected Landscape Areas – Křivoklátsko, Třeboňsko, Pálava, Beskydy mountains, Poodří and Jeseníky mountains; two National Nature Reserves – Řežabinec pond and Lednické rybníky ponds and one Nature Reserve – Věstonická nádrž reservoir (Nové Mlýny middle reservoir IBA). About 90% of the area of the Žehuňský rybník pond IBA is protected, as there are two National Nature Reserves - Žehuňský rybník pond and Žehuňská obora game preserve. Only small parts of three IBAs are protected (Doupov hills, Confluence of the Morava and Dyje rivers and Heřmanský stav pond-Stružka wetlands) and a temporary protected area was established in 1998 in one half of one IBA (Dehtář pond). Since 1992 there has been a proposal for the inclusion of the Lednické rybníky ponds and the Confluence of the Morava and Dyje IBAs within the Pálava Protected Landscape Area. A large number of small-scale protected areas within the existing PLAs have been established or proposed.

Several areas enjoy international protection (Table 4). Five IBAs have Biosphere Reserve status (Krkonoše mountains – 1992, Křivoklátsko – 1977, Šumava mountains – 1990, Třeboňsko – 1977, Pálava – 1986). Out of ten Wetlands of International Importance in the Czech Republic, six are included in the IBAs – Krkonoše mountains mires (since 1993), Šumava peatlands (since 1990), Třeboň fishponds (since 1990), Třeboň peatlands (since 1993), Lednice fishponds (since 1990) and Poodří (since 1993). Two IBAs (Nové Mlýny middle reservoir and the Confluence of the Morava and Dyje rivers) are both a part of one Wetland of International Importance – Floodplain of lower Dyje river (since 1993).

Changes in protection status, decisions on hunting restrictions

- The decision of the České Budějovice district office from 15. 7. 1998 declared the western half of Dehtář pond a temporary protected area for the period between the 15th of July and the 30th of November and reduced the number of waterfowl hunts to two per year (Pykal, Kloubec 1998).
- The decision of the Břeclav district office restricted waterfowl hunting at the Nové Mlýny middle reservoir to eight days a year (of the 181 day hunting season) and allowed hunts every first and third Saturday of September to December in 1998–2002 (Chytil 1998, Vyhnálek et al. 1999).
- The decision of the Třeboňsko PLA Administration from 20. 5. 1999 restricted waterfowl hunting in the area of the PLA (Bureš 2000):
  – hunting migrating ducks and coots is restricted to one day a week (Saturday)
  – geese hunting at ponds and 50 m around the ponds is restricted to one day a week (Saturday)
  – duck hunting at localities where ducks are not released or are released in numbers not exceeding 500 individuals, is restricted to three organised hunts
  – all hunts must end by 3 p.m.
  – the Black-headed Gull is protected throughout the whole year

Activities of caretaker groups

There are caretaker (or patron) groups working in all Czech Important Bird Areas. About a hundred individuals take part in the activities and the caretaker groups vary in size and the scale of work, depending on the number of people involved, their time constraints, and to a large degree by the character of the area. In a military training area, such as the one in the Doupov hills, educational and promotional activities are limited and even research can be hindered. In most Protected Landscape Areas and National Parks, on the other hand, a lot of work is being done by the administrators of these areas in cooperation with the caretaker groups. Research and monitoring are the most common activities of caretaker groups and the educational and promotional activities are on the increase (Table 5 and 6). The largest and most active caretaker groups work in the Poodří IBA (with Karel Pavelka as the head of the group) and in the Křivoklátsko IBA (led by Milan Tichai), but some smaller caretaker groups are also very active, such as the ones in Řežabinec pond IBA (Karel Pecl) and Žehuňský rybník pond IBA (Lubor Urbánek).

News from individual areas is more or less regularly published in the *IBA Newsletter:*

Krkonoše mountains – Flousek 1999, **Žehuňský rybník pond** – Urbánek 1996, 1997, 1998, 2000, **Křivoklátsko** – Tichai 1998, **Doupov hills** – Tejrovský 1996, 1997, 1998, 1999a,b, **Šumava mountains** – Bürger 1995, Bürger et al. 1997, Kloubec 1999a, Bufka, Málková 1999, **Řežabinec pond** – Pecl 1996, 1997, 1999, **Dehtář pond** – Kloubec, Pykal 1996, Pykal, Kloubec 1998, **Třeboňsko** – Ševčík, Bureš 1996, Ševčík 1997, Kloubec 1998, Bureš 1999, Kloubec 1999b, Bureš 2000, **IBAs of Southern Moravia** (Nové Mlýny middle reservoir, Pálava, Lednické rybníky ponds, Confluence of the Morava and Dyje rivers) – Chytil 1996a,b,c,d, Chytil, Macháček 1997, 1998, 1999, **Beskydy mountains** – J. Pavelka 1995, 1996, 1997, 2000a, **Poodří** – K. Pavelka 1996, 1997, 1998, K. Pavelka et al. 2000, Košťál 1997, **Jeseníky mountains** – Bureš 1996, Hajný, Baláž 1999. Apart from the IBA Newsletter, a special annual newsletter summarising the activities and results of the work of the caretaker group in the Poodří IBA is produced by Karel Pavelka. There were three meetings of the caretaker groups where the members had a chance to share their experience and present the results of their work. The first such seminar was organised in 1992 in Třeboň – "Important Bird Areas in the Czech and Slovak Republics," followed by a second seminar in 1995 in Kostelec nad Černými lesy – "Important Bird Areas in the Czech Republic" and with the last seminar "Important Bird Areas at the end of the millenium" taking place in Mikulov in 1999. The concept of caretaker groups proved to be successful and the idea is being implemented in IBA Programmes in many other countries.

Publishing activities

• **Important Bird Areas in Europe, Czechoslovakia** (Hora, Kaňuch et al. 1992)
The book by Jana Hora and Pavol Kaňuch (116 black-and-white and 32 full-color pages) was published by the Czech and the Slovak sections of ICBP in 2500 copies in May 1992. It presented all 36 Czech and Slovak Important Bird Areas. The publishing was supported by the Dutch Ministry of Agriculture, Nature Conservation and Fisheries, the Swiss Society for the Protection

of Birds *(Schweizer Vogelschutz)*, the Ministry of Environment of the Czech Republic, the Slovak Committee for the Environment, the Czech Institute for Nature Conservation, the Slovak Union for the Protection of Nature and Landscape and the Czech Nature Conservation Union. The Czech version of the inventory was followed by an English version which was published in 2000 copies with the support of the Ministry of Environment of the Czech Republic, the Czech Institute for Nature Conservation, the Czech Society for Ornithology, the Moravian Ornithological Society, the South-Bohemian Ornithological Club, the Society for the Protection of Birds in Slovakia, the National Museum in Prague, Zemplínské Múzeum Michalovce and E–Tours travel agency.

- **Proceedings of the seminar Important Bird Areas in the Czech and Slovak Republics, Třeboň, 24–25 March 1992** (Hora et al. 1992)

The book of proceedings was published by the Czech section of ICBP in cooperation with the Ministry of Environment of the Czech Republic, the National Museum in Prague, the Society for the Protection of Birds in Slovakia, Zemplínské Múzeum Michalovce, the Union of cities and towns of the Vranov region and Diana Michalovce. It was edited by Jan Hora, Pavol Kaňuch, Miroslav Thorn, William Safranek, František Pojer, Danuše Přibylová a Ladislav Hajný. Published 1400 copies, 176 pages, 21 contributions.

- **Proceedings of the seminar Important Bird Areas in the Czech Republic, Kostelec nad Černými lesy, 7–8 April 1995** (Hora et al. 1995)

The book of proceedings was edited by Jan Hora, Jan Plesník and Jana Jandová, and it was published by the CSO in cooperation with the Forestry Faculty of the Czech Agricultural University in Prague with the support of the Ministry of Environment of the Czech Republic and the Royal Society for the Protection of Birds. Published 600 copies, 98 pages, 31 contributions.

- **Proceedings of the seminar Important Bird Areas at the end of the millenium, Mikulov, 19–21 November 1999** (Málková, Jandová 2000)

The book of proceedings was published by the CSO with support of *BirdLife/Vogelbescherming Nederland* and it was edited by Petra Málková a Jana Jandová. Published 500 copies, 108 pages, 17 contributions.

- **IBA Newsletter**

Between 1994 and 2000 eleven issues were published – two issues in 1995, 1996, 1999 and 2000 and one issue in 1994, 1997 a 1998. Both 1996 issues were published with the support of the Ministry of Environment of the Czech Republic and the RSPB. The 1998 issue, both 1999 issues and the August issue of 2000 were published with the support of *BirdLife/Vogelbescherming Nederland*. The December 2000 issue was published as a part of the project *Conservation of Forest and Wetland IBAs in the Czech Republic* sponsored by *BirdLife/Vogelbescherming Nederland* with support from the Dutch Ministry of Agriculture, Nature Conservation and Fisheries and from the Dutch Ministry of Foreign Affairs (MATRA Management/Programme International Management).

- **Leaflet Important Bird Areas of the Czech Republic**

The leaflet edited by Petra Málková, Jan Hora and Miloslav Thorn presents all 16 Czech Important Bird Areas and gives basic information about the IBA Programme and its goals, the IBA categories and criteria, problems of bird protection in the Czech Republic and activities of the caretaker groups. It was published with the support of *BirdLife/Vogelbescherming Nederland*.

- **Brochure Important Bird Areas in Europe**. **Priority Sites for Conservation. Summary.**

The original English version was published by *BirdLife International*. It gives a summary of the European inventory of Important Bird Areas published in the same year (Heath, Evans 2000). The Czech translation was published by the CSO in November with support from *Vogelbescherming Nederland*, the Royal Society for the Protection of Birds, the Dutch Ministry of Agriculture, Nature Conservation and Fisheries and from the Dutch Ministry of Foreign Affairs (MATRA Management/Programme International Management). Published 1,000 copies, 16 pages.

Participation in international workshops and conferences

- *IBA Central and Eastern European Workshop* (16–21. 11. 1993 – Sarród, Hungary)
  Meeting of national IBA Project co-ordinators from central and eastern Europe as organised by *BirdLife International* in cooperation with the Royal Society for the Protection of Birds (RSPB). The programme of the workshop covered all aspects of IBA work. Jan Hora was the CSO representative at the workshop (Hora 1994a).

- *Site Management Planning for Conservation* (9–15. 4. 1994, Gdańsk, Poland)
  The workshop, organised by *BirdLife International* in cooperation with RSPB, focussed on the preparation and implementation of management plans for IBAs. Miroslav Šálek and Josef Chytil represented CSO at the workshop (Šálek, Chytil 1994).

- *XXI. World Conference of BirdLife International "Global Partnership for Conservation"* (11–19. 8. 1994, Rosenheim, Germany)
  Over 400 representatives from 79 countries participated in the XXI. World Conference of BirdLife International and the 7th meeting of *BirdLife International* partners. Jan Hora and Josef Chytil represented the Czech Republic. The main topics of the meeting were: "Birds and bio-diversity," "Bird conservation and sustainable development," "Birds and agriculture" and "Strategy and objectives of BirdLife International" (Hora 1994b,c).

- *European Workshop on the Corncrake* (25–27. 10. 1994, Gdańsk, Poland)
  A workshop focussed on the problematics of research and protection of the Corncrake, organised by *BirdLife International* for 40 participants from 22 countries, including two representatives of the CSO – Petr Bürger and Jiří Pykal (Pykal 1995).

- *IBA Inventory Review Workshop* (21–24. 4. 1995, Arnhem, the Netherlands)
  The main task of the workshop was a discussion about the new criteria for IBA selection. 34 participants from 25 European countries also had a chance to work with the IBA database and share their experience in data collection and networking (Hora 1995b).

- *IBA Inventory Review Workshop II* (31. 5. 1996, Lappenranta, Finland)
  A day before the European conference of *BirdLife International* started, the national IBA coordinators met at this workshop to tackle topics that have arisen since the new revision of IBAs. The workshop was divided into four sessions: (1) information for those who did not attend the workshop in Arnhem, (2) criteria, (3) data collection, (4) database (Hora 1996a,b, Hora, Plesník 1996).

- *Workshop Focus on Site Protection – Management of Reserves and other Protected Areas for IBA Protection and BirdLife Partner Development* (26. 9.–1. 10. 1998, Jordan)
  Representatives of 15 countries from various continents participated in this workshop, sharing experience in different approaches to site protection and their importance for the development of BirdLife organisations. A wide range of topics were addressed – the role of sites in protection and the possibilities that they offer, land ownership, site selection, the combination of site protection and the development of an organisation, species and habitat management plans, securing funds, monitoring programs, and many others. Each topic was introduced by one or more participants and then a discussion followed or the participants worked in groups and then they presented their conclusions and a discussion followed. The workshop took place in the Dana reserve, which is managed by the Jordanian Royal Society for Nature Protection. Thus the participants had a chance, not only to see the beauty of Jordanian nature and birds, but also to learn about the approach to nature protection and problems and their solutions in Jordan (Hora 1998).

- *Workshop Focus on Site Protection – Management of Reserves and other Protected Areas for IBA Protection and BirdLife Partner Development* (15–21. 3. 1999, Taiwan)
  This workshop was a follow-up to the workshop in Jordan. In the first session of the meeting the participants informed each other on practical use of the knowledge gained in Jordan. Main topics of the following session included the role of protected areas in the development of an organisation and in recruiting members, visitor facilities, development of volunteer activities, programmes for schools in protected areas, fundraising, action planning, development strategies etc. (Hora 1999).

- *BirdLife International World Conference & Global Partnership Meeting* (10–17. 10. 1999, Malaysia)
  This varied programme consisted of two parts – the Partnership Meeting and the conference itself. News from partners from all parts of the world as well as from the secretariat in Cambridge was presented, followed by 28 workshops on various topics. One of the workshops called Local Support for IBAs dealt with the issue of caretaker groups and was prepared by the CSO representatives. Regional programmes and the global programme for the next five years were discussed and approved, elections for the regional committees and the global committee were held and a fair with each organisation presenting its activities was organised. (Voříšek, Hora 1999).

Perspectives of the programme

- The new European programme of *BirdLife International* – preparation began in 1997 and was approved at the world conference of *BirdLife International* in October 1999 in Malaysia. The programme consists of nine main themes with many tasks, including tasks of the IBA programme. The most important ones include (for a detailed list see Hora, Málková 1999):
- to update the European and the national IBA database
- to use the IBA database at the national level
- to promote the new European IBA inventory
- to develop the network of caretaker groups
- to introduce new effective methods of monitoring the areas
- to ensure the protection of the areas
- to participate in the preparation of the area management plans, to promote, check or even participate in their implementation
- to review EIA procedures, and to ensure adequate evaluation of the areas
- to maintain contacts with the state administration, owners and users of land and other stakeholders
- to promote the establishing of the SPAs *(Special Protection Areas)* according to the Birds Directive of the EU, i.e. the inclusion of IBAs within the Natura 2000 network
- to promote the inclusion of IBAs within areas covered by international agreements
- to use IBAs for educational and promotional activities
- to secure information and training for the network of caretaker groups

At present the most pressing tasks of the national IBA programme in the Czech Republic include the selection of new IBAs and reclassification of the existing sites according to the C criteria (European Union level) and establishing SPAs in these areas. This includes data collection and update, preparation of Natura 2000 data forms, promotion of the Bird Directive (and the Habitats Directive) and other demanding tasks. Another important task is the promotion of IBA protection within projects supported from EU funds. This especially applies to the pre-accession assistance for the rural development and agriculture in the SAPARD programme and the pre-accession instrument for structural policy, ISPA. The funds available within the SAPARD program should be aimed at agricultural management that is beneficial to the environment. The protection of IBAs and thus also SPAs should be promoted where there are conflicts with the development of new and upgraded transport infrastructure.

Table 1. An overview of all Impotant Bird Areas designated in the Czech Republic since 1989

Area name	Inventory			Coordinators
	I	II	III	
Krkonoše mountains	+	+	+	J. Flousek, P. Miles
Šumava mountains	+	+	+	P. Bürger, J. Pykal,
Třeboňsko	+	+	+	J. Janda, J. Bureš
Dehtář pond	+	+	+	B. Kloubec, J. Pykal
Řežabinec pond	+	+	+	K. Pecl
Novozámecký rybník pond	+	+		M. Honců, P. Kurka
Břehyňský rybník pond		+		M. Honců, P. Kurka
Žehuňský rybník pond	+	+	+	L. Urbánek
Pálava	+	+	+	J. Chytil, P. Macháček
Confluence of the Morava and Dyje rivers	+	+	+	
J. Chytil, P. Macháček, D. Horal				
Skařiny		+		J. Chytil
Lednické rybníky ponds	+	+	+	P. Macháček, J. Chytil
Pohořelické rybníky ponds	+	+		K. Hudec, J. Chytil
Nové Mlýny middle reservoir	+	+	+	J. Chytil, P. Macháček
Znojemsko	+	+		K. Hudec, J. Chytil
Poodří		+	+	K. Pavelka
Beskydy mountains		+	+	J. Pavelka
Jeseníky mountains		+	+	L. Hajný, P. Baláž
Křivoklátsko			+	F. Pojer, M. Tichai
Doupov hills			+	V. Tejrovský
Heřmanský stav pond-Stružka wetlands			+	
K. Polášek				
Total number of IBAs	13	18	16	

I – Grimmett, Jones 1989, II – Hora, Kaňuch et al. 1992, III – Heath, Evans 2000

Table 2. Important Bird Areas in the Czech Republic and their size

Area (ha)	Number of IBAs	Names of IBAs
up to. 100	–	
101–500	2	Řežabinec pond, Dehtář pond
501–1,000	1	Lednické rybníky ponds
1,001–5,000	4	Žehuňský rybník pond, Nové Mlýny middle reservoir, Confluence of the Morava and Dyje rivers, Heřmanský stav pond-Stružka wetlands
5,001–10,000	2	Pálava, Poodří
10,001–50,000	–	
50,001–100,000	5	Krkonoše mountains, Křivoklátsko, Doupov hills, Třeboňsko, Jeseníky mountains
100,001–200,000	2	Šumava mountains, Beskydy mountains

Table 3. Important Bird Areas in the Czech Republic and their prevailing habitat types

Habitat type	Number of IBAs	Names of IBAs
Ponds and pond systems	5	Žehuňský rybník pond, Řežabinec pond, Dehtář pond, Lednické rybníky ponds, Heřmanský stav pond-Stružka wetlands
Valley resrvoirs	1	Nové Mlýny middle reservoir
Floodplain forests	1	Confluence of the Morava and Dyje rivers
Large scale areas with various wetland systems	2	Třeboňsko, Poodří
Forest and woodland hills	3	Křivoklátsko, Doupov hills, Pálava
mountains	4	Krkonoše mountains, Šumava mountains, Beskydy mountains, Jeseníky mountains

Table 4. Important Bird Areas in the Czech Republic and their degree of protection

Status	Number of IBAs	Names of IBAs
National Park	2	Krkonoše mountains, Šumava mountains
Protected Landscape Area	6	Křivoklátsko, Třeboňsko, Pálava, Beskydy mountains, Poodří, Jeseníky mountains
National Nature Reserve	3	Žehuňský rybník pond, Řežabinec pond, Lednické rybníky ponds
Nature Reserve	1	Nové Mlýny middle reservoir
Temporary Protected Area	1	Dehtář pond
small part protected only	3	Doupov hills, Confluence of the Morava and Dyje rivers, Heřmanský stav pond-Stružka wetlands
Biosphere Reserve	5	Krkonoše mountains, Křivoklátsko, Šumava mountains, Třeboňsko, Pálava
Wetland of International Importance – whole area	3	Nové Mlýny middle reservoir *, Lednické rybníky ponds, Confluence of the Morava and Dyje rivers *
– part of the area	4	Krkonoše mountains, Šumava mountains, Třeboňsko**, Poodří

* part of the Floodplain of lower Dyje River Ramsar Site
** Třeboň peatlands, Třeboň fishponds

Table 5. Activities of caretaker groups at Important Bird Areas in the Czech Republic

Activity	Level (number of IBAs)			
	High	Middle	Low	None
Research and monitoring	10	6	–	–
Conservation	2	6	8	–
Education	2	4	7	3
Promotion	3	5	8	–

Table 6. Overview of activities undertaken at Important Bird Areas in the Czech Republic

Activity	Number of IBAs
Research and monitoring	
International water bird census	10
Regular bird census	6
Monitoring of water bird breeding populations	6
Monitoring of autumn migration of reedbed birds by mistnetting	4
Research and monitoring of the Corncrake	8
Conservation	
Proposals for protected areas	4
Restrictions on hunting	3
Education and promotion	
International Dawn Chorus Day	up to 5
World/European BirdWatch Festival	up to 8
Summer camp for young ornithologists	2

International Agreements and Programmes

International agreements and programmes concerning nature protection are the key mechanism for site based conservation, especially where international cooperation is needed. Agreements and programmes relevant to the protection of Important Bird Areas in the Czech Republic are listed in the following overview.

Convention on Biological Diversity (CBD)

The convention was negotiated at a UN conference in Rio de Janeiro in 1992. Contrary to most international agreements that are aimed at a concrete and specific area of nature conservancy, the Convention on Biological Diversity covers every aspect of conservation and sustainable use. Thus it became an important framework for conservation-related activities on the regional and national level. The convention has three main objectives:
• the conservation of biological diversity at all levels
• the sustainable use of its components, and
• the fair and equitable sharing of the benefits arising out of the use of genetic resources.

There are five programmes and twenty detailed themes concerning biodiversity that were developed since the convention came into force in 1993.

For the conservation of biodiversity the primary approach is *in situ* conservation. Article 8 outlines a framework for the in situ conservation activities by the parties. They are asked to establish a system of protected areas or areas where special measures need to be taken to conserve biodiversity. As the lists of IBAs have been compiled following strict criteria on a scientific basis, harmonised with existing criteria under the EC Birds Directive and Ramsar Convention, they can serve well as part of a national system of protected areas with a focus on conservation.

The national biodiversity strategies and action plans which have recently been developed in almost all European countries should reflect the role of IBAs as scientifically-based elements of the national implementation of the provisions of the convention. The Czech Republic, a contracting party to CBD, is developing three main documents concerning biodiversity. The Report on the State of Biological Diversity and on the Implementation of CBD in the Czech Republic (First Report) gives basic information on biodiversity in the country. National Biodiversity Strategy and an Action Plan for Biodiversity Protection in the Czech Republic are being prepared.

Pan-European Biological and Landscape Diversity Strategy (PEBLDS)

The strategy was endorsed in 1995 as a pan-European response to the Convention on Biological Diversity. It builds on existing initiatives and programmes, such as the Convention on Biological Diversity, the Bern Convention, the Bonn Convention and the European Conservation strategy. The strategy is defined for a 20 year period, and divided into four five-year Action Plans. Eleven Action Themes run through each Action Plan, of which one is to establish a Pan-European Ecological Network of protected areas.

Ramsar Convention

Convention on Wetlands of International Importance Especially as Waterfowl Habitat

The convention was accepted in February 1971 in Ramsar, Iran at a conference on wetlands and waterfowl, and it came into force in December 1975. Historically, it was the first intergovernmental treaty exclusively concerning habitat conservation. Its aim is the conservation and wise use of wetlands. The main undertakings accepted by the contracting parties to the Ramsar Convention are:

- to designate at least one wetland site to be included in the List of Wetlands of International Importance
- to formulate and implement their planning so as to promote the conservation of the wetlands included in the List, and as far as possible, the wise use of wetlands in their territory
- to promote the conservation of wetlands and waterfowl by establishing nature reserves on wetlands whether they are included in the List or not, and provide adequately for their wardening
- to support the research and management of wetlands
- to cooperate with other contracting parties, above all when transboundary localities are concerned.

The convention has 116 signatories worldwide. In Europe it has been ratified by 39 states, with a total of 636 Wetlands of International Importance (so-called Ramsar Sites) of a total area of 112,186 km². Wetland Important Bird Areas usually fulfil the criteria of Wetlands of International Importance. Three Czech IBAs are Ramsar Sites as a whole, and four other IBAs are partly covered by a Ramsar Site.

Bonn Convention
Convention on the Conservation of Migratory Species of Wild Animals (CMS)

The convention was accepted in 1979 in Bonn, Germany, and it came into force in 1983. The Czech Republic became a member state of the convention in 1994. The main objective of the convention is to protect migratory species (not only birds, but also mammals, fish and invertebrates) in recognition of the fact that protection is needed throughout every part of their migratory ranges, and that this requires international cooperation and action.

The convention has two appendices. Appendix I lists species in danger of extinction throughout all, or a major part, of their ranges. Appendix II lists species that would benefit from international cooperation in their conservation and management. If a party to the convention is a range state of a listed migratory species, it accepts the obligation to provide strict protection for species in Appendix I and to endeavour to conclude agreements with other range states for the conservation and management of species in Appendix II.

For Appendix I species, parties that are range states are obliged to endeavour, amongst other things, to:

- conserve and, where feasible and appropriate, restore those habitats of the species which are of importance in removing the species from danger of extinction (Article III 4a); and
- with regard to the Agreements which parties are encouraged to conclude for Appendix II species, each Agreement should, where appropriate and feasible, provide for the maintenance of a network of suitable habitats appropriately disposed in relation to the migration routes.

Agreement on the Conservation of African-Eurasian Migratory Waterbirds (AEWA)

AEWA is an Agreement under the Bonn Convention which can be signed and ratified by a Range State irrespective of whether the state has signed or ratified the Bonn Convention. It was accepted in 1995 in The Hague and concerns territories of 117 states. AEWA aims to create the legal basis for a concerted conservation policy among the range states of all migratory waterbird species and populations which migrate in the African-Eurasian flyway, irrespective of their current conservation status. The Agreement provides a framework for conservation action, monitoring, research and management of several globally important bird-migration systems. As such, it has close links to the IBA Programme and the Ramsar Convention.

Bern Convention
Convention on the Conservation of European Wildlife and Natural Habitats

The convention was accepted in 1979 in Bern, Switzerland, and it came into force in 1982. The Czech Republic became a member state of the convention in 1998. The main objective of the convention is to protect and maintain populations of wild flora and fauna and give particular emphasis to endangered and vulnerable species, including endangered and vulnerable migratory species. Specifically, each Contracting party undertakes to:

- take appropriate and necessary legislative and administrative measures to ensure the conservation of the habitats of the wild flora and fauna species especially those specified in Appendices I and II, and the conservation of endangered natural habitats
- give special attention to the protection of areas that are of importance for the migratory species specified in Appendix II and III and which are appropriately situated in relation to migration routes, as wintering, staging, feeding, breeding or moulting areas
- prohibit the deliberate damage to or destruction of breeding or resting sites of Appendix II species.

The convention has four appendices. Appendix I is a list of plants. Appendix II is a long list of strictly protected faunal species which includes a high proportion of the European avifauna. Appendix III covers almost all the bird species not included in Appendix II, with the exception of 11 species. Appendix IV lists methods that cannot be used for hunting.

Emerald Network

The Emerald network is an initiative, under the Bern Convention, to extend the Natura 2000 network of protected areas (see 'Habitats Directive', below) beyond the EU to cover member countries of the Council of Europe. Parties are recommended to take steps to designate Areas of Special Conservation Interest (ASCI) to ensure that necessary and appropriate conservation measures are taken for each area situated within their territory or under their responsibility where that area fits one or several of the following conditions:

- It contributes substantially to the survival of threatened species, endemic species, or any species listed in Appendices I and II of the Convention;
- It supports significant numbers of species in an area of high species diversity or supports important populations of one or more species;
- It contains an important and/or representative sample of endangered habitat types;
- It contains an outstanding example of a particular habitat-type or a mosaic of different habitat-types;
- It represents an important area for one or more migratory species;
- It otherwise contributes substantially to the achievement of the objectives of the Convention.

World Heritage Convention

Convention Concerning the Protection of the World Cultural and Natural Heritage

The convention was accepted at a UNESCO conference in Paris in 1972 and came into force in 1975. Its aim is the protection of natural and cultural areas of outstanding universal value. Such sites and monuments are considered of such exceptional value that their protection is the responsibility of all mankind, and thus international cooperation in order to contribute effectively to this protection is sought. Each site nominated by the Parties for inclusion is assessed by a World Heritage Committee, which in the case of natural sites, is advised by the experts from the International Union for the Conservation of Nature (IUCN). The Convention considers as "natural heritage":

- natural features consisting of physical and biological formations or groups of such formations, which are of outstanding universal value from the aesthetic or scientific point of view;
- geological and physiographical formations and precisely delineated areas which constitute the habitat of threatened species of animals and plants of outstanding universal value from the point of view of science or conservation;
- natural sites or precisely delineated natural areas of outstanding universal value from the point of view of science, conservation or natural beauty.

The States Parties undertake, in accordance with the provisions of the Convention, to give their help in the identification, protection, conservation and presentation of the cultural and natural heritage

Man and the Biosphere Programme (MAB)

The Man and the Biosphere programme is a UNESCO programme that was proposed in 1968 and decreed in 1976. It is aimed, amongst other things, to develop within the natural and social services the basis for the rational use and conservation of the resources of the biosphere. Of the

14 international themes and projects of the programme, Project 8 – the conservation of natural areas and the genetic material they contain, is the most important one for the conservation of birds. Its objective is to create a worldwide network of Biosphere Reserves, with each reserve qualifying under one or more of the following categories:

• representative examples of natural biomes
• unique communities or areas with unusual natural features of exceptional interest such as a population of a globally rare species
• examples of harmonious landscapes resulting from traditional patterns of land-use
• examples of modified or degraded ecosystems capable of being restored to more natural conditions

Each Biosphere Reserve needs to be large enough to comprise an effective conservation unit and must have adequate long-term protection.

Parks for Life

This initiative was launched in most European countries in 1994 in a process coordinated by IUCN and WWF together with FNNPE, WCMC and *BirdLife International*. Parks for Life is a response to the call of the IV World Parks Congress (Caracas, February 1992) for regional action plans, and to the conclusions of the Earth Summit in Rio (June 1992). As a plan of action, it sets out the policies and actions needed to ensure an adequate, effective and well-managed network of protected areas in Europe.

The network would be well integrated into all other parts of national life – this means that the protected areas would be embedded in regional planning and that policies for related sectors such as agriculture, forestry and tourism would be environmentally benign. The plan sets out the policies needed to achieve this and shows how its implementation would fulfil some of the commitments governments accepted at Rio, notably to the Convention on Biological Diversity. For example, the plan calls for further 'greening' of the European Union's Common Agricultural Policy, so that environmental protection is one of its central aims, and for combining measures to restrain production with stronger safeguards for protected areas. The plan also calls for more careful use of EU Structural Funds so that they enhance rather than damage the environment. The plan recommends that each country uses a range of different types of protected areas, concentrating in particular on those recorded by IUCN as Category II (national parks, principally of large areas of relatively unmodified vegetation), Category IV (managed nature reserves, mainly for conserving species and ecosystems) and Category V (protected landscapes and seascapes, or lived-in landscapes).

Washington Convention

Convention on International Trade in Endangered Species of Wild Fauna and Flora (CITES)

The convention was accepted in 1973 in Washington and came into force in 1975. It is an international agreement between governments. Its aim is to ensure that international trade in specimens of wild animals and plants does not threaten their survival. The convention concerns not only live animals and plants but also wildlife products derived from them.

Three appendices list species covered by the convention. Appendix I includes species threatened with extinction which are or may be affected by trade. Appendix II lists species that may become threatened with extinction unless trade in specimens of such species is subject to strict regulation and Appendix III includes species which any party identifies as being subject to regulation within its jurisdiction for the purpose of preventing or restricting exploitation, and as needing the cooperation of other parties in the control of trade. All three appendices include a large number of bird species.

The following two documents are 'directives' – binding regulations of the European Union, which have to be transposed into Czech national legislation before the country joins the EU.

Birds Directive

Directive on the Conservation of Wild Birds (79/409/EEC)

This directive was adopted on 2 April 1979, and came into force on 6 April 1981. It contains 19 articles and five annexes. It creates a framework for the protection of wild birds, their habitats, nests and eggs in the territory of the Member States of the European Union. All Member States are committed to providing a sufficient variety of habitats and to preserve, maintain or restore an adequate proportion of these for all wild bird species in their territory.

The Member States of the EU are required to designate Special Protection Areas (SPAs) which are, by their size and number, sufficient to ensure the survival and reproduction of 181 bird species and subspecies listed in Annex I in their area of distribution. This requirement concerns both terrestrial and marine biotopes, and apart from species of Annex I, it is also aimed at regularly occurring migrating species and their wintering, moulting and breeding areas and staging posts along their migrating routes. Special Protection Areas, together with areas designated based on the habitats Directive, create the Natura 2000 network.

Annex I includes 181 protected bird species and subspecies, which are shall be the subject of special conservation measures, Annex II lists 79 protected bird species and subspecies, may be, under certain conditions, hunted under national legislation. Annex III is a list 26 species and subspecies that may be under certain conditions sold within the EC, while Annex IV lists means, arrangements, methods and modes of transport that cannot be used for hunting.

Habitats Directive

Directive on the Conservation of Natural Habitats and of Wild Fauna and Flora (92/43/EEC)

This directive was adopted on 21 May 1992, and came into force two years later – in 1994. It has 23 articles in 9 sections, and 6 annexes. Its goal is the protection of biodiversity in the territory of the Member States of the European Union. The Member States of the EU are required to designate the Special Areas of Conservation (SACs) for all important types of habitats listed in Annex I and habitats of wild plant and animal species listed in Annex II.

Annex I is a list of 253 types of habitats of Community interest, whose protection requires the designation of the Special Areas of Conservation. Annex II gives the list of plant and animal species of Community interest, which require the designation of the Special Areas of Conservation. Annex III describes the criteria for the process of site selection.

Annex IV is a list of plant and animal species of Community interest requiring strict protection. Annex V includes species of Community interest whose taking in the wild and exploitation may be subject to management measures. Annex VI is a list of means, arrangements, methods and modes of transport that cannot be used for hunting.

This chapter was compiled using materials published by the Czech Society for Ornithology and by BirdLife International, namely the following: Damohorský, Stejskal 1998, Grimmett, Jones 1989, Heath, Evans 2000, Hora, Kaňuch et al. 1992, Plesník 1998. Other sources used include Chytil et al. 1999, IUCN CNPPA 1994.

Bird Protection in the Czech Republic

Pavel Marhoul, Jan Plesník

There is a long tradition of bird protection in the territory of today's Czech Republic. The first measures for the protection of certain bird species date back to Middle Ages. The first reserve in the area of the Czech Republic meant for the protection of birds was set almost two centuries ago, when Earl Chotek established a reserve in Veltrusy park in order to protect a nesting colony of the Rook. More information on the history of bird protection in the Czech Republic can be found in the works of Sedláček and Kleschta (1992) or Damohorský and Stejskal (1998). The aim of this chapter is to give an overview of the current state of bird protection in the Czech Republic from the viewpoints of legislature, main threats, main forms of active help to the birds, and future prospects in case the Czech Republic becomes a member state of the European Union.

Legislation on bird protection

Many important changes in nature protection legislature have taken place since the last IBA inventory of Czechosklovakia was published (Hora, Kaňuch et al. 1992). Many laws concerning nature protection, and thus bird protection, have came into force. The most important of them is the **law nr. 114/1992 Sb., on the protection of nature and landscape** and its application-of-law **regulation nr. 395/1992 Sb.,** that replaced the old legislature: law nr. 40/1956 Sb., on the state protection of nature and its application-of-law regulation nr. 80/1965 Sb., on the protection of wild animals.

Law nr. 114/1992 Sb., brings about three main mechanisms directly or indirectly providing the protection of birds. These are: *site-based protection, general protection of flora and fauna* and *specific protection of flora and fauna*. All three approaches function independently while complementing each other.

Site-based protection

Site-based protection is provided by six different categories of protected areas that differ in size and quality of protected values. As for size, the law recognises large-scale protected areas (national parks – NP and protected landscape areas – PLA) and small-scale protected areas (national nature reserves – NNR, national natural monuments – NNM, nature reserves – NR and natural monuments – NM).

The definition of a **national park (NP)**, prepared by the International Union for the Conservation of Nature (IUCN) and accepted in Delhi, India in 1969, first appeared in Czech legislature in the new law on the protection of nature and landscape in 1992. Large areas where there are exceptional values preserved can be established as national parks. The areas of national parks are divided into three zones with different degrees of protection – the strictest regime being in enforced in the first zone. The economical use of the areas of national parks is limited or completely excluded and the access to the public is limited. National parks have their own governance – the administrations of national parks, which coordinate and regulate all main activities concerning interference with natural environment. The national parks are established based on special laws. There are four national parks in the Czech Republic: the Krkonoše (Giant Mountains) NP, Podyjí NP, the Šumava (Bohemian Forest) NP and České Švýcarsko NP. Combined, they cover about 1.5% of the area of the country. All Czech national parks are bilateral – there are similar areas across the border in Poland, Austria and Germany. More areas (such as the central part of Křivoklátsko) are now being surveyed to see if national park status is applicable to them. Two Czech national parks – Krkonoše a Šumava – are UNESCO Biosphere Reserves.

As for bird occurrence and protection, Czech national parks are important, above all, for woodland species. Šumava NP hosts the largest populations of the Capercaillie and the Hazel Hen in the country. The White-backed Woodpecker, Three-toed Woodpecker, Peregrine, Pygmy Owl and Tengmalm's Owl are other important species of forested areas of the national park, while tree-less areas host the Black Grouse and a numerous population of the Corncrake. České Švýcarsko NP is an important breeding area for the Peregrine Falcon and the Eagle Owl, while Krkonoše NP is remarkable for its populations of the Red-spotted Bluethroat, the Alpine Accentor, the Peregrine Falcon, the Corncrake and the random breeding of the Dotterel. Podyjí NP is important for the birds of oak-hornbeam forests and open areas, such as the Wryneck, Turtle Dove and Corn Bunting.

Protected landscape areas (PLA) are meant for the protection of large areas or whole geograph-ical regions with harmonious landscape, characteristic geomorphology and dominance of natural ecosystems. The remnants of historical settlements can be important parts of such areas. According to the degree of protection, PLAs are usually divided into four zones. The first zone usually includes so-called small-scale protected areas. Each PLA has its own administration. PLAs are established by a special government decree. Currently there are 24 PLAs in the Czech Republic, covering about 13% of its territory. Some other areas, such as Novohradské hory, Český les and Střední Poohří, are being surveyed for possible PLA establishment. Several PLAs are of an extraordinary importance for the protection of birds. Pond systems such as those in Třeboňsko and Poodří PLAs, are important for the protection of waterbirds. Pálava, České Středohoří and Bílé Karpaty PLAs are important for termophilous species and Jeseníky, Beskydy, Křivoklátsko a Slavkovský les PLAs are important for woodland species. The importance of several PLAs (Bílé Karpaty, Křivoklátsko, Pálava, Šumava and Třeboňsko) is highlighted by their inclusion within the biosphere reserve network of the Man and Biosphere programme of UNESCO.

The most important category of small-scale protected areas are **national nature reserves (NNR)**, which are being established for the protection of areas of exceptional natural values from the national or international viewpoint. The law prescribes the protection regime which prevents any interference with their environment and limits the access of the public to marked paths. National nature reserves are established by the Ministry of Environment of the Czech Republic, which can, in the case of public interest, significantly exceeding the interest of nature protection, grant an exemption from the protection conditions. Currently there are 117 NNRs in the Czech Republic (of which 70 are included within large-scale protected areas). Of those self-contained areas, the most important NNRs for bird protection are: Bohdanečský rybník pond and Matka pond, Božídarské rašeliniště peatbog, Břehyně-Pecopala, Cahnov-Soutok, Králický Sněžník, Lednické rybníky ponds, Novodomské rašeliniště peatbog, Novozámecký rybník pond, Ranšpurk, Řežabinec pond-Řežabinecké tůně pools, Soos, Žehuňský rybník pond a Žehuňská obora game preserve.

National natural monuments (NNM) usually are areas of small scale. They aim to protect important geological or geomorphological formations (caves, geological profiles), localities of rare minerals, habitats of endangered plants and animals or localities formed by specific human activities (historical park-like landscapes). NNMs are established by the Ministry of Environment of the Czech Republic and their protection regime bans all activities that could lead to damage or destruction of the values protected. There are 100 NNMs established in the territory of the Czech Republic. Chropyňský rybník pond and Pastvisko at Lednice can be named as important examples.

Nature reserves (NR) and **natural monuments (NM)** are meant for the protection of ecosys-tems or their fragments remarkable for a given region or geographical area. They have similar protection regimes as NNMs and NNRs and are established by a decree issued by the relevant district authority or a PLA administration (who can also grant exemptions from their protection regime). There are about 650 nature reserves and 1050 natural monuments in the Czech Republic, but the total area they cover does not exceed 1% of the country's territory.

Apart from specific site-based protection, law nr. 114/1992 Sb. also provides for general site-based protection through so-called Significant Landscape Components and through the Territorial System of Ecological Stability (which consists of ecological centres and ecological corridors of local, regional and supraregional importance).

The third tool of site-based protection available to district authorities and PLA and NP admin-istrations is the establishment of – **temporarily protected areas**. The above-mentioned authorities can grant temporary protection to areas where important species of wild plants and animals occur temporarily or unpredictably. In the case of birds, this tool is used for protecting breeding sites of rare species and important migration stopovers. For example, Dehtář pond is temporarily protected during the time of summer gathering and autumn migration of waterbirds (June – November). The breeding grounds of the Curlew are temporarily protected during the breeding season of the species. Temporarily protected areas combine the approaches of both general and specific protection. The law can under certain conditions allow the payment of compensation to the owners of the land.

General protection of flora and fauna

The law introduces so-called general protection of flora and fauna (and thus birds). Species are protected from destruction, damage, collection, hunting which leads to or could lead to threats of those species, their degeneration, impairment of their breeding abilities, extinction of their populations or destruction of their ecosystems. Only the permission of nature conservancy authorities can allow for hybridisation and release of hybrid individuals or non-native species into the environment. The law's definition of a non-native species is a species that is not part of native ecosystems of a given region.

Specific protection of flora and fauna

In a practical sense, specific protection is much more important for birds. An important part of the law on the protection of nature and landscape is the possibility to grant special protection to certain plant and animal species that are endangered or rare and scientifically or culturally important. The law offers three categories of special protection: critically endangered (CE), severely endangered (SE) and endangered (E) species. **Regulation nr. 395/1992 Sb.** gives the lists of the taxa for each of the categories and it includes 35 critically endangered, 58 severely endangered and 30 endangered bird species. The law sets the conditions for the protection of listed species and they cover all developmental stages as well as those species' natural and artificial dwellings. It is forbidden to interfere with their natural development – to catch them, keep them in captivity, disturb them, hurt or kill them. It is also not allowed to collect them and damage them, damage or remove their developmental stages or their dwellings. The three categories differ in the degree of protection. The protection of endangered species is excluded in cases where the interference is necessary for the proper management of buildings and other property or for hygienic reasons. The nature conservancy authorities can grant exemptions from the protection conditions in cases of public interest significantly exceeding the interest of nature protection. The Ministry of Environment is the relevant authority in cases of critically and severely endangered species. District authorities and PLA or NP administrations can grant exemptions in cases of endangered species. In military training areas, the relevant nature conservancy authority dealing with endangered species is the regional department of the Ministry of Environment.

The law also introduces so-called rescue programmes aimed at protecting selected species. Within such programmes special protection regimes are designed and enforced using rescue breeding, reintroduction, removal and other acceptable methods leading to the deserved state. Rescue programmes for critically endangered species are approved by the Ministry of Environment.

Trade in endangered plant and animal species is regulated by **law nr. 16/1997 Sb., on conditions of exports and imports of endangered species of wild flora and fauna**, which fulfils within Czech legislature the obligations arising from ratifying the Convention on International Trade in Endangered Species of Wild Fauna and Flora (Washington Convention, CITES). The objective of the law is protection and improvement of the conservation status of wild plant and animal species that are subject to international trade. The law sets conditions for the import and export of listed endangered species and measures aimed to ensure protection (including the registration and non-transferrable identification of individuals of listed species. There are three lists of targeted species: 1) species directly threatened by extinction, 2) species that need protection by regulating their import and export so that they do not become threatened with extinction and 3) species identified by a party of the Washington Convention as needing the cooperation of other parties in the control of trade. The lists of species are provided by the Ministry of Environment in regulation nr. 82/1997 Sb., in the wording of regulation nr. 264/1998 Sb. The first list includes the following wild birds of the Czech republic: the Imperial Eagle, the White-tailed Eagle and the Peregrine Falcon. The second list includes, for example, the Black Stork, the Spoonbill, the Common Crane and all birds of prey and owls not mentioned in the first list.

The protection of selected animal species that are problematic from the viewpoint of specific stakeholders is ensured **by law nr. 115/2000 Sb., on the compensation for damage caused by selected protected animals.** The only bird species concerned is the Cormorant and the aim is to protect breeding populations of this species against illegal interference from affected owners and users of water bodies where the Cormorant causes damage to fish-stocks. The law grants compensation for damage caused by the Cormorant between 1 April and 15 July of a given year. No compensation is granted for damage outside this period.

Another law concerning bird protection is **law nr. 246/1992 Sb., on the protection of animals against cruelty**. The aim of this law is to protect animals (vertebrates only) from cruelty, damage to their health, and their putting to death without reason, when these acts are done by man (even through neglect). The law bans any cruelty to animals, both wild and domesticated, and it also bans all forms of promotion of cruelty.

Institutional provision of state nature protection

The central authority in state nature protection in the Czech Republic is the **Ministry of Environment** (MoE). The ministry's scope of activities is vast. One of the most important tasks is the elaboration of the conception of the strategy of nature and landscape protection in the country (Mlčoch et al. 1998, Plesník, Prchalová in prep.). MoE also ensures international cooperation in nature conservation, performs legislative activities (issues application-of-law instructions – regulations, decrees, initiates and works on law and decree proposals submitted by the government of the Czech Republic, issues binding internal instructions for interpretation of legislature in nature and landscape protection) and other tasks. For specially protected animals it grants exemptions from the law; for critically and severely endangered species it safeguards rescue programmes. It also permits the import and export of internationally protected species and it allows for the research of critically and severely endangered species.

Protected Landscape Area and National Park administrations provide for state nature protection in their areas of authority. They are authorised to establish, by issuing regulations, small-scale protected areas in nature reserve and natural monument categories. They provide for protection and research of the areas. As opposed to the independent National Park administrations, the individual PLA administrations are centrally coordinated by the **Administration of Protected Landscape Areas of the Czech Republic** (with headquarters in Prague), which separated in 1995 from the Czech Institute for Nature Protection.

Outside the large-scale protected areas, the environmental departments of **district offices** have analogous responsibilities to those of NP and PLA authorities in large-scale protected areas. Some responsibilities in nature protection (such as issuing tree-logging permission) are delegated further to towns and township administrations. The **Czech Environmental Inspection** oversees the abidance to environmental regulations. It is a government body authorised to issue fines.

The **Agency for Nature Conservation and Landscape Protection of the Czech Republic** is another government body that originated in the 1995 break up of the Czech Institute for Nature Protection. It is a scientific institution providing methodical, informational, educational and scientific services, as well as research, documentation and advisory in the field of nature and landscape management. The main task of this institution is maintaining a central database and documentation in nature protection, issuing judgements and expert opinions for other governmental bodies, enterprises and citizens, performing inventory surveys and preparing management plans for protected areas.

Main threats to birds

Fragmentation, destruction and contamination of the environment

Contrary to past decades, the problem of pesticide use has somewhat receded. This is the result of changes brought about after 1989. The introduction of market principles into agriculture resulted in a strong increase of prices of all chemical compounds used in farming – herbicides, insecticides, rodenticides, seed dressing and inorganic fertilisers. Those, until then "essential" applications, became too expensive and unavailable for many farming entities, causing a sudden drop in their usage. The use of plant-protection compounds dropped from about 2.42 kg per hectare in 1985 to 0.9 kg in 1997; similarly the use of inorganic fertilisers decreased from 230 kg per hectare in 1989 to 73.2 kg ten years later.

However, the load of chemical components and compounds in the environment has a long-term effect. Even now, more than twenty years after the ban of organic carbohydrates based on DDT, DDE and HCB, it is possible to detect traces of these compounds in various agricultural products. Striking examples of negative effects brought on by chemical pollution, such as mass poisonings of corvids or low breeding success in birds of prey, are, fortunately, much less common than in the past. Nevertheless, in the past few years the use of some chemical compounds, including PCBs, has been on the rise again, giving reason for concern.

As in agriculture, dramatic changes took place in heavy industry and other parts of the economy. The pressure from neighbouring countries and ecological initiatives forced the introduction of effective desulphurisation at fossil-fuelled power stations, mainly in the northern part of the country, where their impact on the forest ecosystems in surrounding mountain regions was disastrous. The quality of surface water has improved considerably due to the changes in farming and due to improved sewage treatment as many sewage treatment plants were built in the past decade. Partial improvements can be traced even to road traffic. The ban on leaded fuel and the requirement of catalytic converters has led to the decreased impact of car use on the environment.

Although the list of improvements is long, many problems in bird protection, mainly in agricultural landscape, remain. The most prominent issue is the structure of the modern agricultural landscape. The vanishing of hedgerows, field margins and unused patches of land, has in the past few decades reached such a degree that only very few bird species find nesting opportunities. On the other hand, many fields were abandoned and are left for succession to develop. Unfortunately, such areas are suitable for birds only for a short period of time or not at all. Numerous studies show enduring negative effects of modern farming methods on many bird species. The decrease in nesting opportunities and food sources is, among other things, caused by a considerable shift from winter to spring crops and by more and more common stubble ploughing in the autumn.

Casualties in birds nesting in fodder crops represent another problem difficult to solve. Of interest is the case of a 50 ha field of alfalfa on the border of Prague where after the harvest 13 destroyed pheasant nests and at least two destroyed partridge nests were counted.

The past decade also brought about changes in the landscape caused by the construction boom. Habitats of many bird species are threatened by the construction of transport infrastructure, industrial parks and similar projects. For example, the construction of a highway bypass around the town of Strážnice is threatening possibly the last locality hosting the Curlew in Moravia.

Many changes in landscape have been brought about by recreational use and fast-growing tourism. As tourists concentrate in certain areas (often those that are valuable for birds) it is necessary not to undervalue this trend and consider it when looking to protect birds. Sensitive species concentrated in areas affected by tourism during the breeding season and the winter, such as the Capercaillie or the Black Grouse, are the most threatened. Disturbance caused by mountain climbing is another specific threat (eg. for the Peregrine).

A little known but apparently serious problem are the deaths caused by road traffic. Although detailed studies from large areas are lacking, local surveys show alarming results. Šafránek (1999) evaluated the effect of road traffic on birds in a 2 km segment of a category III road in the Přerov district. He found 159 dead birds over 280 inspections. The mortality rate was higher in areas with scattered greenery (gardens and wood patches in fields) and in the summer months (main reason for this probably being the presence of just fledged young and the vagrancy of grain-feeding birds). By applying the results to the road network of the whole Czech Republic, the author estimates that between 1.03 to 2.57 million birds die every year on category III roads only.

Similarly, there is little information about the numbers of birds killed through collisions with glass surfaces. Glass components are more and more often used in the construction of buildings and other structures such as bus stops, phone booths and noise-prevention barriers. There are two reasons why such surfaces are dangerous to birds: they are either not seen by the birds or they reflect the surrounding landscape and confuse the birds. The Czech Society for Ornithology has started a project aimed at detecting the numbers of birds killed by glass surfaces and evaluating the danger of such structures to birds (Pavelka 2000b).

Both the road traffic and glass surface problems should be given maximum attention.

Direct harassment

One of the most serious threats to birds is direct harassment. In 1996, regulation nr. 134/1996 Sb. of the Ministry of Agriculture of the Czech Republic came into force. This regulation guides the application of the Hunting Law and it sets the hunting seasons or year-round preservation for all bird species that the Hunting Law considers game. Based on this regulation, hunters can kill the Crow and the Magpie all-year round and many other species in defined hunting seasons: the Mallard, Pochard, Tufted Duck, Coot, Pheasant, Reeves's Pheasant, Wild Turkey, Turtle Dove, Woodpigeon, Jay, Rook and geese.

Other species have defined hunting seasons, but as they are specially protected species, an exemption granted by the relevant authority is needed for their hunting. There are six such species: exemptions are not granted at all for the Black Grouse and the Partridge; they are rarely granted for the Eagle Owl and the Woodcock, but they have been regularly granted for the Cormorant in the past few years.

The hunting regulation includes statements that are in direct conflict with the interests of nature protection. One such statement is that the hunting season of geese ends at the end of February (which is when the Greylag Goose has already started nesting). The negative effects of this part of the regulation could fully be seen at the Nové Mlýny middle reservoir. The site had gradually become the most important wintering site of geese in the Czech Republic, hosting tens of thousands of birds. When the regulation came into force the numbers dropped to about 4,000 individuals, and the number of breeding also decreased significantly – 150 nests were recorded in the middle of the 1990's while only 189 nests were found in 1999 (Chytil, Macháček 2000a). The situation only improved after the district office in Břeclav banned hunting in January and February in 1999.

The regulation also allows for daily hunting of the Coot, ducks and migrating geese. Before 1996, this was restricted to Saturdays only.

Another controversial part of the regulation allows the hunting of the Black-headed Gull all year round at fingerling and rearing ponds and ponds with intensive duck breeding. The regulation also allows for hunting the Black-headed Gull in pheasantries, and localities hosting the Capercaillie, Black Grouse, Hazel Hen and Great Bustard, or where the above mentioned species and the Partridge are released. Grey Heron hunting is also allowed at rearing and fingerling ponds. Entirely groundless and unacceptable is the section of the regulation allowing for the hunting of the Common and Rough-legged Buzzards all year round. This, in theory, concerns only birds "repeatedly attacking domestic poultry and pigeons" but in reality hundreds of both buzzard species are killed each year under this absurd pretext. 221 buzzards were killed in 1999 according to hunter's - statistics, but this figure can be taken as undervalued.

Apart from the above-mentioned species, which can be hunted under certain conditions, all other species are protected by the law on nature and landscape protection or hunting legislature. Nevertheless, many such species are being killed or their nests and eggs are being destroyed. The "Free Wings" project directed by the Czech Society for Ornithology focuses on all illegal activities concerning birds. Data is being collected by return cards and during the first nine months of the project 120 cases were recorded. The primary targets of illegal activities are birds of prey and owls (most common victim being the Common Buzzard, followed by the Marsh Harrier, Goshawk, Sparrowhawk and Long-eared Owl). Apart from those relatively common species, shootings of several rare species were recorded as well: the White-tailed Eagle, Honey Buzzard, Great White Egret, Hobby, Red and Black Kites, Hen Harrier and Ural Owl (the latter was included in a research project and had a miniature radio transmitter attached to its body). CSO also monitors nest robberies of the Peregrine, Saker and both Kite species. Quite a common target of attacks by hunters and fishermen is the Mute Swan. Recorded cases obviously represent just a fragment of the real situation regarding direct harassment. The threat is highlighted by the fact that the Czech legislature does not (unlike in the US or several EU countries) consider killing a protected animal an offence.

Power lines

Pylons of high-voltage power lines (22 and 35 kV) represent a major risk, above all to diurnal raptors, owls and waders. Dozens of deaths and injuries resulting from birds attempting to land on the horizontal consoles of the pylons have been recorded. This risk increases when it is raining. It is obvious that most cases remain undisclosed, as dead birds are quickly removed by raptors and other carnivores. The characteristics of the landscape in the Czech Republic highlight this problem. In the agricultural landscape of lowlands with little or no trees, the pylons are often the only objects towering above the land and are inviting for birds to sit there. The problem is difficult to tackle as there are about 750,000 pylons of a dangerous type throughout the country and their exchange is hard to be reached quickly. In the past few years, the state nature conservancy authorities together with NGOs and electric companies have aimed at securing the most dangerous pylons with protective elements (so-called combs) that prevent birds from landing on the pylons, or plastic components covering the insulators and surrounding parts of the wires. Priority is given to pylons in high-risk areas (nesting areas of critically endangered species, migration routes and stop-overs, etc.). Over 6,600 pylons have been adjusted this way since 1998. In the future, the best way to protect birds from injuries is building electric pylons of safe designs only.

Threats to avifauna in the Czech Republic

According to the Red List of Birds of the Czech Republic (Šťastný, Bejček *in prep.*) which is based on IUCN criteria from 1994, it is possible to say that almost 46% of bird species nesting in the Czech Republic are threatened. The authors evaluated the degree of threats to 223 species that nested in the country at least once. Ten species are considered extinct. A total of 70 species (31.4% of all nesting species) belong to the critically endangered (CR), endangered (EN) and vulnerable (VU) categories, i.e. categories signifying a high degree of threats (CR – 23, EN – 24 a VU – 23). A total of 34 species (14.3%) fit in the lower categories (conservation dependent – CD, near-threatened – NT, little concerned – LC, rare – R). The most vulnerable group of species is birds of wetland ecosystems followed by birds of agricultural landscape. Of the 70 species in the higher categories, 27 are waterbird species (38.6%), relatively less threatened are woodland bird species – 12 species (17.1%). The Great Bustard, Stone Curlew, Capercaillie, farmland waders (the Curlew, Black-tailed Godwit, Redshank and Snipe) and several raptor species (the Imperial Eagle, Peregrine and Saker) are among the most threatened birds in the Czech Republic.

Practical protection of birds in the Czech Republic

Governmental nature protection institutions, various non-governmental non-profit organisations and numerous individuals cooperate in the practical protection of birds in the Czech Republic.

Changes in landscape

The Ministry of Environment has introduced several programmes aimed at increasing the diversity of the landscape and thus indirectly at increasing biodiversity, birds included.

A programme of revitalisation of river systems started in 1992. It is an investment programme supporting renewal, stabilisation and water regime management of the landscape. The programme pays for the building and renewal of ponds and other water bodies and removal of unwelcome adjustments of streams and others.

The landscape management programme is a non-investment programme started in 1996. It supports measures aimed at erosion protection, maintenance of the traditional use of the landscape and an increase in biodiversity of certain localities. Within this programme the ministry supports the establishment of hedgerows and permanent grasslands, the introduction of extensive management, environmentally sound grazing, renewal and care of artificial habitats for protected animal species etc. A project aimed at increasing nesting and feeding opportunities for the Partridge in the Českomoravská vrchovina hills is an example of a measure supported within the programme.

In 2001, 290 million CZK was spent on the programme of revitalisation of river systems and 230 million CZK was spent on the landscape management programme. Similar programmes devoted to landscape management are administered by the Ministry of Agriculture. Resources are available for pond mud extraction, the use of organic fertilisers, establishment of the components of the System of Ecological Stability and the management of agricultural landscape. In 2000, more than 3.5 billion CZK of state budget funds was used for the above-mentioned purposes.

Protection of nests and artificial nests

Pressure from various groups makes it necessary to physically protect nests of certain bird species. The danger comes from falconers, hunters and also from uninformed forest workers. Nest guarding is a common measure even outside the Czech Republic. In Western Europe, electronic systems installed in the vicinity of nests connected with the nearest police posts are often used. In Poland special zones are established around the nests of some bird species (such as the Peregrine or White-tailed Eagle) and entry is possible only by special permission. Nest protection in the Czech Republic is organised mainly by non-governmental organisations and it focuses primarily on the Peregrine and Saker – critically endangered species favoured by falconers and fanciers. Illegal nest robberies represent a much larger problem in neighbouring Slovakia. Paradoxically, this concerns the Czech Republic as well. Thirteen Golden Eagle nests were robbed in Slovakia in 2000 and at least two Czech citizens were caught at this illegal activity.

The construction of artificial nests is another important activity, mainly of some non-governmental organisations. Both stork species, cavity nesting birds of prey, owls and songbirds are the most common target species. State nature conservation bodies support such activities through the landscape management programme and through subsidies for non-governmental non-profit organisations. The Ministry of Environment also supports the building of islets for waterbirds. Two islets are being built in the Nové Mlýny middle reservoir, several islets for the Common Tern are being built at ponds in Třeboňsko. Nest boxes for various bird species are also being installed as part of programmes aimed at biological protection of farmland and forests.

Stations for handicapped animals

Stations for handicapped animals are meant for the care of animals unable to live independently in nature, injured and diseased individuals and abandoned young. As these institutions often deal with specially protected animal species, for their activities they need an exemption granted according to law nr. 114/1992 Sb., on nature and landscape protection. The Ministry of Environment has about 50 such stations from all over the country in its database. Some of them are associated in so-called national network of stations, which is managed by the Czech Union of Nature Conservationists and supported by the ministry.

Captive breeding and reintroduction programmes

Reintroduction of captive-bred individuals is one of the ways of active bird protection. The history of such activities shows some very successful examples. The release of captive-bred White-tailed Eagles by Klaus Fentzloff from Germany helped to establish a breeding population of the species in Třeboňsko.

The law on nature and landscape protection introduced so-called rescue programmes and the Ministry of Environment is commissioned to guarantee such programmes for critically endangered animal and plant species.

The rescue programme for the Capercaillie started in 1998. Individuals bred in captivity are released in selected areas of favourable conditions. Some of the birds are bred in the Czech Republic, but the majority is being imported from Germany and Sweden. The species is being released in the Šumava mountains, Brdy hills, Jeseníky mountains, Krkonoše mountains and Český les area. Several hundred birds have been reintroduced, and some of them were equipped by miniature radio-transmitters for further survey. Unfortunately, preliminary results show a very high mortality rate of released birds.

Another rescue program covering the whole country deals with the Peregrine and Saker. A smaller programme focused on the area of the Šumava mountains deals with the Ural Owl. The former is a modern and complex rescue program that does not only deal with the release of the birds, but also ensures management and guarding of nesting sites, adaptation of electric pylons and monitoring of the birds. The programme is directed by a standing committee under the patronage of the Agency for Nature Conservation and Landscape Protection of the Czech Republic, central office in Havlíčkův Brod. A decade ago, only sporadic nesting of both species was recorded, but the numbers of nesting pairs have increased and today the country hosts 10–15 nesting pairs of the Peregrine and 5–10 pairs of the Saker.

The reintroduction of the Ural Owl in the Šumava mountains is implemented by the Šumava NP and PLA administrations in cooperation with specialists from other institutions. Released young birds are either imported from Eastern Slovakia or captive-bred in Czech zoos and stations for handicapped animals. Breeding in nature has already been recorded (Kloubec 1999a).

Other reintroduction projects are managed by NGOs, hunter's associations and amateurs.

Although partial success has been accomplished in several reintroduction projects, many questions remain unanswered and the results of many other projects are dubious. Experience from abroad shows a very low success in reintroduction projects. For example, an analysis of the *US Fish and Wildlife Service,* which is responsible for planing and management of so-called species action plans in the United States, showed that after twenty years and several hundred projects, only five species can be considered rescued. Other detailed studies on released individuals showed very high mortality rates and negligible participation in reproduction. For these reasons the reintroduction of captive-bred individuals should be used only when other solutions have been ruled out. The protection and management of appropriate habitats should be given priority. A similar viewpoint is held by the IUCN, a prestigious international organisation.

The future of bird protection in the Czech Republic

For the past few years the Czech Republic has been preparing to join the European Union. Apart from many other conditions that need to be fulfilled, the country has to align its legislative with that of the European Communities. In nature conservancy this means the transposition and implementation of two key directives: the Council Directive on the conservation of wild birds – 79/409/EEC (Birds Directive) and the Council Directive on the conservation of natural habitats of wild fauna and flora – 92/43/EEC (Habitats Directive).

The main result of the implementation of both directives will be the creation of a network of protected areas known as NATURA 2000. The network will be composed of two types of areas: *Special Areas of Conservation* (SACs) based on the Habitats Directive and *Special Protection Areas* (SPAs) based on the requirements of the Birds Directive. Annex I of the Birds Directive lists 181 bird species and subspecies threatened in the EU. Of this list, 58 species regularly or irregularly nest in the Czech Republic, 58 other species have never been recorded in this country and the rest of the species and subspecies have only been recorded during migration or as rare vagrants. It is important that SPAs do not protect just the breeding grounds of Annex I species and subspecies, but they are also meant for the protection of localities vital for the migration and wintering of birds. Emphasis is given to wetlands, as they are important habitats for many bird species as well as other animal and plant species.

Areas of the NATURA 2000 network are selected based on a sound scientific approach and objective criteria – the presence of species or habitats or both. It is expected that at the end of the process of establishing the NATURA 2000 network it will cover between 15% and 20% of the Czech Republic's territory (i.e. the same or bigger area than the sum of current protected areas in the country). Apart from the task of establishing SPAs, the Birds Directive will introduce several other changes to Czech legislature. Article 5 of the directive bans deliberate killing or capture by any method, deliberate destruction of, or damage to, their nests and eggs or removal of their nests, taking their eggs in the wild and keeping these eggs even if empty, deliberate disturbance of these birds particularly during the period of breeding and rearing and keeping in captivity all birds native to the environment of the European territory of the EU Member States.

The directive also concerns bird hunting, which is possible only with species mentioned in Appendix II of the Directive. The Appendix has two lists: species of the list II/1 may be hunted in the whole territory of the EU, only if the national legislative of a given state allows for it. Of the species commonly hunted in the Czech Republic, the list includes for example the Greylag Goose, Bean Goose, Mallard, Pochard, Tufted Duck, Pheasant, Coot and Woodpigeon. Of the species that are not permissable to hunt without an exemption from law nr. 114/1992 Sb., on nature and landscape protection, the list includes for example the Partridge, Snipe, Gadwall, Teal and Garganey.

Annex II/2 contains more than 50 bird species. They can be hunted in all EU Member States that have asked the European Commission and are indicated in the list. Again this has to be in agreement with the national legislative of a given state. Hunting of all species is not allowed during the breeding season and at the time of arrival at the breeding grounds. Many waterbirds, fowl-like birds, waders and songbirds are included in this Annex. Among others, it includes the Mute Swan, Hazel Hen, Black Grouse, Capercaillie, but also the Blackbird and the Corn Bunting. There are no birds of prey or owls included in the Annex.

Governments can issue so-called derogation when there is no other satisfactory solution for the following reasons: in the interest of public health and safety; in the interest of air safety; to prevent serious damage to crops, livestock, forests, fisheries (the case of the Cormorant) and water; for the protection of flora and fauna; for the purposes of research and teaching, of re-population, of re-introduction and for the breeding necessary for these purposes; to permit, under strictly supervised conditions and on a selective basis, the capture, keeping or other judicious use of certain birds in small numbers. Member States are obliged to inform the European Commission about issued derogations.

It is important that the European Commission emphasises the implementation of the Directive. The Commission brought to the European Court of Justice the Member States of which it decided did not fulfil the responsibilities arising from the Directive. The emphasis on effective nature conservation is given by the amount of funds the Commission makes available for this area. The European Commission introduced various programmes supporting conservation projects. The most important ones include the LIFE programme and so-called agri-environmental programmes (Plesník 2000, Plesník, Žáková 2000). The ways the Directives are used in nature conservation give us hope for the future.

Ornithological Importance
of the Czech Republic

Karel Šťastný, Vladimír Bejček

An article of similar name was published in the 1992 IBA inventory (Hora 1992b), an overview of former Czechoslovakia. In 1993 the country divided and since then some changes have occurred in ornithology as well. This is why a new complete list of the avifauna of the Czech Republic was written up in 1995 (Hudec et al. 1995). It names all the bird species recorded in the wild between 1800 and 1994. In the area of what is now the Czech Republic, 390 bird species have been recorded. Of those, 186 were regular nesters, another eight were irregular ones. 14 more species nested only exceptionally, and with eight other species (the Great White Egret – *Egretta alba*, the Wigeon – *Anas penelope*, the Scaup – *Aythya marila,* the Smew – *Mergus albellus*, the Ringed Plover – *Charadrius hiaticula,* the Herring Gull – *Larus argentatus,* the Hawk Owl – *Surnia ulula* and the Citrine Wagtail – *Motacilla citreola)* nesting has been recorded only once. Six species nested in the country only in the 19th century (the Golden Eagle – *Aquila chrysaetos)* or disappeared during the 20th century (the Lesser Kestrel – *Falco naumanni,* the Roller – *Coracias garrulus,* the Rock Thrush – *Monticola saxatilis,* the Lesser Grey Shrike – *Lanius minor* and the Woodchat Shrike – *L. senator).* Altogether 222 bird species have nested in the Czech Republic, of which the status is still unclear for three of those: the Baillon's Crake *(Porzana pusilla),* the Scops Owl *(Otus scops)* and the Aquatic Warbler *(Acrocephalus paludicola).*

184 bird species regularly migrate through the Czech Republic and 41 others migrate irregularly. Rare vagrants with less than ten sightings during the period include 79 species, 33 of which were recorded only once.

Regularly wintering birds include 133 species, 53 more wintered irregularly. (One bird species may be included in all three categories – as nesting, migrating and wintering birds, thus the total is lower than the sum of the three categories.)

Let us look at the changes of the past six years so that our overview can cover two centuries, ending in the year 2000. First of all there are seven new breeding species. In 1996, with the help of foreign experts, the nesting of *(Aquila clanga)* was unambiguously confirmed, as erratic determination of specimens of two fully-fledged nestlings shot at a nest near Pardubice in 1847 was uncovered (Lemberk 1997). The Imperial Eagle *(Aguila heliaca)* first nested in the country in 1998 and then again in 1999 and 2000 at the same site in Southern Moravia (Horák 1998, *in litt.).* For the Yellow-legged Gull *(Larus cachinnans)* the first breeding was confirmed in 1990 at the Nové Mlýny reservoirs. In 1999 the breeding of at least five, but probably seven, pairs was confirmed there (Chytil, Macháček 1999). The breeding of one pair of this species was confirmed even for Třeboňsko in 1998 (Cepák, Ševčík 1998). The nesting of one pair of the Little Tern was proven in 1995 near Karviná-Darkov (Kondělka 1996). The successful breeding of the Scops Owl *(Otus scops)* was confirmed for the first time in 1998 in Bílé Karpaty (Pavelčík 2000). The breeding attempt of the Moustached Warbler *(Acrocephalus melanopogon)* was recorded based on sightings and the trapping of a singing male and discovery of its nest. (Procházka, Musil 1999). Apart from that, there is a forgotten record of the breeding of the Wood Duck *(Aix galericulata)* which escaped from the Plzeň zoo and nested in 1978 near Bolevec. There is still some uncertainty in the nesting of the Baillon's Crake *(Porzana pusilla)* and the Aquatic Warbler *(Acrocephalus paludicola).*

Of the group of the eight once-only nesting species, the Wigeon *(Anas penelope)* nested the second time in Northern Bohemia in 1997 (Tejrovský 1998/99). Also the breeding of the Herring Gull *(Larus argentatus),* now clearly distinguished from the Yellow-legged Gull *(L. cachinnans),* was reconfirmed for 1990. Thus, the number of breeding bird species in the Czech Republic rose to 227.

To the 33 recorded species in the Czech Republic, more have been added: the Blue-winged Teal

(Anas discors) in 1996 near Tovačov (Polčák 1997), the King Eider *(Somateria spectabilis)* also in 1996 near Nymburk (Jelínek in Chytil 1997), the Purple Sandpiper *(Calidris maritima)* in 1997 near Bzenec (Šimeček 1998a) and the Siberian Jay *(Perisoreus infaustus)* found as a stuffed specimen from 1968 in Vysoké Mýto (Chytil *in verb*). Thus the total number of bird species occuring in the Czech Republic rose to 394. If we include two newly approved species- the Rock Pipit *(Anthus petrosus)* and the Iberian Chiffchaff *(Phylloscopus brehmii)*, it comes to 396.

In the article from 1992 (Hora 1992b), population estimates from 1973–77 (Šťastný et al. 1997) were used. By the end of the 20th century new quantitative estimates and population trends for individual bird species were updated (Šťastný, Bejček 1993, Hudec et al. 1995, Šťastný et al. 1997). The following overview lists the most interesting changes within individual systematic groups.

Grebes *(Podicipediformes)*

A dramatic decline has been recorded in all regularly nesting Grebe species, the strongest decline in the Black-necked Grebe (at least by 50% in comparison to the 1970s).

Pelicans and allies *(Pelecaniformes)*

The Cormorant is the only regularly breeding species and its numbers declined from 599–682 pairs in 1989–91 to 319 pairs in 1994 and to 150–200 pairs (Martincová et al. 2000) at the end of the 1990s, the main reason being the allowance to hunt them outside of breeding season.

Herons, Storks and allies *(Ciconiiformes)*

Many species of this group, just like many other water and wetland species from other groups, declined dramatically. This applies to the Bittern and the Little Bittern whose numbers dropped to 20–30 pairs and 50–90 pairs in 1985–89 and their population has not recovered since. The same applies to the Purple Heron with 1–5 breeding pairs in 1990–94. The population of the Night Heron with about 400 breeding pairs is quite stable. The numbers of the Grey Heron are rising constantly (about 1400 pairs in 1993). The numbers of the Black Stork (200–300 pairs) and the White Stork (931 pairs in 2000) are quite high in comparison to other Central European countries, and Western European countries especially. Since the middle of the 1980s, the Spoonbill, a threatened species in Europe, has been nesting in the Czech Republic regularly.

Waterfowl *(Anseriformes)*

The situation is critical with some species: the Teal - 150–250 pairs, the Garganey - 100–180 pairs, the Shoveler - 140–200 pairs. The Pintail and the Ferruginous Duck (last breeding recorded in 1988) may be considered extinct in this country. A population decline of 25–50% has been recorded in all other duck species with the exception of the Gadwall. The Red-crested Pochard with 160–180 pairs, has a stable population in the Czech Republic. Pleasing are the relatively high numbers of breeding Greylag Geese - 580–670 pairs in 1985–89. The breeding of the Goosander was recorded for the fourth time.

Birds of prey *(Falconiformes)*

The situation of birds of prey in the Czech Republic has improved considerably, even if shootings of protected species are still recorded (such as the two cases of the White-tailed Eagle in the past few years). A stable population or a population increase has been recorded in most species. The most important is the small population of the White-tailed Eagle, a species endangered in Europe, with 10–15 pairs in 1994 and about 25 pairs in 2000 (J. Procházka *in verb*). The Saker (5–10 pairs) reaches the northern limit of its breeding range in Northern Moravia, but in 1993 the breeding area of the species stretched westwards up to the city of Znojmo, which was the western limit of the species's breeding range back then. At the end of the 1990s, the species bred even further west right over the Czech Republic's western border, in Germany. The numbers of the Peregrine Falcon, until quite recently a globally threatened species, have been rising as well. This species did not nest here before the 1970s, but its population grew to 10–15 pairs by the end of the century. Perhaps the only raptor species demonstrating a population decline in the Czech Republic is the Black Kite with 70–90 pairs nesting in 1985–89 and only 30–50 pairs nesting in 1994.

Fowl-like birds *(Galliformes)*

Practically all species of this Order (with the exception of the Quail, whose fluctuating population is peaking) show a population decline. Even numbers of such a common species as the Pheasant have dropped by about 50%. The situation of three threatened wood species is worth mentioning:

the Capercaille with only 100–150 birds, the Black Grouse with 800–1000 cocks in 2000 (Málková 2000) and the Hazel Hen with 800–1600 pairs.

Cranes, Rails and allies *(Gruiformes)*
The wetland species of this Order show a fast decline, which includes common species such as the Coot and the Moorhen – a drop of 25–50% in the numbers of both species. The Common Crane, reaching its southern distribution limit in the Czech Republic, is an exception to this trend. It started nesting here at the beginning of 1980s and the population reached 10–15 pairs in 1999. A globally threatened species, the Corncrake counted 200–400 pairs in 1985–89; by 2000, its numbers rose to at least 1500 pairs. On the other hand, the Great Bustard will have to be included in the list of extinct species. It has not nested in the Czech Republic for many years, a single female was recorded wintering in Southern Moravia in the second half of the 1990s, but there are no wintering birds there now.

Shorebirds, Gulls and allies *(Charadriiformes)*
There has been a drastic decline in the numbers of waders inhabiting wet meadows. This applies to the Black-tailed Godwit (30–45 pairs in the second half of the 1990s), the Redshank (40–50 pairs in the second half of the 1990s) and the Curlew (most probably only two pairs in 2000), but also to the Snipe (at most 500 pairs in 1995–97). Quite similar is the situation with another species preferring a dry environment – the Stone Curlew, which rarely nests in Southern Moravia. The numbers of the Green Sandpiper have been rising since the early 1970s with the population reaching 15–30 breeding pairs in 1994. As for gulls, the population of the Black-headed Gull has declined by about 50%. On the other hand, the numbers of the Mediterranean Gull (25 pairs at the end of the 1990s) and the Common Gull (3–7 pairs at the end of the 1980s) keep on rising. The Black Tern numbers have declined by 25–50%.

Parrots *(Psittaciformes)*
Although this is not a native group to the Czech Republic, the viable population of the Monk Parakeet in the country is worth mentioning. The colony in the Sázava river valley started in 1986 and it reached 34 individuals in 1994 and about 100 birds in 2000 – of it 10–20 juveniles hatched that year (Žoha *in verb.*).

Owls *(Strigiformes)*
The decline in the population of the Barn Owl is alarming (only 300–350 pairs in 1990) and there is a strong decline in the numbers of the Little Owl (500–1000 pairs at the end of the 1990s – Schröpfer 2000). Nevertheless, the populations of the Pygmy Owl (900–1300 pairs) and the Tengmalm's Owl (550–800 pairs) are quite strong. In comparison to the rest of Europe, the Czech Republic has a very strong Eagle Owl population (600–950 pairs). Important owl species of mountain regions include the Ural Owl with 5–10 breeding pairs in the Beskydy and Šumava mountains. The occurrence of the species in Šumava is a result of an undergoing reintroduction programme.

Rollers, Kingfishers and allies *(Coraciiformes)*
The numbers of the Hoopoe are still quite low (60–120 pairs). With the fluctuating breeding range of the Bee-eater at the southern border of the Czech Republic, the country's breeding population numbers are volatile as well. The population of the species has been growing since the 1980s, reaching its peak in 1996 with 115–120 breeding pairs and then declining to only 36–40 pairs in 2000 (Šimeček 1997, 1998b, 1999, Viktora *in litt.*).

Woodpeckers and allies *(Piciformes)*
Reaching its western (and until quite recently also its northern) distribution range in the Czech Republic, the Syrian Woodpecker's population grew to 300–400 pairs 1990–94. Another important woodpecker species is the Three-toed Woodpecker with 300–500 breeding pairs. The White-backed Woodpecker population counts 150–250 pairs. Both latter mentioned species have their western distribution limit in the Czech Republic.

Perching birds *(Passeriformes)*
One of the most important songbird species experiencing a declining population is the Tawny Pipit (40–80 pairs). At the northern limit of its breeding range, with only 15–20 pairs, the Alpine Accentor nests in the Krkonoše a Hrubý Jeseník mountains. The western limit of the breeding range of the Thrush Nightingale stretched to the Czech Republic in the past decade (first breeding in

1989). Two subspecies of the Bluethroat breed here – ssp. *cyanecula* with 190–210 pairs in 1994 and ssp. *svecica* with 30–40 pairs. The Greenish Warbler has been breeding in the Czech Republic since 1992 when its outermost southern and western breeding-range limit reached this country (1–5 breeding pairs each year). The Scarlet Rosefinch population has been spreading westwards and southwards, and so its numbers are rising (from 350–450 pairs in 1985–89 and more than 1400 pairs at the end of 1990s). The Ortolan is a rare and continuously declining species. It's numbers apparently dropped from 200–300 pairs in 1985–89.

When reviewing the situation of the past decade (1991–2000) the results are as follows: of the 202 regularly nesting species (17 irregularly nesting and seven introduced or escaped species not included), populations of 31% of species are increasing, populations of 37% of species are declining and the remaining 32% of bird species populations are stable (Hudec et al. 2000).

The avifauna of the Czech Republic consists mainly of common, inland, typically European species. From the zoogeographic viewpoint, the country can be divided into two zones: the zone of broad-leaved forests covering most of the Czech Republic and the steppe zone covering part of Southern Moravia. Typical species of the Central-European broad-leaved forest zone include the Chaffinch *(Fringilla coelebs)* and the Greenfinch *(Carduelis chloris)*, while the Bee-eater *(Merops apiaster)* and the Imperial Eagle *(Aquila heliaca)* are typical for the steppe zone. Due to the geo-morphology of the Czech Republic, two other zones are present here: the zone of boreal coniferous forests (taiga) and the zone of alpine tundra in the upper parts of high mountains. The Pygmy Owl *(Glaucidium passerinum)* and the Three-toed Woodpecker *(Picoides tridactylus)* are typical species of the former, while the Dotterel *(Charadrius mirinellus)* and the Alpine Accentor *(Prunella collaris)* are typical for the latter. Because of the Central-European location of the country, there are many species breeding at their breding range limits. The Imperial Eagle *(Aquila heliaca)* breeds here at its northern and western breeding range, the Saker *(Falco cherrug)* at its northern (and until quite recently also its western) breeding range. The Goldeneye *(Bucephala clangula)* and the Meadow Pipit *(Anthus pratensis)* reach their southern breeding range limits in the Czech Republic.

In general, the country can be divided into three types of environment important for its avifauna. These are woods, wetland and agricultural landscape with fields and meadows. The woods cover about 33% of the area, and the most important ones are primeval and native forests in mountain regions with characteristic bird inhabitants such as the Ural Owl *(Strix uralensis)*, the Capercaillie *(Tetrao urogallus)*, the Three-toed Woodpecker *(Picoides tridactylus)* and the White-backed Woodpecker *(Dendrocopos leucotos)*. Some areas are secondarily tree-less due to logging and forest die-out caused by air pollution. Such areas host some rare bird species such as the Black Grouse *(Tetrao tetrix)* and the Meadow Pipit *(Anthus pratensis)*. Open agricultural landscape with a mosaic of ecotones, solitary trees and bushes and scattered greenery along streams is important for Shrikes *(Lanius* sp.), the Ortolan *(Emberiza hortulana)* and the Corn Bunting *(Miliaria calandra)*. Wet, extensively managed meadows are important for the Corncrake *(Crex crex)*, the Redshank *(Tringa totanus)* and the Black-tailed Godwit *(Limosa limosa)*. Dry fields host the Stone Curlew *(Burhinus oedicnemus)* and the Tawny Pipit *(Anthus campestris)*. Wetlands – mainly fishponds and other shallow reservoirs serve not only as breeding sites of many water birds, but also as migration stopovers and wintering sites. For example, the reservoirs in Southern Moravia have held up to 100,000 geese over the past several years.

Site Selection

Jan Hora

The rationale behind the Important Bird Areas Programme is that many bird species concentrate in specific areas for part of the year or part of their life cycle. On the one hand this makes such species especially vulnerable whilst, on the other, it provides opportunities for implementing site-specific conservation measures for quite a number of species. Important Bird Areas are those areas where a significant part of these species' populations can be found on a regular basis.

The first pan-European IBA inventory was published by ICBP *(International Council for Bird Preservation,* now *BirdLife International)* in 1989 (Grimmett, Jones 1989) and it presented information on 2,444 areas in 39 European states and autonomous regions. This inventory was a follow up to an ICBP report for the European Commission (Osieck, Mörzer Bruyns 1981) covering 694 IBAs in the then nine Member States of the European Community. It was later supplemented with site lists for Greece, Spain and Portugal. In 1989 a new report describing 1,525 areas in the then 12 Member states of the European Community (Grimmett, Gammell 1989). National inventories of 15 European states, including an inventory for the former Czechoslovakia (Hora, Kaňuch et al. 1992) followed. In 1994 BirdLife International started a five-year project aimed at a thorough revision of the IBA inventory, which was necessitated by hundreds of newly identified areas, mainly in Eastern Europe, and extensive new data on the numbers and threats to bird species in (Collar a kol. 1994, Tucker, Heath 1994, Rose, Scott 1994, 1997, Scott, Rose 1996, Heredia a kol. 1996). The result of the project was the second pan-European IBA inventory covering 3,619 sites in 51 states or autonomous regions (Heath, Evans 2000).

This major IBA revision was preceded by a re-formulation of IBA criteria with a global validity (BirdLife International 1995). IBAs are selected based on quantitative ornithological criteria arising from the knowledge of bird population sizes and trends. These criteria ensure the selection of sites important for the international protection of bird populations and allow their comparability on national, continental and global levels.

To this end, the criteria build upon existing international legal instruments such as the EC Birds Directive, which obliges the designation of Special Protection Areas in the European Community, and the Ramsar Convention under which contracting parties must designate at least one Ramsar Site.

Twenty IBA criteria have been developed for the selection of IBAs in Europe (in detail: Heath, Evans 2000, *Zpravodaj IBA, červen 1995: 3, listopad 1995: 2–5).* These allow for the identification of IBAs, based on a site's international importance for: (1) threatened bird species, (2) congregatory bird species, (3) assemblages of restricted-range bird species, and (4) assemblages of biome-restricted species. Criteria have been developed such that, by applying different numerical thresholds, the international importance of a site for a species may be categorised at three distinct geographical levels:

1. Global importance (A criteria)

A1. Species of global conservation concern

The site regularly holds significant numbers of a globally threatened species, or other species of global conservation concern.

Under this criterion, sites are identified for those species most threatened with extinction at a global level. This includes species classified as 'Critical', 'Endangered' and 'Vulnerable', according to the most recent, universally recognised criteria for global threat status (Collar a kol. 1994, IUCN 1994, Plesník 1995), as well as those species classified as 'Conservation Dependent', 'Data Deficient' or 'Near-threatened'. These latter types of species, although not strictly globally threatened, are considered here to be of sufficient global conservation concern to merit the identification of Important Bird Areas at the global level. All of these types of species are listed in Table 2 and in *Birds to Watch 2* (Collar *et al.* 1994).

This category thus allows the identification of IBAs for 35 species in Europe (Table 2). All of these species are also species of European conservation concern (see Box 1). The regular presence of a Critical or Endangered species at a site, irrespective of its abundance at the site, is considered sufficient to propose the site as an IBA. The only such species in Europe are *Pterodroma madeira* and *Numenius tenuirostris*. The remaining 33 species have to be present at a site in 'significant' numbers for a site to qualify under this criterion. The relevant numerical threshold for each species is calculated from the size of the species' global population and also depends on whether the species has a relatively large or small body-size, and whether it has primarily dispersed or colonial nesting habits.

The words 'regular' and 'significant' in these definitions are intended to exclude instances of vagrancy, marginal occurrence, and ancient or historical records. 'Regularly' includes seasonal presence (and presence at longer intervals, if suitable conditions themselves only occur at extended intervals, e.g. at temporary wetlands). Also, sites prospective for holding endangered species (such as restored sites or localities with re-introduced species) are not excluded from this category.

A2. Restricted-range species

The site is known or thought to hold a significant component of the restricted range species whose breeding distributions define an Endemic Bird Area or Secondary Area (SA). EBA is defined as a region to which two or more restricted-range bird species are confined, with 'restricted range' defined as a world distribution of less than 50,000 km². SA supports one or more restricted-range species, but does not qualify as an EBA because only a single species is confined to it.

In Europe, there are three EBAs (Madeira and Canary Islands with nine restricted-range species, Caucasus with three such species and Cyprus with two such species) and three Secondary Areas (Corsican mountains, Azores, and Caledonian pine forest in Scotland).

A3. Biome-restricted assemblages

The site is known or thought to hold a significant component of the group of species whose distributions are largely or wholly confined to one biome.

Five biomes have been treated under this criterion in Europe: the Arctic/tundra biome (32 species), the boreal biome (15 species), the Mediterranean biome (21 species), the Eurasian high-montane biome (10 species) and the Eurasian steppe biome (9 species).

A4. Congregations

(i) The site is known or thought to hold, on regular basis, 1% or more of a biogeographic population of a congregatory waterbird species.

(ii) The site is known or thought to hold, on regular basis, 1% or more of the global population of a congregatory seabird or terrestrial species.

(iii) The site is known or thought to hold, on regular basis, at least 20,000 waterbird, or at least 10,000 of seabird of one or more species.

(iv) The site is known or thought to be a 'bottleneck site' where at least 20,000 storks (Ciconiidae), raptors (Accipitriformes and Falconiformes) or cranes (Gruidae) pass regularly during spring or autumn migration.

This category was applied to those species that are vulnerable, at the population level, to the destruction or degradation of sites, by virtue of their congregatory behaviour when breeding, wintering or on passage. A total of 160 species were treated when applying these criteria in Europe. A few species of waterbird and raptor that are not considered to be congregatory (in Europe), or which have small, marginal populations in Europe, are not treated under this criteria category. This category embraces sites over which flying migrants concentrate, e.g. at narrow sea-crossings, along mountain ranges or through mountain passes. Although it is the airspace here that is important, conservation of the land beneath may be necessary to protect the site and its birds from threats such as shooting and the construction of lethal obstacles such as power-lines and high radio-masts. Also included are migratory stop-overs and nocturnal roosts which may not hold large numbers at any one time but which, nevertheless, do hold such numbers over a relatively short period due to the rapid turnover of birds on passage.

2. European importance (B criteria)

B1. Congregations

(i) The site is known or thought to hold 1% or more of a flyway population or other distinct population of a waterbird species.

(ii) The site is known or thought to hold 1% or more of a distinct population of a seabird species.

(iii) The site is known or thought to hold 1% or more of a flyway population or other distinct population of a congregatory species other than a waterbird or seabird.

(iv) The site is a 'bottleneck site' where 5,000 or more storks (Ciconiidae), or 3,000 or more raptors (Accipitriformes and Falconiformes) or cranes (Gruidae) pass regularly on spring or autumn migration.

Flyway or other distinct populations in Europe have been identified by Wetlands International (Rose, Scott 1994, 1997).

B2. Species with an unfavourable conservation status in Europe

The site is one of the 'n' most important sites in a country for a species with an unfavourable conservation status in Europe (endangered, vulnerable, rare, declining, localised or insufficiently known in Europe), and for which the site-protection approach is thought to be appropriate.

SPEC 2: Species concentrated in Europe (species with more than 50% of their global population or range lying within Europe) and with an unfavourable conservation status.

SPEC 3: Species not concentrated in Europe, but with an unfavourable conservation status there.

The 'n' figure is determined by the minimum size of the national population relative to the minimum estimate of the total European population. For each country holding 1% or more of the minimum European breeding population of a given species, those sites which support 1% or more of the minimum national breeding population should be selected.

This criterion addresses the problem of identifying IBAs for species that are widely dispersed across the landscape but which are amenable to conservation through site protection, and is framed so as to limit the maximum number of qualifying sites in countries with large total populations of any species. The criterion should, however, be used with caution, for example in countries where absolute populations of a species are low (e.g. 100 pairs or less), since use of the 1% level loses meaning if a site qualifies on the basis of a single pair. Also, for countries which hold less than 1% of the European population of a given species, or for countries which comprise less than 1% of the land area of Europe (i.e. less than c.100,000 km^2), sites may still be selected under this criterion if they support similar numbers of the species as sites in other countries which meet this criterion in a standard fashion.

B3. Species with a favourable conservation status but concentrated in Europe

The site is one of the 'n' most important sites in a country for a species with a favourable conservation status in Europe but with its global range concentrated in Europe, and for which the site-protection approach is thought to be appropriate.

SPEC 4: Species with a favourable conservation status in Europe but with more than 50% of their global range lying within Europe, for which the site-protection approach is thought to be appropriate.

The principles and methods used for setting thresholds, calculating the maximum number of sites per species in each country, and applying the criteria, are the same as for the B2 criterion.

3. European Union importance (C criteria)

Seven categories of criteria have been applied for the selection of IBAs at the EU level. Several of them emulate the higher categories under the global (A) and European (B) level criteria. The C criteria categories are based on those used in the most recent inventory of IBAs in the European Community (Grimmett, Gammell 1989), introducing some additional quantitative thresholds. Full details of the development of the C criteria are presented in Osieck (2000).

C1. Species of global conservation concern

The site regularly holds significant numbers of a globally threatened species, or other species of global conservation concern.

This criterion is identical to the A1 criterion, and the same thresholds apply.

C2. Concentrations of species threatened at the European Union level

The site is known to regularly hold at least 1% of the flyway or EU population of a species considered to be threatened in the EU.

'Threatened species' refers to species, subspecies and populations listed in Annex I of the EC Birds Directive, for which Special Protection Areas (SPAs) are designated under Article 4.1 of the Directive. The definition of 'flyway population' is the same as that given for the B1 criteria. Flyway or other distinct populations in waterbirds are defined according to the standards of Wetlands International (Rose, Scott 1994, 1997). Thresholds for flyway populations can be used for various seasons. For a small number of species where the European breeding population is significantly larger than the EU breeding population, lower numerical thresholds have been set. The thresholds were also revised when populations of EU candidate countries were included. No other bird other than the Corncrake (45 pairs) meets the thresholds in the Czech Republic.

C3. Migratory non-threatened species

The site is known to regularly hold at least 1% of a flyway population of a migratory species that is not considered threatened in the EU.

'Migratory species not considered threatened' refer to species considered under Article 4.2 of the Birds Directive (i.e. regularly occurring migratory species not listed in Annex I). 'Migration' is defined as seasonal long-distance movements to and from breeding areas. A more exact legal definition of a migratory species can be found in the Bonn Convention: *"The entire population or any geographically separate part of the population of any species or lower taxon of wild animals, a significant proportion of whose members cyclically and predictably cross one or more national jurisdictional boundaries."* The word 'migratory' therefore excludes populations which are largely sedentary or short-distance dispersive (e.g. *Larus argentatus* and *Cepphus grylle* in Western Europe, or *Cygnus olor* in the Czech Republic) as those species are not implicated in the context of Article 4.2 of the Birds Directive. This criterion covers wetlands of international importance (Ramsar Sites) identified under Ramsar criteria category 6, to which reference is made in Article 4.2 of the Birds Directive. Wetlands of international importance uniquely qualifying for waterbirds listed in Annex I of the Birds Directive are covered by IBA criterion C2. The definition of 'flyway population' is the same as that given for the B1 criteria. Lower numerical thresholds (than those used for B1 criteria) have not been set.

C4. Large congregations

The site is known to regularly hold at least 20,000 migratory waterbirds, or at least 10,000 pairs of migratory seabird, of one or more species.

This criterion is the same as the A4iii criterion and is used for the same species. It covers all wetlands of international importance identified under Ramsar criteria category 5. This category is used for species that are vulnerable because they concentrate at valuable or sensitive localities when breeding, wintering or on passage.

C5. Large congregations – bottleneck sites

The site is a 'bottleneck' site where at least 5,000 storks (Ciconiidae), or at least 3,000 migratory raptors (Accipitriformes and Falconiformes) or cranes (Gruidae), regularly pass on spring or autumn migration.

This criterion is the same as the B1iv criterion. As most of the species concerned are listed in Annex I of the Birds Directive, this criterion refers mainly to sites important in the context of Article 4.1.

C6. Species threatened at the European Union level

The site is one of the five most important in the European region in question for a species or subspecies considered threatened in the European Union.

'Threatened species' refers to species, subspecies and populations listed in Annex I of the EC Birds Directive. 'European region' refers to what are known as NUTS regions (Appendix 5). The Nomenclature of Territorial Units for Statistics (NUTS) was established by Eurostat-the EC Statistical Office-to provide a single uniform breakdown of approximately equal territorial units for the production of regional statistics for the European Union. Although the NUTS has no legal value *per se*, it has been used since 1988 in Community legislation.

In general, up to five sites per NUTS region may be identified for a species. However, in exceptional cases, there may be grounds for increasing the number of sites per NUTS region to slightly more than five. Sometimes the identification of five sites for a given species is not possible or practical. This applies especially to species with small populations, dispersed species or species with limited range only.

If two or more sites in a given region hold the same number of pairs or individuals of a particular taxon, the relative priority of the sites for selection as IBAs is ranked according to the overall number of threatened (Annex I) species that occurs at each site. The C6 criterion has generally been applied to breeding populations, but may also be applied for non-breeding occurrences if these are not covered well by other criteria in the country concerned. The rationale of the criterion, overall, is to achieve a wide geographical coverage of sites throughout the species' range in the European Union.

The ruling of the European Court of Justice requires that SPAs are designed for all Annex I species: "...*each Member State has to designate such areas for all Annex I species occurring on its territory.*" Although this wording does not exclude vagrants and accidental occurrence, only areas for species with regular and predictable presence can be designed. Thus the best approach is to start with completing a list of Annex I species suiting this condition.

Sites meeting C6 should hold appreciable numbers (appreciable at the EU level) of the species or subspecies concerned. This additional condition is necessary to exclude irregular occurrences and sites holding a low number of birds (1% of the regional breeding population or 0.1% of the biogeographical population are suggested as minimum levels), although different countries have adopted different approaches in their definition of 'appreciable'. Sites holding non-viable populations of any species (e.g. one pair) should not be selected.

C7. Other ornithological criteria

A site which has been designated as a Special Protection Area (SPA), or has been selected as a candidate SPA, based on ornithological criteria (similar to, but not equal to, C1–C6) in recognised use for identifying SPAs .

Application of this criterion is confined to designated SPAs, and to sites which have been selected as SPAs in the framework of a national inventory which has been used by government agencies as such (although not necessarily officially accepted). This criterion should be applied only to a minority of exceptional cases where it would be inadvisable to exclude the sites concerned from the IBA inventory. This criterion is not applicable in EU candidate countries.

How do the IBA criteria relate to the identification of SPAs?

As the Birds and Habitats Directives are the most important international legal instruments for site protection in the European Union, all sites which qualify under Article 4 of the Birds Directive should be listed as IBAs.

Article 4 requires that:

"*The species mentioned in Annex I shall be the subject of special conservation measures concerning their habitat in order to ensure their survival and reproduction in their area of distribution.*"

"*Member States shall classify in particular the most suitable territories in number and size as special protection areas for the conservation of these species, taking into account their protection requirements in the geographical sea and land area where this Directive applies.*" (C1, C2, C5 and C6).

"*Member States shall take similar measures for regularly occurring migratory species not listed in Annex I, bearing in mind their need for protection in the geographical sea and land area where this Directive applies, as regards their breeding, moulting and wintering areas and staging posts along their migration routes.*" (C3, C4 and C5).

All potential Special Protection Areas (SPAs) should meet at least one of the criteria of the IBA criteria category C. Although the IBAs selected based on these criteria cannot be considered an official list of potential SPAs, the IBA inventory can be recognised as the best scientific reference for identifying SPAs. This was confirmed in a ruling by the European Court of Justice against the government of the Netherlands in 1988. From the viewpoint of BirdLife International, it is possible to say that IBAs qualifying under one of the C criteria should be also designed as SPAs so that the requirements of the Birds Directive are fulfilled. When selecting IBAs in European countries outside the EU, the following species, which are SPEC but are not listed in the Annex I of the Birds Directive, were not considered:

1. Slavonian Grebe *(Podiceps auritus)*
2. Little Egret *(Egretta garzetta)*
3. Great White Egret *(Egretta alba)*
4. Bewick's Swan *(Cygnus columbianus bewickii)*
5. Whooper Swan *(Cygnus cygnus)*
6. Marsh Harrier *(Circus aeruginosus)*
7. Merlin *(Falco columbarius)*
8. Capercaillie *(Tetrao urogallus)*
9. Hazel Grouse *(Bonasa bonasia)*
10. Black-winged Stilt *(Himantopus himantopus)*
11. Avocet *(Recurvirostra avosetta)*
12. Dotterel *(Charadrius morinellus)*
13. Common Tern *(Sterna hirundo)*
14. Arctic Tern *(Sterna paradisea)*
15. Pygmy Owl *(Glaucidium passerinum)*
16. Tengmalm's Owl *(Aegolius funereus)*
17. Black Woodpecker *(Dryocopus martius)*
18. White-backed Woodpecker *(Dendrocopos leucotos)*
19. Bluethroat *(Luscinia svecica)*
20. Moustached Warbler *(Acrocephalus melanopogon)*
21. Red-breasted Flycatcher *(Ficedula parva)*

Criteria used for the selection of Important Bird Areas in the Czech Republic

A1. Species of global conservation concern

Of the 35 species, for which this criterion is used in Europe, 21 are named in the list of bird species of the Czech Republic (Table 7), but the condition of "regularly holding significant numbers" is met only for the White-tailed Eagle *(Haliaeetus albicilla)* and the Corncrake *(Crex crex)*. Two sites fulfil the criteria in the case of the White-tailed Eagle (5 breeding pairs or 15 wintering birds) – Třeboňsko (for both breeding and wintering) and the Nové Mlýny middle reservoir (wintering). There are more than a dozen sites with 20 calling male Corncrakes, (which is the threshold for the species). It was assumed that the strict use of the threshold would not make any sense in Central Europe (also considering the situation in Poland or Russia, where hundreds of sites would qualify). Thus a stricter criterion, at least 40 calling males, was used. Four sites met such a threshold – Krkonoše mountains, Doupov hills, Šumava mountains, Beskydy mountains and Jeseníky mountains. Recent data show that two more sites fulfil this criterion for the Corncrake – the Libavá military training area and the region of Králický Sněžník.

A4. Congregations

(i) Regular congregation of 1% or more of a biogeographic population of a congregatory waterbird species.

(iii) Regular congregation of at least 20,000 waterbird, or at least 10,000 of seabird of one or more species.

This category is of a limited use in the Czech Republic. Only the Bean Goose *(Anser fabalis)*, Greylag Goose *(Anser anser)*, White-fronted Goose *(Anser albifrons)* and Gadwall *(Anas strepera)* reach the IBA A4i designation thresholds of 3,800, 3,500, 12,800 and 1,300, respectively. The Nové Mlýny middle reservoir meets the thresholds for all three goose species, Třeboňsko satisfies the thresholds for the Greylag Goose and Gadwall. As for the criterion A4iii, it is again met by the Nové Mlýny middle reservoir, Poodří and, recently only irregularly, by Třeboňsko.

B1. Congregations

(i) Regular congregation of 1% or more of a flyway population or other distinct population of a waterbird species.

The only species in the Czech Republic regularly fulfilling at several sites the thresholds for IBA designation (Table 8) is the Greylag Goose *(Anser anser),* with the minimum of 200 birds. The Řežabinec pond, Dehtář pond and Lednické rybníky ponds were selected under this criterion.

B2. Species with an unfavourable conservation status in Europe

The Czech Republic, as a small country, had the option to use the threshold of 0.5% (species with a minimal national population at least 0.5% of the minimal European population) rather than the 1% threshold (Table 9). The following species were not considered when selecting IBAs: the Kestrel *(Falco tinnunculus),* the Turtle Dove *(Streptopelia turtur),* the Skylark *(Alauda arvensis),* and the Swallow *(Hirundo rustica).* Based on this criterion, five sites were designated in the Czech Republic: Žehuňský rybník pond, Křivoklátsko, Pálava, the Confluence of the Morava and Dyje rivers, and Heřmanský stav pond-Stružka wetlands. Apart from Dehtář pond, all Czech IBAs selected in higher categories (A1, A4, B2) meet this criterion as well.

B3. Species with a favourable conservation status but concentrated in Europe (i.e. species with more than 50% of their global population or range lying within Europe)

No IBA was selected in the Czech Republic based solely on this criterion and selected species (Table 10) were used additionally to support the importance of a higher category.

Criteria Species

Table 7. **Numerical thresholds for species of global conservation concern in Europe. List of birds found in the Czech Republic with thresholds for IBA category A1. (According to Heath & Evans 2000)**

Species	Global threat status	Threshold (pairs)
Pygmy Cormorant *(Phalacrocorax pygmeus)*	NT	10
Lesser White-fronted Goose *(Anser erythropus)*	VU	5
Red-breasted Goose *(Branta ruficollis)*	VU	60[2]
Marbled Teal *(Marmaronetta angustirostris)*	VU	5
Ferruginous Duck *(Aythya nyroca)*	VU	20
White-headed Duck *(Oxyura leucocephala)*	VU	5
White-tailed Eagle *(Haliaeetus albicilla)*	NT	5
Cinereous Vulture *(Aegypius monachus)*	NT	5
Pallid Harrier *(Circus macrourus)*[1]	NT	10
Greater Spotted Eagle *(Aquila clanga)*[1]	VU	2
Imperial Eagle *(Aquila heliaca)*	VU	2
Lesser Kestrel *(Falco naumanni)*	VU	10
Corncrake *(Crex crex)*	VU	20
Little Bustard *(Tetrax tetrax)*	NT	60[2]
Great Bustard *(Otis tarda)*	VU	30[2]
Black-winged Pratincole *(Glareola nordmanni)*[1]	NT	10
Sociable Plover *(Chettusia gregaria)*[2]	VU	10
Great Snipe *(Gallinago media)*	NT	20
Slender-billed Curlew *(Numenius tenuirostris)*	CR	P
Audouin's Gull *(Larus audouinii)*	CD	20
Aquatic Warbler *(Acrocephalus paludicola)*	VU	10

[1]   *not a species of Annex I of the Birds Directive*
[2]   *number of individuals, all other figures in pairs – to convert between pairs and individuals, the figure has to be multiplied by 3*
R   *regular presence of the species irrespective of its abundance is sufficient for a site to qualify under this criterion*
CR   *Critical*
VU   *Vulnerable*
CD   *Conservation Dependent*
NT   *Near Threatened*

Table 8. Numerical thresholds for selected congregatory species. List of birds found in the Czech Republic with thresholds for IBA categories A4 and B1. (According to Heath & Evans 2000)

Species	Population	A4	B1
Little Grebe *(Tachybaptus ruficollis)*		1,000	
	Western Palearctic		1,000
Black-necked Grebe *(Podiceps nigricollis)*		1,000	
	Western Palearctic		1,000
Cormorant *(Phalacrocorax carbo)*		4,200	
	N Europe/Central Europe		2,000
Night Heron *(Nycticorax nycticorax)*		1,500	
	Europe/NW Africa (B)		1,500
Great White Egret *(Egretta alba)*		120	
Grey Heron *(Ardea cinerea)*		4,500	
	N Europe (B)		4,500
Black Stork *(Ciconia nigra)*		210	
	Central/E Europe (B)		200
White Stork *(Ciconia ciconia)*		4,850	
	Central/E Europe (B)		4,000
Mute Swan *(Cygnus olor)*		2,900	
	NM Mainland and Central Europe		2,100
Bean Goose *(Anser fabalis)*		3,800	
	W Siberia/NE & NW Europe		800
	W & Central Siberia/NE & SW Europe		3,000
White-fronted Goose *(Anser albifrons)*		12,800	
	Central Europe/W Siberia		1,000
Greylag Goose *(Anser anser)*		3,500	
	Central Europe/N Africa		200
Gadwall *(Anas strepera)*		1,300	
	NW Europe		300
	NE Europe/Black Sea/Med		1,000
Teal *(Anas crecca)*		14,000	
	NW Europe		4,000
	W Siberia/NE Europe/Black Sea/Med		10,500
Mallard *(Anas platyrhynchos)*		83,000	
	NW Europe		50,000
Garganey *(Anas querquedula)*		20,000	
	W Siberia/Europe/W Africa		20,000
Shoveler *(Anas clypeata)*		4,900	
	NW Europe/Central Europe		400
Red-crested Pochard *(Netta rufina)*		750	
	SW/Central Europe & W Med		250

Species	Population	A4	B1
Pochard *(Aythya ferina)*		13,500	
	Central & NE Europe/ Black Sea/Med (W)		10,000
Tufted Duck *(Aythya fuligula)*		16,000	
	Central Europe/Black Sea/Med		6,000
Goldeneye *(Bucephala clangula)*		4,200	
	NW Europe/Central Europe		3,000
Smew *(Mergus albellus)*		900	
	NW Europe/Central Europe		250
Goosander *(Mergus merganser)*		2,200	
	NW Europe/Central Europe		2,000
	Central Europe (B))		30
Corncrake *(Crex crex)*		45p	45p
Coot *(Fulica atra)*		40,000	
	NW Europe (W)		15,000
Crane *(Grus grus)*		1,550	
	NE Europe/Central Europe (B)		600
Little Ringed Plover *(Charadrius dubius)*		3,200	
	Europe/W Africa		3,200
Lapwing *(Vanellus vanellus)*		70,000	
	Europe/W Africa		70,000
Spotted Redshank *(Tringa erythropus)*		720	
	Europe/W Africa		720
Black-headed Gull *(Larus ridibundus)*		65,000	
	NW Europe (B)		60,000
Common Tern *(Sterna hirundo)*		7,800	
	S Europe/W Europe (B)		1,800
	N Europe/E Europe (B)		6,000
Black Tern *(Chlidonias niger)*		1,700	
	Europe/Asia (B)		1,700
Bee-eater *(Merops apiaster)*		40,000	13,000
Sand Martin *(Riparia riparia)*		120,000	60,000

(B) – breeding, (W) – wintering

Table 9. **List of SPEC 2 and SPEC 3 species, whose Czech national population exceeds 0.5% of their total European population**

Species	A	B
Night Heron *(Nycticorax nycticorax)*	0.6	3
Black Stork *(Ciconia nigra)*	3.1	2
White Stork *(Ciconia ciconia)*	0.5	6
Gadwall *(Anas strepera)*[1]	2.0	15
Red-crested Pochard *(Netta rufina)*[1]	1.5	2
Kestrel *(Falco tinnunculus)*[1]	3.1	90
Saker *(Falco cherrug)*[2]	2.0	0
Turtle Dove *(Streptopelia turtur)*[1]	2.2	600
Eagle Owl *(Bubo bubo)*	5.3	6
Kingfisher *(Alcedo atthis)*	0.7	3
Wryneck *(Jynx torquilla)*[1]	0.7	25
Grey-headed Woodpecker *(Picus canus)*	4.2	30
Green Woodpecker *(Picus viridis)*[1]	2.6	90
Three-toed Woodpecker *(Picoides tridactylus)*	0.6	3
Skylark *(Alauda arvensis)*[1]	2.1	8,000
Sand Martin *(Riparia riparia)*[1]	0.6	800
Swallow *(Hirundo rustica)*[1]	3.0	4,000
Radstart *(Phoenicurus phoenicurus)*[1]	2.0	300
Red-backed Shrike *(Lanius collurio)*	1.1	250

[1] *Not a species of Annex I of the Birds Directive*
[2] *Species proposed for inclusion Annex I of the Birds Directive*
A *Proportion of the Czech national population on the total Eurpean population (%)*
B *1% of national population (in pairs)*

Table 10. **List of selected SPEC 4 species, whose Czech national population exceeds 0.5% of their total European population**

Species	A	B
Honey Buzzard *(Pernis apivorus)*	0.6	6
Stock Dove *(Columba oenas)*[1]	0.6	30
Middle Spotted Woodpecker *(Dendrocopos medius)*	1.9	10
Ring Ouzel *(Turdus torquatus)*[1]	0.8	15
Barred Warbler *(Sylvia nisoria)*	0.7	15
Collared Flycatcher *(Ficedula albicollis)*	7.3	250

[1] *Not a species of Annex I of the Birds Directive*
A *Proportion of the Czech national population on the total Eurpean population (%)*
B *1% of national population (in pairs)*

Table 11. The European Union level IBA criteria for selected species regularly occurring in the Czech Republic

Species	C1	C2	C3	C4	C5	C6
Cormorant *(Phalacrocorax carbo sinensis)*	–	–		W	–	–
NW Europe			1,200			
N/Central Europe			2,000			
Black Sea/Med	–	–	1,000			
Bittern *(Botaurus stellaris)*	–	15p	–	W	–	*
Little Bittern *(Ixobrychus minutus)*	–	55p	–	W	–	*
Night Heron *(Nycticorax nycticorax)*	–	270p	–	W	–	*
Purple Heron *(Ardea purpurea)*	–	50p	–	W	–	*
Little Egret *(Egretta garzetta)*	–	1,000	–	W	–	*
Great White Egret *(Egretta alba)*	–	120	–	W	–	*
Black Stork *(Ciconia nigra)*	–	200	–	W	*	*
White Stork *(Ciconia ciconia)*	–	4,000	–	W	*	*
Spoonbill *(Platalea leucorodia)*	–	100	–	W	–	*
Bean Goose *(Anser fabalis)*	–	–	3,000	W	–	–
White-fronted Goose *(Anser albifrons)*	–	–	1,000	W	–	–
Greylag Goose *(Anser anser)*	–	–	200	W	–	–
Gadwall *(Anas strepera)*	–	–	300	W	–	–
Shoveler *(Anas clypeata)*	–	–	400	W	–	–
Red-crested Pochard *(Netta rufina)*	–	–	250	W	–	–
Ferruginous Duck *(Aythya nyroca)*	20p	–	–	W	–	*
Pochard *(Aythya ferina)*	–	–	10,000	W	–	–
Tufted Duck *(Aythya fuligula)*	–	–	6,000	W	–	–
Spotted Crake *(Porzana porzana)*	–	100p	–	W	–	*
Honey Buzzard *(Pernis apivorus)*	–	–	–	–	*	*
Black Kite *(Milvus migrans)*	–	200p	–	–	*	*
Red Kite *(Milvus milvus)*	–	220p	–	–	*	*
White-tailed Eagle *(Haliaeetus albicilla)*	5p	–	–	–	*	*
Marsh Harrier *(Circus aeruginosus)*	–	–	–	–	*	*
Hen Harrier *(Circus cyaneus)*	–	–	–	–	*	*
Montagu's Harrier *(Circus pygargus)*	–	–	–	–	*	*
Lesser Spotted Eagle *(Aquila pomarina)*	–	–	–	–	*	*
Imperial Eagle *(Aquila heliaca)*	2p	–	–	–	*	*
Peregrine Falcon *(Falco peregrinus)*	–	–	–	–	*	*
Hazel Hen *(Bonasa bonasia)*	–	–	–	–	–	*
Black Grouse *(Tetrao tetrix)*	–	–	–	–	–	*
Capercaillie *(Tetrao urogallus)*	–	–	–	–	–	*
Spotted Crake *(Porzana porzana)*	–	100p	–	W	–	*
Little Crake *(Porzana parva)*	–	55p	–	W	–	*
Corncrake *(Crex crex)*	20p	45p	–	W	–	*
Coot *(Fulica atra)*	–	–	15,000	W	–	–
Crane *(Grus grus)*	–	600	–	W	*	*
Lapwing *(Vanellus vanellus)*	–	–	70,000	W	–	–
Mediterranean Gull *(Larus melanocephalus)*	–	45p	–	W	–	*
Black-headed Gull *(Larus ridibundus)*	–	–	60,000	W	–	–
Common Tern *(Sterna hirundo)*	–	–	6,000	W	–	*
Black Tern *(Chlidonias niger)*	–	40p	–	W	–	*

Species	C1	C2	C3	C4	C5	C6
Eagle Owl *(Bubo bubo)*	–	–	–	–	–	*
Pygmy Owl *(Glaucidium passerinum)*	–	–	–	–	–	*
Ural Owl *(Strix uralensis)*	–	–	–	–	–	*
Short-eared Owl *(Asio flammeus)*	–	–	–	–	–	*
Tengmalm's Owl *(Aegolius funereus)*	–	–	–	–	–	*
Nightjar *(Caprimulgus europaeus)*	–	–	–	–	–	*
Kingfisher *(Alcedo atthis)*	–	–	–	–	–	*
Grey-headed Woodpecker *(Picus canus)*	–	–	–	–	–	*
Black Woodpecker *(Dryocopus martius)*	–	–	–	–	–	*
Syrian Woodpecker *(Dendrocopos syriacus)*	–	–	–	–	–	*
Middle Spotted Woodpecker *(Dendrocopos medius)*	–	–	–	–	–	*
White-backed Woodpecker *(Dendrocopos leucotos)*	–	–	–	–	–	*
Three-toed Woodpecker *(Picoides tridactylus)*	–	–	–	–	–	*
Woodlark *(Lullula arborea)*	–	–	–	–	–	*
Tawny Pipit *(Anthus campestris)*	–	–	–	–	–	*
Bluethroat *(Luscinia svecica)*	–	–	–	–	–	*
Barred Warbler *(Sylvia nisoria)*	–	–	–	–	–	*
Red-breasted Flycatcher *(Ficedula parva)*	–	–	–	–	–	*
Collared Flycatcher *(Ficedula albicollis)*	–	–	–	–	–	*
Red-backed Shrike *(Lanius collurio)*	–	–	–	–	–	*
Ortolan Bunting *(Emberiza hortulana)*	–	–	–	–	–	*

*p – pairs, W – winter, * – yes*

Comments on Data Processing

Petra Málková, David Lacina

The format of data presentation is based on the form used in the European inventory (Heath, Evans 2000). Revised data was used with updates from 1996–2000. New important sources were added to the list of references as well. Table 12 gives the overview of all current 16 Czech IBAs, while Tables 13 and 14 list authors of texts and photographs for each area chapter.

Table 12. Important Bird Areas in the Czech Republic

Cod	Code 1992	Name	Categori	Area (ha)	Protection
001	001	Krkonoše montains	A1, B2, B3	54,800	NP, BR, RS
002	008	Žehuňský rybník pond	B2	1,639	NNR
003	-	Křivoklátsko	B2, B3	69,792	PLA, BR
004	-	Doupov hills	A1, B2, B3	60,000	partial – SSPA
005	002	Šumava mountains	A1, B2, B3	163,000	NP, PLA, BR, RS
006	005	Řežabinec pond	B1i, B2	111	NNR
007	004	Dehtář pond	B1i	260	partial – TPA
008	003	Třeboňsko	A1, A4i, B1i, B2, B3	70,000	PLA, BR, RS
009	014	Nové Mlýny middle reservoir	A1, A4i, A4iii, B1i, B2	1,080	PR, RS
010	009	Pálava	B2, B3	8,300	PLA, BR
011	012	Lednické rybníky ponds	B1i, B2, B3	653	NNR, Rs
012	010	Confluence of the Morava and Dyje rivers	B2, B3	5,000	partial – SSPA, RS
013	017	Beskydy mountains	A1, B2, B3	116,000	PLA
014	016	Poodří	A4iii, B2, B3	8,150	PLA, RS
015	-	Heřmanský stav pond-Stružka wetlands	B2	3,000	partial – SSPA
016	018	Jeseníky mountains	A1, B2, B3	74,391	PLA

Code – international IBA code, **Code 1992** – code as used in the previous inventory for Czechoslovakia (Hora, Kaňuch et al. 1992); **Protection: NP** – National Park, **PLA** – Protected Landscape Area, **BR** – Biosphere Reserve, **RS** – Wetland of International Importance (Ramsar Site), **SSPA** – Small-scale Protected Area, **TPA** – Temporary Protected Area

Table 13. Authors of texts

Code	Important Bird Area	Authors of texts
001	Krkonoše	Flousek J.
002	Žehuňský rybník	Urbánek L.
003	Křivoklátsko	Tichai M., Nedozrálová E., Pochová Š.
004	Doupovské hory	Tejrovský V.
005	Šumava	Pykal J., Kloubec B.
006	Řežabinec	Pecl K.
007	Dehtář	Kloubec B., Pykal J.
008	Třeboňsko	Bureš J., Ševčík J.
009	Střední nádrž	Chytil J.
010	Pálava	Chytil J.
011	Lednické rybníky	Macháček P.
012	Soutok	Horal D., Horák P.
013	Beskydy	Pavelka J.
014	Poodří	Pavelka K.
015	Heřmanský stav-Stružka	Polášek Z.
016	Jeseníky	Baláž P.

Table 14. Authors of photographs

Code	Important Bird Area	Authors of photographs
001	Krkonoše mountains	Hník K. (1–5,7), Hlásek J. (6)
002	Žehuňský rybník pond	Urbánek L. (1,2), Ševčík J. (3)
003	Křivoklátsko	Pochová Š. (1–3,5), Červený J. (4)
004	Doupov hills	Tejrovský V. (1–4,6), Macháček P. (5)
005	Šumava mountains	Červený J. (1–6)
006	Řežabinec pond	Pecl K. (1–4)
007	Dehtář pond	Kloubec B. (1,2), Macháček P. (3)
008	Třeboňsko	Ševčík J. (1,2,4–6), Macháček P. (3)
009	Nové Mlýny middle reservoir	Macháček P. (1–4)
010	Pálava	Macháček P. (1–6)
011	Lednické rybníky ponds	Macháček P. (1–4)
012	Confluence of the Morava and Dyje rivers	Macháček P. (1,2), Horák P. (3)
013	Beskydy mountains	Pavelka J. (1,3,5), K. (2), Formánek J. (4)
014	Poodří	Pavelka K. (1–3,5,6), Macháček P. (4)
015	Heřmanský stav pond-Stružka wetlands	Boucný L. (1), Boucný D. (2)
016	Jeseníky mountains	Boucný D. (1, 2), Baláž P. (3,5), Formánek J. (4)

Area chapters have the following structure:

Headings include the following data:
- Name of the IBA
- IBA code – new international identification code of the area as used by Heath and Evans (2000)
- Criteria used for selection of the site
- Administrative regions – list of administrative regions the site covers
- Coordinates of the centre of the area
- Area of site in hectares, percentage of the area protected
- Altitude
- Map of the Czech Republic with blue or green dots indicating the location of the area within the country (blue = sites with prevailing wetlands, green = sites with prevailing forests)
- Map of the locality – schematic with water in blue, forests in green and IBA boundaries in red.

Site description provides information about the area from the viewpoints of geomorphology, geology, history, and biology.

Protection lists all types of large and small-scale Protected Areas, Biosphere Reserves, and Wetlands of International Importance, with their dates of establishment and names as used in relevant Czech legislation.

Threats list current and potential negative factors threatening the bird populations and habitats of the IBA.

Research gives an overview of research activities with special regard to the works of local caretaker groups.

Land use gives information about the type of activities represented in the area, as a percentage of the whole IBA in the following categories: forestry, hunting, agriculture, fisheries/aquaculture, tourism/recreation, urban/industrial/transport and military.

Habitats, again as percentage of the area, are listed in the following categories: forest and woodland, scrub, grassland, wetland, rocky areas and others, categories marked with "+" are represented in less than 1% of the area.

Ornithological importance provides an overview of the area as a bird breeding site, wintering site and migration stopover and lists the most important species. IBA criteria species are presented in a table with data on numbers and the criteria used.

Flora and fauna mentions other important rare or endangered animal and plant species typical for the area.

References

The first section of references lists sources quoted in the general chapters. The following sections list sources concerning the area chapters. Some titles may thus appear in more than one section.

Figures

The following figures (Figure 1 and 2) express the importance of the IBAs in nature conservation on the national and international scale. They show an overlap of IBAs with protected areas established based on national legislation (National Park, Protected Landscape Area, National Nature Reserve or Monument, Nature Reserve or Monument) or based on international agreements (Wetland of International Importance, Biosphere Reserve). IBAs with more than 90% of their area protected are considered high protection status. Those with 10–90% of their area protected are considered partial protection status, and low protection status is given to those with less than 10% of their area protected.

The national protection status of IBAs in the Czech Republic

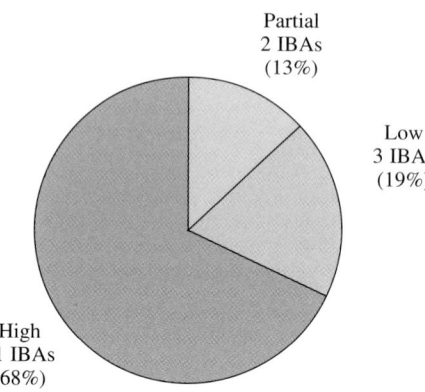

Partial
2 IBAs
(13%)

Low
3 IBAs
(19%)

High
11 IBAs
(68%)

Figure 1. Total area overlap between IBA network in the Czech Republic and national protected-area system is about 5,600 km² (89% of total IBA area).

The international protection status of IBAs in the Czech Republic

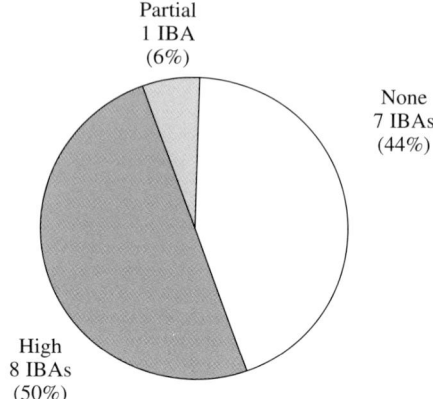

Partial
1 IBA
(6%)

None
7 IBAs
(44%)

High
8 IBAs
(50%)

Figure 2. Total area overlap between IBA network in the Czech Republic and international protected-area system is 3,750 km² (59% of total IBA area).

Habitats at IBAs in the Czech Republic

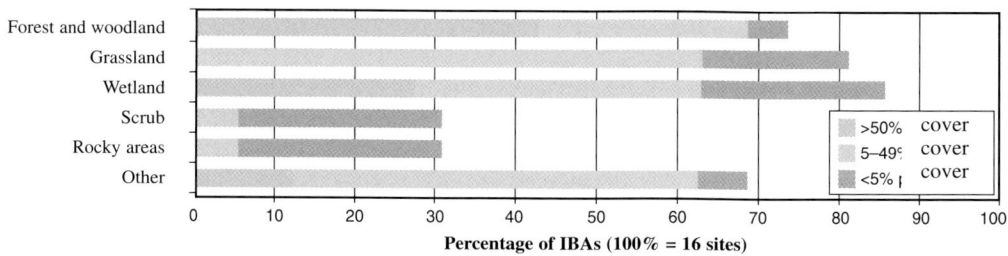

Figure 3. The prevailing types of habitats of Czech IBAs are forests, grasslands, and wetlands. Forests cover over 50% of the land area of seven Czech IBAs, and predominate in mountainous and hilly regions. Meadows and pastures are found in 13 IBAs, but they do not represent a dominant habitat type in any of them. Wetland habitats are present in the majority of Czech IBAs and four sites have wetlands covering more than 50% of their area.

Land-uses at IBAs in the Czech Republic

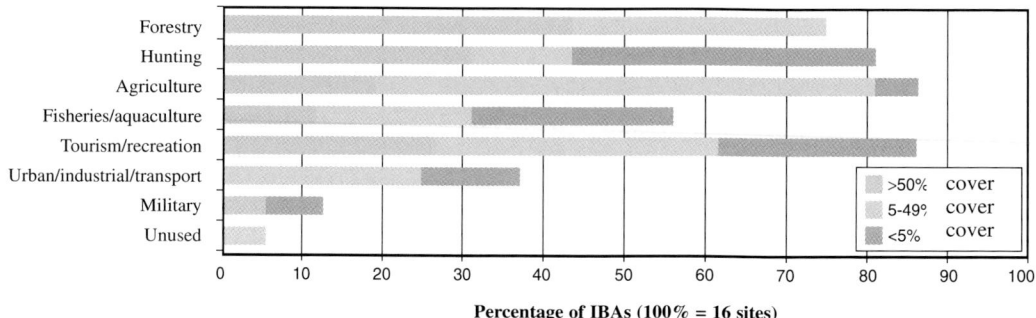

Figure 4. Forestry is the dominant land-use in mountainous regions, and together with hunting and recreation, these activities take place in more than 75% of IBAs. Thirteen IBAs support some form of agricultural activity, at three IBAs agriculture is the prevailing type of land use. Fisheries are present at 12 IBAs and form the major land-use in four of these.

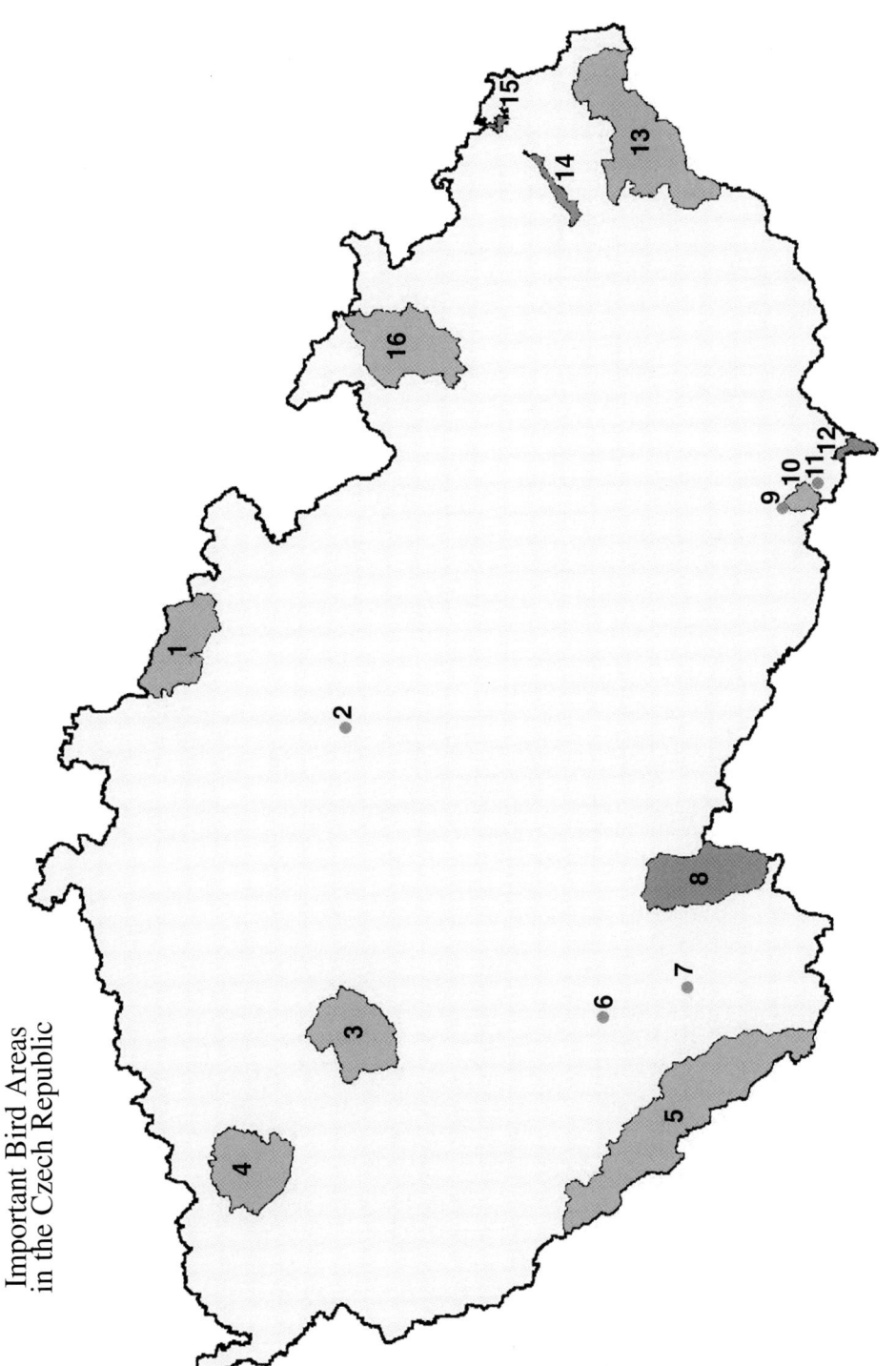

Important Bird Areas in the Czech Republic

1. Krkonoše mountains (Giant mountains), 2. Žehuňský rybník pond, 3. Křivoklátsko (Křivoklátsko region), 4. Doupov hills, 5. Šumava mountains (Bohemian forest), 6. Řežabinec pond, 7. Dehtář pond, 8. Třeboňsko (Třeboň region), 9. Nové Mlýny middle reservoir, 10. Pálava, 11. Lednické rybníky ponds (Lednice fish-ponds), 12. Confluence of the Morava (March) and Dyje (Thaya) rivers, 13. Beskydy mountains, 14. Poodří, 15. Heřmanský stav pond-Stružka wetlands, 16. Jeseníky mountains

KRKONOŠE MOUNTAINS
(GIANT MOUNTAINS)

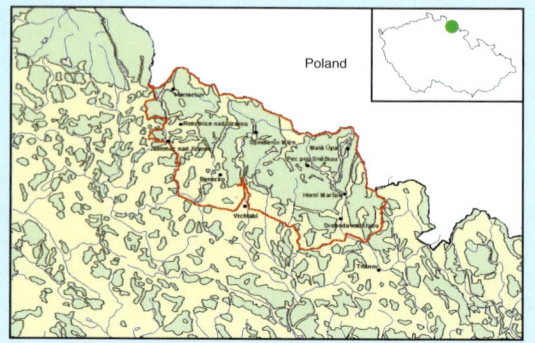

IBA code: 001
Criteria: A1, B2, B3
Administrative regions: Trutnov and Semily
Coordinates: 50°42' N 15°38' E
Area: 54,800 ha, 100% protected
Altitude: 380–1,602 m

Site description

The highest mountain range in the Czech Republic is situated in the north-eastern part of the country, sharing a border with Poland. The dominant rocks of the area are granite, gneiss, mica schist and phyllite. Brown podsolic soils are the prevailing type of soils. River headwaters and streams are present in the area, water is also present in the form of several ponds, small glacial lakes and numerous peatbogs. As for climate, the whole area belongs to the temperate region with high levels of precipitation (about 800 mm in the foothills and up to 1,400 mm at the summits) with low yearly average temperatures (between 6.1 °C in the foothills and 0.2 °C at the highest summit). The altitude range the Krkonoše mountains cover divides the area into four altitudinal vegetation belts and it is the only Czech mountain range significantly exceeding the treeline, which reaches the altitude of 1,200–1,300 m there. Dominant tree species of the broadleaved and mixed forests of the submontane belt (400–800 m) include European beech *(Fagus sylvatica)*, Sycamore *(Acer pseudoplatanus)* and Norway Spruce *(Picea abies)*. Secondary monocultures of spruce are also very common. Alders *(Alnus glutinosa)* and willows *(Salix* spp.) form an important part of vegetation surrounding watercourses. Montane belt (800–1,200 m) is covered mainly by secondary, and only to limited degree by primary spruce forests. All forests in this belt are influenced by about 30 years of air pollution fallout. This has damaged most trees at lower altitudes and killed the ones at the upper levels. Enclaves without trees with species-rich alpine meadows are very characteristic, and are there as a result of the farming practices of the 18th century. The most valuable ecosystems are concentrated in 16 km of arcto-alpine tundra in the subalpine

The mosaic of biotopes at the foot of the mountains is quite rich with human settlements, arable fields, meadows, pastures, and scattered greenery

(1,200–1,450 m) and alpine (1,450–1,602 m) belts. It contains a shrub layer dominated by Swiss mountain pine *(Pinus mugo),* virgin and secondary mat-grasslands, subarctic petbogs and species-rich azonal ecosystems of glacial cirques.

Relatively intact spruce-covered mountains host common avifauna of coniferous forests

Protection

Krkonoše National Park (36,400 ha) and its buffer zone (18,400 ha) was established in 1963. 54,800 ha of IBA covered by Biosphere Reserve (Krkonoše / Karkonosze BR) since 1992 and 210 ha covered by Ramsar Site (Krkonošská rašeliniště – Krkonoše Mountains Mires) since 1993.

Threats

Large-scale destruction of forests due to air pollution (all forests above the altitude of 900 meters are damaged to some degree) leads to changes in the composition of the fauna of the area. In the long term, forest species communities give way to the communities of open areas. The impact of tourism is not insignificant either; the mountains are visited by 6 to 8 million people each year. The area hosts about 6,000 houses (both permanently occupied and recreational), about 360 funiculars and ski-tows and about as many pistes. There are also 700 km of marked hiking paths in the area. Therefore, bird populations are influenced by a wide range of activities – from building new skiing resorts to almost permanent disturbance by tourists at attractive localities.

Research

Faunistic and inventory surveys are the basic research activities in the area. Special attention is

Wet meadows in lower parts of Krkonoše are preferred by the Corncrake

In the tundra of Krkonoše (1,500–1,550 m) the only nesting bird species include the Dotterel, Skylark, Meadow and Water Pipits, and Wheatear

Interior of a virgin spruce forest damaged by air pollution – the Wryneck nests even in such areas

given to Capercaillie *(Tetrao urogallus),* Black Grouse *(Tetrao tetrix),* Corncrake *(Crex crex),* Red - spotted Bluethroat *(Luscinia s. svecica),* birds of prey and owls. The atlas work in the whole area of both the Polish and Czech part of Krkonoše gives up-to-date information about the breeding ranges, numbers and population trends of all bird species. Other quantitative studies monitior the relationship between forests dying out due to air pollution and the composition of bird communities in variously damaged areas. Since 1911, bird ringing has been an important part of the ornithological research in the area. Such activities have focused on ringing migrating birds (the Balt action 1970–1983, night trapping since 1980) as well as local breeding populations.

Land use	
Forestry	70%
Hunting	80%
Agriculture	20%
Tourism/recreation	85%

Habitats	
Forest and woodland (broadleaved, deciduous forest, native coniferous forest, mixed forest, tree-line ecotone)	73%
Grassland (alpine, subalpine and boreal)	7%
Wetland (raised bog)	+
Other (highly improved reseeded grassland, arable land, urban and industrial areas)	20%

Ornithological importance

The most important bird communities dwell above the tree line. No significant negative trends have been recorded for these populations. Forest bird communities of similar importance are more vulnerable due to forests dying out. A total of 148 breeding species (proven, probable, and possible breeding) were recorded during a 1991–1994 regional survey in the Czech part of the national park.

Criteria species		
Black Stork	12–16 p.	B2
Honey Buzzard	3–5 p.	B3
Kestrel	110–140 p.	B2
Corncrake	> 120 males	A1
Stock Dove	90 p.	B3
Eagle Owl	8–10 p.	B2
Redstart	700 p.	B2
Ring Ouzel	240 p.	B3
Red-backed Shrike	1,200 p.	B2

Flora and fauna

Over 320 species of vertebrates were recorded in Krkonoše – among them almost 60 mammal species, 250 bird species (both nesting and migrating), six amphibian and six reptile species, two species of fish, and one species of lamprey.

Invertebrate fauna of Krkonoše includes two endemic subspecies – snail *(Cochlodina dubiosa corcontica)* and butterfly *(Torula quadrifaria sudetica)* and a range of relic species of spiders, dragonflies, beetles, two-winged flies and water mites. The flora of Krkonoše includes dozens of endemic and relic species as well. These are found especially in glacial corries, alpine and subalpine meadows, and subarctic peatbogs.

The Dotterel regularly bred in Krkonoše until 1946, after more than half a century breeding was confirmed again in 1999

Subarctic peatbogs with scattered dwarf pines host breeding populations of the Red-spotted Bluethroat, Ring Ouzel, and Redpol

ŽEHUŇSKÝ RYBNÍK POND

IBA code: 002
Criteria: B2
Administrative region: Nymburk
Coordinates: 50°10' N 15°19' E
Area: 1,639 ha, 90% protected
Altitude: 203–235 m

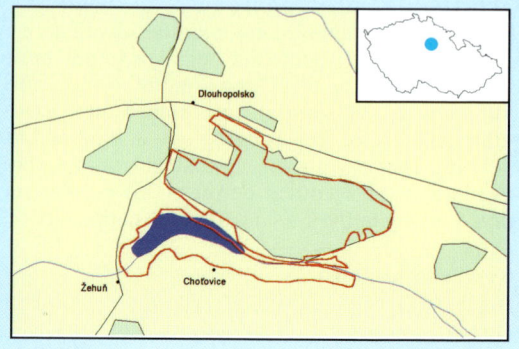

Site description

The Žehuňský rybník pond IBA covers both the pond and an adjacent game preserve. It is situated within the municipalities of Dlouhopolsko, Žehuň, Choťovice, and Zbraň in the Nymburk administrative region. The large shallow pond (258 ha) was established at the Cidlina river in 1492. There are several islets in the pond and it is surrounded by extensive reed beds.

The pond is used for the production of fish and for recreational purposes; it also serves as protection against floods. Surrounduing wet meadows, which are regularly mowed, host many species of wetland plants. One tenth of the area is covered by arable land. The game preserve, established in 1840, is used for breeding fallow deer and mouflons. In the past, wild boars were bred there as well. The preserve lies on the Cidlina river terrace of turonic age. The main tree species include oak and hornbeam with some stands of Pubescent Oak *(Quercus pubescens)* in the eastern part of the preserve which is linked to steppe slopes with vegetation typical for very dry conditions.

Protection

National Nature Reserve Žehuňský rybník pond (511 ha) established in 1948;
National Nature Reserve Žehuňská obora game preserve (928 ha) established in 1948;
Natural Monument (4.8 ha).

Threats

Intensification of managment and an increase of the fishstock in the pond limits the source of food for waterbirds and as a result, their numbers decrease. Other negative factors include the use of fertilizers in the pond and on surrounding meadows and the use of pesticides. The increase in recreational use of the pond (windsurfing, yachting) and adjacent slopes (cycling) represents a serious threat as well. Other negative factors include high stocks of game in the preserve and illegal hunting on the pond. The planned construction of a highway connecting Prague and Hradec Králové is a serious potential threat to the area. The pollution of the Cidlina river and replacement of original broad-leaved forests by conifers are examples of problems from the past that have been successfully eliminated.

Research

The caretaker group's research activities focus mainly on monitoring changes in the bird communities and their habitats. At present the caretaker group promotes specific measures, such as cutting reed beds and scrubs which cover half of the area of slopes and quickly spread around the pond. The group also wants to limit the number of vehicles

National Nature Reserve Žehuňský rybník pond

and people approaching the northern edge of the pond and to install educational tables at notable places. There are plans to enlarge the IBA so that it also covers the natural monument Báň and the Dlouhopolský rybník pond.

Land use

Forestry	60%
Hunting	55%
Agriculture	20%
Fisheries/aquaculture	15%
Tourism/recreation	5%

Habitats

Forest and woodland (broadleaved deciduous forest)	60%
Scrub	+
Grassland (dry siliceous grassland, humid grassland)	10%
Wetland (standing freshwater, river/stream, water-fringe vegetation)	20%
Artificial landscape (arable land, forestry plantation, urban parks/ gardens, other urban/industrial areas)	10%

Ornithological Importance

The area is an important nesting site of 130 bird species (1996–2000) as well as a passage site of waterbirds and raptors. During the 20th century, 248 bird species were recorded in the area. It hosts important breeding populations of the Bearded Tit *(Panurus biarmicus)*, Bittern *(Botaurus stellaris)*, Little Crake *(Porzana parva)*, and Marsh Harrier *(Circus aeruginosus)*. In the year 2000, one pair of White-tailed Sea Eagles *(Haliaetus albicilla)* nested in the area. Other migrating and breeding species of the area include the Black-throated Diver *(Gavia arctica)*, Red-throated Diver *(G. stellata)*, Great White Egret *(Egretta alba)*, Spoonbill *(Platalea leucorodia)*, Black Tern *(Chli-*

National Nature Reserve Žehuňská obora game preserve

donias niger), Whiskered Tern *(Ch. hybridus)*, Caspian Tern *(Sterna caspia)*, Bean Goose *(Anser fabalis)*, Whitefront Goose *(A. albifrons)*, Greylag Goose *(A. anser)*, Peregrine Falcon *(F. peregrinus)* and Osprey *(Pandion haliaetus)*.

Criteria species

Gadwall	14 p.	B2
Kingfiisher	3 p.	B2

Flora and fauna

Eight species of amphibians were recorded in the area – the Green Toad *(Bufo viridis)*, European Tree Frog *(Hyla arborea)*, Agile Frog *(Rana dalmatina)* and Marsh Frog *(R. ridibunda)* among them – as well as five species of reptiles, which include the Smooth Snake *(Coronella austriaca)* and Dice Snake *(Natrix tesselata)*. Rare plant species of the area include the Spring Adonis *(Adonis vernalis)*, the Branched Saint-Bernard's Lily *(Anthericum ramosum)*, the White Helleborine *(Cephalantera alba)*, the Lady Orchid *(Orchis purpurea)*, the Early Marsh Orchid *(Dactylorhiza incarnata)*, and the Lesser Butterfly Orchid *(Platanthera bifolia)*.

Gadwall

59

KŘIVOKLÁTSKO

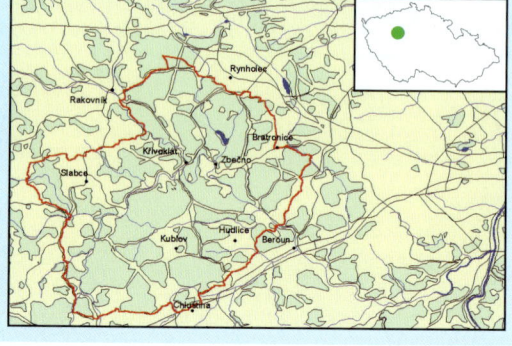

IBA code: 003
Criteria: B2, B3
Administrative region: Rakovník, Beroun, Kladno,
Rokycany, Plzeň - sever
Coordinates: 50°00' N 13°49' E
Area: 69,792 ha, 100% protected
Altitude: 223–616 m

Site description

A large area of varied topography about 30 km
west of Prague. Its axis is the Berounka river, with
its deeply carved valleys and canyons. The geology of the area is very diverse, which results in
a very diverse vegetation. Forests of various types
cover 62% of the area and they contain more than
80 species of woods. The most common tree species include the spruce (32%), pine (20%), oak
(16%), beech (9%), and larch (8%). Native beech-
oak forest is the most valuable and most abundant
type of forest in the area (56%) and it acts
as a transitional biotope between species-rich and
acidophilous communities. Limes and maples are
common in boulder and scree-woods, while the
stunted scrub stands of the Sessile Oak (*Quercus
petrea*) are typical for steep dry slopes and rocky
ridges. Xerophilous grassland communities and
various bush and herb communities of ecotones
are also considered valuable. Regularly mowed
species-rich flowering meadows are typical for the
area as well.

Protection

Protected Landscape Area Křivoklátsko (62,792
    ha) established in 1978;
Biosphere reserve Křivoklátsko (62,792 ha) since
    1977;
National Nature Reserves – 4 (775 ha) Kohou-
    tov (30.1 ha), Týřov (420.6 ha), Velká Pleš
    (95.7 ha), Vůznice (231.2 ha);
Nature reserves – 15 (395 ha)
    Brdatka (34 ha), Čertova skála (2.3 ha), Červený

*Typical oak forest – a species-rich habitat of the
Křivoklátsko Protected Landscape Area*

A view of the north-western part of the Týřov National Nature Reserve

kříž (12.6 ha), Dubensko (4.8 ha), Jezírka (59.5 ha), Jouglovka (3.4 ha), Kabečnice (25.5 ha), Lípa (24.9 ha), Na Babě (24 ha), Nezabudické skály (22.9 ha), Prameny Klíčavy (47.8 ha), Stará Ves (1.9 ha), Svatá Alžběta (8.1 ha), Stříbrný luh (106.6 ha), U Eremita (7.8 ha), Vysoký Tok (8.8 ha);
Natural Monuments – 4 (10 ha)
Valachov (3 ha), Vraní skála (2.6 ha), Trubínský vrch (3.9 ha), Zdická skalka u Kublova (0.6 ha).

Threats

Intensive farming and forestry as well as an increase in tourism and recreation (camping, water sports, weekend-house building) and connected increase in transport through the area represent the biggest threats to it. Water is still polluted in many municipalities due to the absence of sewage treatment. High stocks of deer cause damage to the woods.

Research

The caretaker group works mainly in the central and north-western parts of the area and their main tasks include the inventory of species in reserves, and the monitoring of woodpeckers and wintering birds on the Berounka river. Kingfisher *(Alcedo atthis)* and Dipper *(Cinclus cinclus)* counts are carried out in the area and potential nest sites of these two species are being adjusted. The caretaker group started a program focusing on the return of the Sand Martin *(Riparia riparia)*. Plans to establish two new nature reserves are being prepared.

Land use	
Forestry	60%
Hunting	+
Agriculture	30%
Fisheries/aquaculture	1%
Tourism/recreation	20%
Urban/industrial/transport	5%

Habitats	
Forest and woodland (broadleaved deciduous forest, native coniferous forest, mixed forest)	62%
Scrub	2%
Grassland (dry siliceous grassland, humid grassland, mesophile grassland)	5%
Wetland (standing freshwater, river/stream)	2%
Rocky areas	1%
Artificial landscape (highly improved reseeded grassland, arable land, perennial crops/orchards/groves, urban parks/gardens, other urban/industrial areas)	28%

Ornithological Importance

The area is important for birds of broadleaved deciduous forests, namely raptors. More than 120 breeding bird species were recorded over the past century. The hoopoe *(Upupa epops)* and the Sand Martin *(Riparia riparia)* disappeared from the area in the 1990's.

Criteria species		
Black Stork	6–12 p.	B2
Honey Buzzard	10–15 p.	B3
Kestrel	100–200 p.	B2
Stock Dove	80 p.	B3
Woodpigeon	1,300–2,600 p.	B3
Turtle Dove	600–1,200 p.	B2
Eagle Owl	15–30 p.	B2
Tawny Owl	80–120 p.	B3
Kingfisher	20–30 p.	B2
Wryneck	50–100 p.	B2
Grey-headed Woodpecker	60–120 p.	B2
Green Woodpecker	200–400 p.	B2
Middle Spotted Woodpecker	100–200 p.	B3
Skylark	8,000 p.	B2
Swallow	8,000 p.	B2
Redstart	1,000–1,500 p.	B2
Grasshopper Warbler	900–1,800 p.	B3
River Warbler	200–400 p.	B3
Barred Warbler	40–100 p.	B3
Collared Flycatcher	4,000–8,000 p.	B3
Red-backed Shrike	500–1,000 p.	B2

The ruins of the Týřov castle in the reserve of the same name

Eagle Owl

Flora and fauna

The fauna of Křivoklátsko is typical for warm woodlands. It includes many orders of invertebrates – molluscs, spiders, and butterflies are the best-surveyed groups. The Lady Bird Spider *(Eresus niger)* and two species of the genus *Atypus* are found in steppe localities. Two species of crayfish are found in Křivoklátsko – *Astacus torrentium* inhabits the cleanest streams of the area, while *A. fluviatilis* is also found in many other places, ponds included. Various beetles and butterflies are abundant in the area as well. Stag Beetle *(Lucanus cervus)* and Great Capricorn Beefle *(Cerambyx cerdo)* are comparatively common there. The Swallowtail *(Papilio machaon)*, Scarce Swallowtail *(Iphiclides podalirius)*, and Large Blue Butterfly *(Maculinea arion)* are typical butterfly species found in Křivoklátsko. The vertebrates are represented by the Brook Lamprey *(Lampetra planeri)*; the River Trout *(Salmo trutta m. fario)*, Bullhead *(Cottus gobio)*, and Minnow *(Phoxinus phoxinus)* can be found in the clean side streams of the Berounka river. The main amphibian species of the area are the Great Crested Newt *(Triturus cristatus)*, Alpine Newt *(T. alpestris)*, the Agile Frog *(Rana dalmatina)*, and the Yellow-bellied Toad *(Bombina variegata)*. Sunny slopes

The Berounka river valley

offer ideal conditions for reptiles. A typical species of the area is the rare Green Lizard *(Lacerta viridis)*. The Dice Snake *(Natrix tessellata)* feeds on small fish in the Berounka river. Red Deer *(Cervus elaphus)* and Wild Boar *(Sus scropha)* are two very common native species of large mammals of the area, while the Fallow Deer *(Dama dama)* and Mouflon *(Ovis musimon)* were introduced there. Small mammals are represented by common species of rodents and insectivores. From the botanical point of view, the communities of regularly mowed grasslands and termophilous grasslands are the most species-rich. At localities that are not easily accessible, flowering meadows with species such as the Siberian Iris *(Iris sibirica)*, the White Cinquefoil *(Potentilla alba)*, and the Marsh Gentian *(Gentiana pneumonanthe)* have been preserved. Stands of Grey-sheathed Feather-grass *(Stipa joannis)* and Dwarf Sedge *(Carex humilis)* are typical for the termophilous grasslands. Woodland species prevail even among plants. Probably the most typical woodland flower of the area is the Bitter-cress *(Dentaria eneaphyllos)*. An image of the flower is pictured on the PLA logo.

DOUPOV HILLS

IBA code: 004
Criteria: A1, B2, B3
Administrative regions:
Karlovy Vary, Chomutov, Louny
Coordinates: 50°15' N 13°10' E
Area: 60,000 ha, 0.4% protected
Altitude: 280–928 m

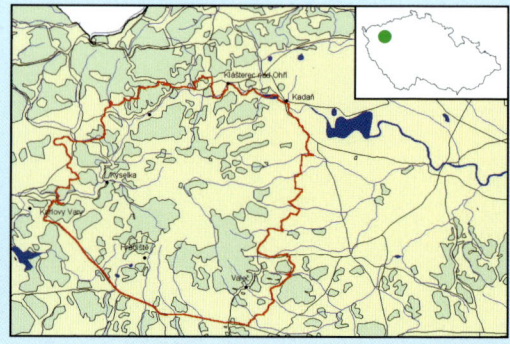

Site description

The Doupov hills lie on the right riverbank of the Ohře. Only a small part of the area between the towns of Ostrov nad Ohří and Perštejn reaches to the left bank of the river. The hills are interposed between the Sokolovská and Mostecká plateaux. In the north they reach the Krušné mountains and in the south they border the hilly areas of Karlovarsko and Plzeňsko. The flat volcanic massif of the Doupov hills represents what is left from a Tertiary volcano of a 30 km diameter. Now fragmented, the hills occupy an area of about 650 km² (Doupovský bioregion has the area of 674 km²). From the geomorphologic point of view, the Doupov hills can be divided into three units – The Hradišťská hills, Jehličenská hills and Rohozecká uplands. Flowering beech woods represent the native vegetation of this area. Extensive remains of such woods, especially on the steep slopes of the Odra river valley, are found between the towns of Kyselka and Kadaň. Beech woods, at some places of primeval forest character, also cover the hillsides of Pustý zámek. The ground cover is extremely rich in species. Extensive fields of debris and scree resulting from weathering and disintegration of the volcanic ground are at most places covered by scree-woods. A mosaic of flowering meadow communities, stands of bushes, and small patches of broadleaved woods (which are the result of succession on abandoned farmland) is the most typical cover in the Doupov hills, especially in the central part of the area. Even though water areas are restricted to small patches at the edge of the hills, they represent important localities from the ornithological point of view. Part of the area is currently being used for military training.

Úhošť National Nature Reserve

The Pstružný creek valley with remaining beech stands

Meadows at Himlštejn

Protection

Úhošť National Nature Reserve (206 ha);

Nature Reserves – 5 (292 ha)

Ostrovské rybníky (62 ha), Vinařský rybník (15 ha), Sedlec (59 ha), Dětaňský chlum (36 ha), Valeč (120 ha);

Natural Monuments – 6 (51 ha)

Orchidejová louka pod Himlštejnem (1 ha), Čedičová žíla Boč (2 ha), Orchidejová louka Černýš (1 ha), Mravenčák (3 ha), Rašovické skály (35 ha), Skalky skřítků (8.5 ha).

Threats

As a result of the reduction in military use of some parts of the area, the communities of flowering meadows, steppes, and forest steppe formations are being overgrown by thorny shrubs. The overexploitation of hillside beech forests and the devastation of peripheral areas by the construction of recreational buildings are other potential threats. At present, wetland communities are insufficiently protected. There are efforts to use the ponds for intensive fishfarming and for releasing semi-wild Mallards for hunting purposes. The stocks of Wild Boars are too high in the area. Uncontrolled hunting as well as poaching are other significant problems of the area.

Research

The research activities of the caretaker group are mainly aimed at monitoring Corncrake (*Crex crex*) breeding population, researching beech wood avi-

fauna and inventorying wetland biotopes. Every year a winter census of water birds is carried out on the Ohře river and breeding waterbirds are monitored at several ponds. The population of the Capercaillie *(Tetrao tetrix)* is also being monitored and sites of critically and severely endange-red bird species such as the Black Stork *(Ciconia nigra)*, Hobby *(Falco subbuteo)*, the Tengmalm's Owl *(Aegolius funereus)*, the Red Kite *(Milvus milvus)*, the Bluethroat *(Luscinia svecica)*, and Nightjar *(Caprimulgus europaeus)* are being identified.

Land use

Forestry	30%
Hunting	100%
Agriculture	5%
Fisheries/aquaculture	5%
Tourism/recreation	5%
Military	55%

Habitats

Forest and woodland (broadleaved deciduous forest, native coniferous forest, mixed forest)	30%
Scrub	15%
Grassland (humid grassland, mesophile grassland)	20%
Wetland (standing freshwater, river/stream, water-fringe vegetation)	5%
Rocky areas (scree/boulders, inland cliff)	5%
Artificial landscape (highly improved reseeded grassland, arable land, ruderal land)	25%

Woods at the upper course of the Liboc

Ornithological Importance

The Doupov hills are the nesting area of 148 bird species, mainly birds of woodland and grassland communities. The Scarlet Rosefinch *(Carpodacus erythrinus)*, Corn Bunting *(Miliaria calandra)*, Ortolan *(Emberiza hortulana)*, Yellow Wagtail *(Motacilla flava)*, and Tawny Pipit *(Anthus campestris)* are the typical nesting species of open areas with scattered greenery. The Pygmy Owl *(Glaucidium passerinum)*, Tengmalm's Owl *(Aegolius funereus)*, Middle Spotted Woodpecker *(Dendrocopos medius)*, Woodlark *(Lullula arborea)*, and Red-breasted Flycatcher *(Ficedula parva)* are typical nesting species of forests.

Criteria species

Black Stork	12–14 p.	B2
Honey Buzzard	15–20 p.	B3
Corncrake	40–50 p.	A1
Stock Dove	300–500 p.	B3
Eagle Owl	25–30 p.	B2
Kingfisher	5–8 p.	B2
Wryneck	80–100 p.	B2
Barred Warbler	150–200 p.	B3
Red-backed Shrike	300–400 p.	B2

Flora and fauna

Invertebrates have not been sufficiently studied in the area, so the knowledge of local invertebrate species is very poor. The presence of the Ladybird Spider *(Eresus niger)* has been recorded in the area. Typical vertebrates of the area are the Fire

Salamander *(Salamandra salamandra)*, Spade-foot Toad *(Pelobates fuscus)*, Dice Snake *(Natrix tesellata)*, Smooth Snake *(Coronella austriaca)*, Aesculapian Snake *(Elaphe longissima)*, Adder *(Vipera berus)*, the Watershrew *(Neomys fodiens)* and the Miller's Watershrew *(N. anomalus)*, Barbastelle *(Barbastella barbastellus)*, Large Mouse-eared Bat *(Myotis myotis)*, European Suslik *(Spermophilus citellus)*, Garden Dormouse *(Eliomys quercinus)*, Edible Dormouse *(Glis glis)*, the Hazel Dormouse *(Muscardinus avellanarius)*, Otter *(Lutra lutra)*, Badger *(Meles meles)*, and Lynx *(Lynx lynx)*. The most important plant communities are the communities of broad-leaved forests with species such as the Coralroot *(Dentaria bulbifera)* and meadow communities with species such as the Small Pasque Flower *(Pulsatilla pratensis)*, the Eastern Pasque Flower *(P. patens)*, the Globe Flower *(Trollius europaeus)*, the Siberian Iris *(Iris sibirica)*, the Large Pink *(Dianthus superbus)*, and the Burning Bush *(Dictamnus albus)*.

Black Stork

A pond and wet meadows at Jeseň

ŠUMAVA MOUNTAINS (BOHEMIAN FOREST)

IBA code: 005
Criteria: A1, B2, B3
Administrative regions:
Český Krumlov, Prachatice, Klatovy
Coordinates: 49°00' N 13°40' E
Area: 163,000 ha, 100% protected
Altitude: 660 – 1378 m

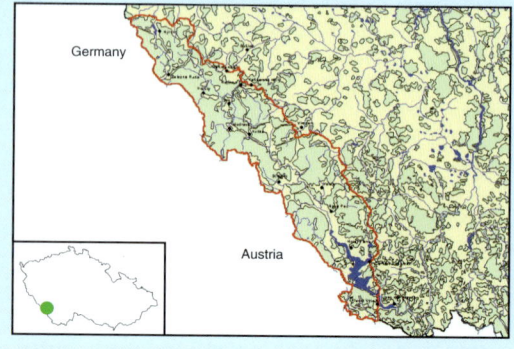

Site description

An extensive 120 km-long mountain range bordering Bavaria and Austria. It is one of the largest and oldest mountain ranges in central Europe. Secondary spruce forests are the dominating cover, but remnants of virgin spruce forests are still present at altitudes above 1,200 m. Other primary types of forests in the Šumava mountains, flowering beech forests and fir forests, have remained in their primeval form only locally at altitudes between 600 and 1,100 m. Following the near-complete evacuation of the population of the Šumava mountains after the World War II, a mosaic of secondary treeless areas and different vegetation succession stages emerged at lower altitudes. A large number of streams and numerous raised and valley bogs are typical for the area. Five of the eight Šumava glacial lakes, which are more than

10,000 years old, are found on the Czech side of the mountains. Many water reservoirs were built there; the Lipenská dam in the southern part of Šumava is the biggest of them.

Protection

Šumava National Park (69,030 ha) established in 1991;
Šumava Protected Landscape Area (94,448 ha) established in 1963;
Šumava Biosphere reserve (167,000 ha) since 1990;
Ramsar Site "Šumavská rašeliniště" – since 1990 (6,371 ha);
National Nature Reserves – 3 (931 ha)
  Bílá strž (79 ha), Boubínský prales (677.3 ha), Černé a Čertovo jezero (174.9 ha);
Blanice National Natural Monument
(281.7 ha + 5,962 ha of buffer zone);
Nature Reserves – 17 (3,763 ha)
  Amálino údolí (80.9 ha), Čertova stráň (20.3 ha), Hamižná (14.9 ha), Chřepice (16.9 ha), Kepelské mokřady (67.9 ha), Kyselovský les (6.8 ha), Losenice (2.7 ha), Městišťské rokle (170.6 ha), Milešický prales (8.3 ha), Nebe (13.9 ha), Pod Popelní horou (6.1 ha), Prameniště (335.3 ha), Rašeliniště Borková (47.5 ha), Svobodova niva (8.6 ha), Zátoňská hora (40.3 ha), Zhůřské pláně (131.9 ha), Zhůřský lom (0.8 ha);
Natural Monuments – 13 (2,629 ha)
  Házlův kříž (69.9 ha), Jasánky (105.2 ha), Jilmová skála (8.1 ha), Královský hvozd (2072 ha), Křišťanov – Vyšný (4.6 ha), Lipka (1 ha), Malý Polec (11.2 ha), Multerberské rašeliniště (9.1 ha), Pestřice (106.6 ha), Poušť (47.2 ha), Prameniště Hamerského potoka (54.8 ha), Svatý Tomáš (53.1 ha), Velké Bahno (85.8 ha).

Threats

In the past, the majority of primeval broadleaved and mixed forests in lower altitudes (below 1,000 m) have been replaced by the less resistant

Rokytecká fen with the Bavarian Mt. Roklan in the background

68

![Mountain ridge from the valley of Zlatý potok brook](top image)

*Mountain ridge from the valley
of Zlatý potok brook*

Interior of a secondary spruce forest

and less stable spruce monocultures. At present these forests succumb to many adverse conditions, including an invasion by the Eight-toothed Spruce Bark Beetle *(Ips typographus)*. While dealing with the consequences of the invasion and preventing the further spread of the beetle, logging in the originally inviolable core zone of the national park was allowed. The ever-increasing pressure from tourism associated with the building of hiking and cycling paths, as well as recreational houses is one of the principal present threats to the area. Unregulated farming, namely the intensive use of pastures, is another negative factor there.

Research

The avifauna inventory work in core zones of the National Park, in small-scale protected areas of the PLA, and in secondarily treeless areas are the main

aims of the research there. The composition of bird communities in relation to forest dieback is also monitored in the virgin spruce forests. Monitored species include the Corncrake (*Crex crex*), the Black Grouse (*Tetrao tetrix*), the Hazel Hen (*Bonasa bonasia*), the Capercaillie (*Tetrao urogallus*), the Tengmalm's Owl (*Aegolius funereus*), the Pygmy Owl (*Glaucidium passerinum*), the Scarlet Rosefinch (*Carpodacus erythrinus*), and the Three-toed Woodpecker (*Picoides tridactylus*). Hand-reared Capercaillies (*Tetrao urogallus*) are released in the territories of the National Park and

A view of the Luzenské valley from Březník

the Protected Landscape Area in order to strengthen the native population. Ural Owls (*Strix uralensis*) are also being reintroduced there.

Ornithological Importance

The area is an important nesting site of 145 species of predominantly meadow and forest birds. Grouse are the most important forest birds. The local population of the Capercaillie *(Tetrao urogallus)* comprises 90% of the Czech Republic's population. The area also holds relatively strong populations of the Black Grouse *(T. tetrix)* and the Hazel Hen *(Bonasa bonasia)*. Two species of mountain woodpeckers, the Syrian Woodpecker *(Dendrocopos leucotos)* and the Three-toed Woodpecker *(Picoides tridactylus)* are important as well. The Šumava mountains is one of the two breeding sites of the Ural Owl *(Strix uralensis)* in the country. The Tengmalm's Owl *(Aegolius funereus)*, relatively rare bird in other areas, is the most abundant owl species there. The quite numerous population of the Corncrake *(Crex crex)* is also worth mentioning.

Land use

Forestry	50%
Hunting	+
Agriculture	15%
Fisheries/aquaculture	3%
Tourism/recreation	+
Military	1%

Habitats

Forest and woodland (broadleaved deciduous forest, native coniferous forest, mixed forest, alluvial/very wet forest)	58%
Grassland (humid grassland, mesophile grassland)	10%
Wetland (standing fresh water, river/stream, raised bog, fen/transition mire/spring)	12%
Rocky areas (scree/boulders, inland cliff)	+
Artificial landscape (highly improved reseeded grassland, arable land, perennial crops/orchards/groves, other urban/industrial areas, ruderal land)	20%

Criteria species

Honey Buzzard	10–20 p.	B3
Corncrake	100–200 p.	A1
Eagle Owl	10 p.	B2
Kingfisher	5 p.	B2
Three-toed Woodpecker	200 p.	B2
Ring Ouzel	450 p.	B3
Firecrest	abundant	B3
Red-backed Shrike	abundant	B2

Flora and fauna

The fauna of the Šumava mountains includes many rare and endangered species. Peatbogs with a high number of relict species of spiders and insects are amongst the most important eco-systems there. Glacial lakes and cirques, boulder-screes, and forests are sites important for inverte-brates. The Lynx (*Lynx lynx*) or Bechstein's Bat (*Myotis bechsteini*) are found in the primary mixed forests. The Otter *(Lutra lutra)* is found along streams. The banks of small brooks at higher altitudes are sought by the Alpine Shrew (*Sorex alpinus*). The Northern Birch Mouse (*Sicista betulina*) also inhabits the area. Small water beds are crucial for the reproduction of amphibians, mainly the Smooth Newt (*Triturus vulgaris*), the Alpine Newt (*T. alpestris*), the Common Frog (*Rana temporaria*), the Common Toad (*Bufo bufo*), and at lower altitudes even the Tree Frog (*Hyla arborea*). Apart from numerous species of wood plants, the fauna of the Šumava mountains also includes many glacial relicts, such as the Three-leaved Rush (*Juncus trifidus*), the Dwarf Birch (*Betula nana*), and in glacial lakes also the Spring Quillwort (*Isoëtes echinospora*) and the Quillwort (*I. lacustris*).

A typical representative of the fauna of the Šumava mountains – the Capercaillie

Highland stream belonging to the Danube catchment area

REŽABINEC POND

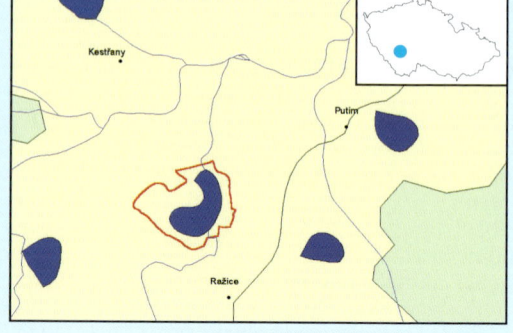

IBA code: 006
Criteria: B1i, B2
Administrative region: Písek
Coordinates: 49°15' N 14°06' E
Area: 111 ha, 100% protected
Altitude: 371 m

Site description

The pond was established in 1530 in a shallow valley of the Otava river. It is the largest pond of the Písek administrative region (104.5 ha) and it is situated about 10 km southwest of the city of Písek. It is a comparatively shallow fish-farming pond with a depth of about 1 m and extensive reedbeds and sedge stands. It is surrounded by an extensively managed agricultural landscape. East of the pond, behind an wind-deposited sand dam, there are pools (6.2 ha), which is what remained after the extraction of stucco-type sands in the area. Percolating water from the pond has created a unique mosaic of various environments in the pools.

Protection

Režabinec pond – Režabinecké tůně pools National Nature Reserve (110.7 ha) established in 1949

Threats

Intensive farming together with fish-farming leads to excessive nutrient enrichment. Fish-farming is regulated by the management plan of the Agency for Nature Conservation and Landscape Protection in České Budějovice. The management plan sets the species composition and the amount of fish released to the pond in order to help the natural recovery of water plant growth and to preserve the varied community of water organisms. In the area there are other tasks urgently needed and they include cutting self-sowing bushes and trees, dredging silted pools, and extracting mud sediments from the bottom of the pond.

Research

Ornithological research of the area started in 1977. At present, a monthly census is carried out at several transects. Every summer ornithological training camps for young people (about 50 participants take part in it each year) are organised around the *"Action Acrocephalus"* project.

Land use	
Agriculture	2%
Fisheries/aquaculture	90%

Habitats	
Grassland (humid grassland)	1%
Wetland (standing freshwater, water fringe vegetation, pools)	99%

Aerial picture of Řežabinec pond – view from the north

The northern pond bank with Pikárna hill in the background

Ornithological Importance

During the 1990's 166 bird species were recorded in the area, 87 of which were nesting species. The most numerous species of the area is the Black-headed Gull *(Larus ridibundus)*, with the biggest nesting colony situated in Southern Bohemia. Režabinec pond lies at the western distribution range of the Greylag Goose *(Anser anser)* in the Czech Republic. Many wader species use the pond as a migration stopover site. Large flocks of geese and ducks concentrate in the area at the end of the summer. In the winter the White-tailed Eagle *(Haliaeetus albicilla)* is regularly recorded in the area.

The pools behind the wind-deposited sand dam on the eastern side of the pond

A young Reed Warbler

Criteria species		
Greylag Goose (M)	1,300 – 2,100 ex.	B1i
Gadwall	10 – 20 p.	B2

Flora and fauna

Extensive reedbeds host many species of beetles and dipteran insects, such as the rare Ground Beetle *Pterostichus aterrimus* and the Hover Fly *Anasimyia lineata*. Režabinec pond is the only Czech locality hosting the rare parasitic fly *Trimerina microchaeta*, whose larvae develop in the egg clutches of certain spiders. The reserve hosts 11 species of amphibians and three reptile species. The reedbeds are dominated by the Reed *(Phragmites communis)*, and to a lesser extent by Reed Manna-grass *(Glyceria aquatica)* and the Broadleaved Cattail *(Typha latifolia)*.

DEHTÁŘ POND

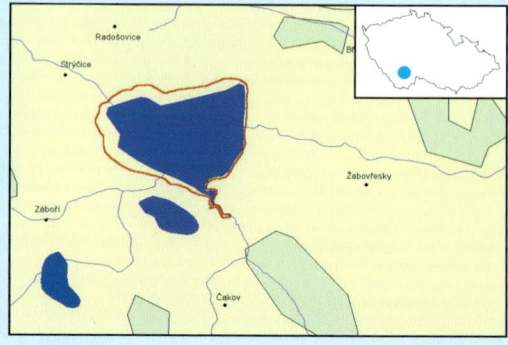

IBA code: 007
Criteria: B1i
Administrative region: České Budějovice
Coordinates: 49°00' N 14°17' E
Area: 260 ha, 46% protected temporarily
Altitude: 406 m

Site description

Dehtář pond is one of the largest ponds in Southern Bohemia. It is situated in the Českobudějovická pond plateau formed from Quarternary sediments, in the midst of extensive agricultural land not far from the forested Šumava foothills. The pond lies in a shallow depression of the terrain and is surrounded by narrow belts of littoral vegetation receding to surrounding grassland and further to arable land. Also surrounding the pond are stands of bush communities with a majority of willows and patches of woods dominated by pines and oaks. At two places near the pond bank there are dozens of weekend houses. The pond itself is used for intensive fish farming. The water level often changes and the pond is left dry for up to several months in the autumn of every other year due to fish harvesting. The water level is also usually lower the year after the harvest. The bare bed of the pond and areas with shallow water are overgrown with low vegetation. The eastern part of the pond is, especially in the summer, used for recreation (swimming, boating, and windsurfing), yet the western part is relatively undisturbed throughout the whole year. Thus, the western part is an ideal site for waterbirds thanks to its size and the pattern of the terrain surrounding it.

Protection

Temporary Protected Area (120 ha) instituted since 1998 for the period between the 15th of July and the 30th of November.

Threats

The situation at the western part of the pond has improved, as hunting is restricted due to its temporary protected area status. Most proposals meant to better the state of this locality were fulfilled by the end of the 1990's. It is possible to say that there are no known significant threats that could change the state of the locality in near future.

A view of the pond from the east

An artificial islet serves as a regular nesting site of Black-headed Gulls and Common Terns

Grey Herons in a nesting colony

Research
Regular census of waterbirds.

Land use	
Hunting	+
Fisheries/aquaculture	100%
Tourism/recreation	50%

Habitats	
Forest and woodland (mixed forest)	3%
Wetland (standing freshwater, water-fringe vegetation)	97%

Ornithological Importance
The pond serves as a stopover for many migrating birds in the spring and then also as an important summer-gathering and passage site for geese. Even though the conditions of the area are not favourable for the nesting of large quantities of birds, some species of waterbirds and wetland birds nest in the grassland surrounding the pond. Important nesting sites include a small wood at the southern peninsula – a nesting site of about 100 pairs of Grey Herons *(Ardea cinerea)*, and an artificial islet in the middle of the pond – a nesting site of several hundreds of pairs of Black-headed Gull *(Larus ridibundus)* and about 50–100 pairs of Common Tern *(Sterna hirundo)*.

Criteria species		
Greylag Goose (M)	50–2,000 ex.	B1i

Flora and fauna
The prevailing flora of the area is typical water and wetland vegetation. The Otter *(Lutra lutra)* is regularly found there.

TŘEBOŇSKO

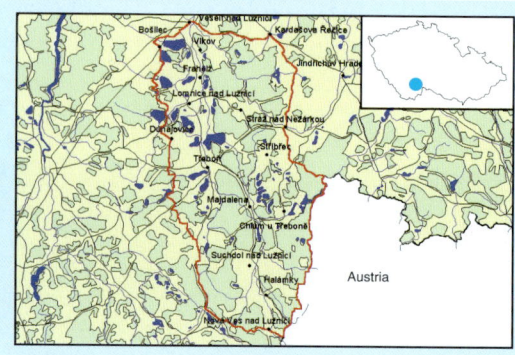

IBA code: 008
Criteria: A1, A4i, B1i, B2, B3
Administrative regions: Jindřichův Hradec,
České Budějovice, Tábor
Coordinates: 49°00' N 14°46' E
Area: 70,000 ha, 100% protected
Altitude: 410–550 m

Site description

The Třeboňsko IBA covers a part of the Třeboňsko plateau between the cities of Veselí nad Lužnicí and České Velenice in the south-eastern part of Southern Bohemia on the border with Austria. The area has changed dramatically since the Middle Ages. The forests were logged, land drained and a complex of more than 500 fishponds of various sizes connected by a network of drains, canals and artificial streams (Nová řeka river, Zlatá stoka – Golden Canal) was created. Different types of biotopes of shallow ponds have since evolved at the original locations of primeval floodplain forests and wetlands, reaching a secondary ecological equilibrium. Other large wetlands lie in the floodplains of the Lužnice and Nová řeka rivers. The numerous peatbogs are considered to be the most valuable ecosystems of Třeboňsko. They originated during the last glaciation at sites with favourable conditions and limited permeabi-

lity of the base. The prevailing types of forests are pine forests with spruce or oak; floodplain oakwoods and wetland alderwoods dominate the floodplains. Stands of Swiss Mountain Pine (*Pinus rotundata*) in peatbogs are also considered valuable.

Protection

Třeboňsko Protected Landscape Area – established in 1979 (70,000 ha);
Třeboňsko Biosphere Reserve – since 1977 (70,000 ha);
Ramsar sites Třeboňské rybníky (Třeboňsko Fish-Ponds) – since 1990 (10,165 ha), and Třeboňská rašeliniště (Třeboňsko Peatlands) – since 1993 (1,100 ha);
National Nature Reserves – 5 (1,835.6)
Červené blato (331.4 ha), Ruda (14.7 ha), Stará

A lagoon in the flooded area of Nová řeka

The Velký Tisý pond with the large peninsula called "Lůsy"

řeka (745.0 ha), Velký a Malý Tisý (615.5 ha), Žofinka (129.0 ha);
National Natural Monument Vizír (10.2 ha).

Nature Reserves – 20 (1,932.4 ha)
Bukové kopce (10.4 ha), Dračice (8.1 ha), Horní Lužnice (414.1 ha), Horusická blata (53.7 ha), Krabonošská niva (36.3 ha), Losí blato u Mirochova (201.0 ha), Meandry Lužnice (90.3 ha), Na Ivance (132.4 ha), Novořecké močály

A Little Bitern pair in the nest

Threats

The threat of eutrophication brought on by intensive agriculture (mainly pig farming) is now
receding. The main fish species bred in the
fishponds is the carp *(Cyprinus)*. The overly
intensive management of the ponds causes hyper-
trofication and results in a decrease in biodiversity
at these wetland localities. It is probably the
biggest problem of the area threatening the quality
of wetland biotopes. Other threats include
unsuitable forest management and hunting (which
includes the release of semi-wild Mallards for
hunting purposes). The PLA administration is
currently implementing a management plan for
small-scale areas, which should help to change the
use of ponds and agricultural land and improve the
management of the area.

Research

Research is aimed at waterfowl censuses and the
monitoring of the White-tailed Eagle *(Haliaeetus
albicilla)* and owls. The breeding biology of the
Greylag Goose *(Anser anser)*, the Cormorant *(Phalacrocorax carbo)*, and the Marsh Harrier *(Circus
aeruginosus)* is being studied. Other surveyed species include the Goldeneye *(Bucephala clangula)*,
Great Crested Grebe *(Podiceps cristatus)*, Little
Grebe *(Tachybaptus ruficollis)*, Common Tern
(Sterna hirundo), Black Tern *(Chlidonias niger)*,
and Little Ringed Plover *(Charadrius dubius)*.

Land use

Forestry	43%
Hunting	+
Agriculture	28%
Fisheries/aquaculture	11%
Tourism/recreation	5%
Urban/industrial/transport	14%

Habitats

Forest and woodland (broadleaved deciduous forest, native coniferous forest, mixed forest, alluvial/very wet forest)	45%
Grassland (humid grassland, mesophile grassland)	5%
Wetland (standing freshwater, river/stream, water-fringe vegetation, fen/transition mire/spring)	24%
Artificial landscape (highly improved reseeded grassland, arable land, perennial crops/orchards/groves, urban parks/gardens, other urban/industrial areas)	36%

Ornithological Importance

Almost 280 bird species have been recorded in
Třeboňsko; at least 182 of them nest there regularly. A large complex of ponds, water streams, and
wetlands makes Třeboňsko one of the most
important areas for waterbirds in central Europe.
In some years the quantities of waterbirds using
the area as a stopover during autumn migration
exceed 20,000 individuals.

Criteria species		
Night Heron	50–120 p.	B2
Black Stork	10–15 p.	B2
White Stork	10–15 p.	B2
Greylag Goose (M)	5,000–10,000 ex.	A4i, B1i
Gadwall	1,000 p.	A4i, B1i, B2
Gadwall (M)	2,000–3,000 p.	A4i, B1i
Red-crested Pochard	20–40 p.	B2
Pochard	790 p.	B3
Honey Buzzard	10–20 p.	B3
White-tailed Eagle	10–13 p.	A1
White-tailed Eagle (W)	30–40 p.	A1
Eagle Owl	10–15 p.	B3
Tawny Owl	100–200 p.	B3
Grey-headed Woodpecker	80–100 p.	B2
Green Woodpecker	80–150 p.	B2
Middle Spotted Woodpecker	50–70 p.	B3
Sand Martin	500–1,000 p.	B2

Flora and fauna

Due to the enormous diversity of sites in Třeboňsko, its flora and fauna are extremely diverse as well. Ecosystems of peatbogs, wind-deposited sand dunes, and fragmented virgin forests are important for invertebrates. The peatbogs host many invertebrate glacial relicts such as the Moorland Clouded Yellow Butterfly *(Colias palaeno)*. Vertebrates inhabit different types of wetlands and large forests. Large populations of nearly all central-European vertebrate species are

The Middle Spotted Woodpecker is a typical species of pond-dyke oaks

A subadult White-tailed Sea Eagle

Remains of primeval floodplain forest in the Stará řeka National Nature Reserve

found in the area. The Třeboňsko population of the Otter *(Lutra lutra)* is the largest one in Central Europe. Extensive coniferous and broadleaved deciduous forests are the most important parts of the area from a botanical standpoint as they hold native tree and bush species – the Swiss Mountain Pine *(Pinus rotundata)* and Labrador-tea *(Ledum palustre)* occurring in peatbogs.

NOVÉ MLÝNY MIDDLE RESERVOIR

IBA code: 009
Criteria: A1, A4i, A4iii, B1i, B2
Administrative region: Břeclav
Coordinates: 48°52' N 16°37' E
Area: 1,080 ha, 100% protected
Altitude: 169–170 m

Site description

The Nové Mlýny Middle Reservoir (VDNM) is situated at the confluence of three Moravian rivers: the Dyje, Svratka, and Jihlava, surrounded by the towns of Dolní Věstonice, Strachotín, Ivaň, and Pasohlávky. The area that was once covered by floodplain forests. The only remaining part of the village of Mušov, now covered by water, is a small church with Romanesque foundations, which catches the eye as it emerges from the middle of the reservoir. The bottom of the reservoir was flattened only at some places before the reservoir was filled up with water. Thus the reservoir varies in depth and small islets emerge whenever the water level drops by just a little. At the current constant level (170.35 m above sea level), about 20 ha of islets in two main groupings emerge above the water: nine islets at Dolní Věstonice (so-called Písky) covering about 10 ha, and islets Kostelní, Hřbitovní, Ivaňský and a complex of six depositions surrounding the Mušov church and covering about 8 ha. At the above-mentioned constant water level, the area of the reservoir is 1,013 ha.

Protection

Nature Reserve Vestonická nádrž – established in 1994 (1,017 ha);

The area is a part of the Floodplain of lower Dyje River Ramsar site (1,080 ha of the Ramsar Site's 11,500 ha) established in 1993.

Threats

Fishing is not very intensive and so does not represent a serious threat. Electro-fishing from boats is used in some parts, while angling is allowed on the southern bank. Hunting, on the other hand, was intensive there, and the ill-judged amendment to the hunting regulation in 1996 called for immediate action by nature conservancy bodies. In the fall of 1996 hunting at the reservoirs took place almost every day throughout the hunting season (September – February). Even the hunting of the Greylag Geese *(Anser anser),* already nesting at the end of February, was recorded. In consequence, the administrative region's authority in Břeclav restricted the hunting season to a period between September 1 and December 31, and allowed hunting only every first and third Saturday of these months. Negotiations concerning the setting of an optimal water level in the middle reservoir and the water management of the middle and lower reservoirs are being carried out.

Research

A number of studies concerning waterbirds have been carried out in the area.

The area is the country's most important gathering site for three species of geese

As the water level was lowered, the bare parts of the reservoir became overgrown by willow, poplar, and numerous herbal species

Land use	
Forestry	+
Fisheries/aquaculture	97%

Habitats	
Wetland (standing freshwater)	97%
Artificial landscape (ruderal land)	3%

Criteria species		
Bean Goose (W)	20,000–80,000 ex.	A4i, B1i
White-fronted Goose (W)	5,000–25,000 ex.	A4i, B1i
Greylag Goose (M)	1,000–5,000 ex.	A4i, B1i
Red-crested Pochard	30–40 p.	B2
White-tailed Eagle (W)	20–40 ex.	A1

Ornithological Importance

Up until 1995 the Nové Mlýny Middle Reservoir was the most important breeding site of the Greylag Goose *(Anser anser)* and it is still the most important breeding site of the Common Tern *(Sterna hirundo)* and the Black-headed Gull *(Larus ridibundus)* in the Czech Republic. It is the only regular breeding site of the Mediterranean Gull *(L. melanocephalus),* the Common Gull *(L. canus),* and the Yellow-legged Gull *(L. cachinnans)* in the country. The locality is the largest regular wintering site of the Smew (Mergus albellus), the Bean Goose *(Anser fabalis),* the Whitefront Goose *(A. albifrons)* and it is also one of the biggest wintering sites of the White-tailed Eagle *(Haliaeetus albicilla)* in the Czech Republic. The area is the country's most important passage site for many duck, gull, tern, and wader species, as well for many passerines, such as the Yellow Wagtail *(Motacilla flava),* the Sedge Warbler *(Acrocephalus schoenobaenus),* and the Reed Bunting *(Emberiza schoeniclus).*

The Middle Reservoir is the only regular nesting site of the Mediterranean Gull in the Czech Republic

Flora and fauna

Because of pollution and eutrophication of the water, no important plant and animal species (with the exception of several mollusc species) are found in the reservoir. At islets and in lagoons at the islets, the Tree Frog *(Hyla arborea)* and the Edible Frog *(Rana esculenta)* have been recorded.

PÁLAVA

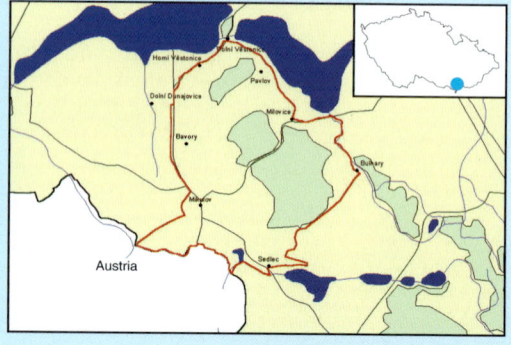

IBA code: 010
Criteria: B2, B3
Administrative region: Břeclav
Coordinates: 48°50' N 16°40' E
Area: 8,300 ha, 100% protected
Altitude: 165–550 m

Site description

Pálava is from a geological and geomorphological point of view an extremely diverse area situated within the towns of Dolní Věstonice, Mikulov, Bulhary, and Milovice. The limestone outcrops between Dolní Věstonice and Mikulov are the most remarkable formations dominating an otherwise undulating lowland landscape. The eastern part of the area is covered by calcareous Milovická pahorkatina hills with deep gorges. The vegetation composition reflects the various conditions of the area. The most important habitat types include forest and forest-steppe plant communities of hills. These are represented by woods of Pubescent Oak in the warmest parts of the area. More humid localities host termophilous oakwoods and oak-hornbeam woods. Other important bio-

Rocky and forest steppes are the most typical biotopes of Pálava

topes are represented by steppe grasslands (which are found even at sites with extreme conditions). Extensive bush stands (with hawthorn, wild rose, and blackthorn) cover areas with thick layers of soil. The plant communities of the Dyje river floodplain represent entirely different types of habitats: hardwood floodplain forests with ash and oak, softwood floodplain forests with willow and poplar, and humid floodplain meadows. An extensive part of the area is covered with farmland; only a small fraction of it is covered with ponds, reed-beds, rocky slopes and old quarries, but these are very important for the local avifauna.

The Black Redstart and the Swift are examples of bird species otherwise bound to human settlements, that nest at limestone outcrops in Pálava

Pálava holds the largest population of the Hoopoe in the Czech Republic

Protection

Protected Landscape Area Pálava – established in 1976 (8,300 ha);

Biosphere Reserve Pálava – since 1986 (8,300 ha);

National Nature Reserves – 4 (614 ha)
   Děvín (383.0 ha), Křivé jezero (119.0 ha), Slanisko u Nesytu (6.7 ha), Tabulová (104.9 ha);

Nature Reserves – 6 (167 ha)
   Liščí vrch (10.0 ha), Milovická stráň (88.4 ha), Růžový vrch a Sirotčí hrádek (10.9 ha), Svatý kopeček (35.9 ha), Šibeničník (3.7 ha), Turold (18.3 ha);

Natural Monuments – 4 (12 ha)
   Annenský vrch (0.6 ha), Kienberg (6.4 ha), Kočičí kámen (0.6 ha), Růžový kopec (4 ha).

A proposal for enlarging the Protected Landscape Area was prepared in 1992. If approved, the PLA would include the area of Lednice and Valtice as well as the floodplain forest complex at the confluence of the Morava and Dyje rivers.

Threats

As the whole IBA has Protected Landscape area status and its most important parts are reserves, there are no known major threats at present.

Research

Long-term monitoring of many bird species is performed in the area. A regular bird census is taken at two transects and long-term atlas work is carried out there.

Land use	
Forestry	30%
Hunting	25%
Agriculture	55%
Fisheries/aquaculture	2%
Tourism/recreation	10%
Urban/industrial/transport	4%

Habitats	
Forest and woodland (broadleaved deciduous forest, alluvial/very wet forest, wooded steppe)	32%
Scrub	4%
Grassland (steppe, dry calcareous grassland)	5%
Wetland (saltmarsh, standing freshwater, water-fringe vegetation)	2%
Rocky areas (inland cliff, caves)	+
Artificial landscape (arable land, perennial crops/orchards/groves, other urban/industrial areas)	57%

Ornithological Importance

The area is important for forest and forest-steppe species. Several raptor species, such as the Common Buzzard *(Buteo buteo)*, Goshawk *(Accipiter gentilis)*, and Honey Buzzard *(Pernis apivorus)* are quite common there. The most important part of the area, from the ornithological point of view, is the Křivé jezero NNR, an oxbow in the floodplain on the right side of the Dyje river, where the Greylag Goose *(Anser anser)* used to nest regularly on the heads of pollarded willows. The White-tailed Eagle *(Haliaeetus albicilla)* attempts to breed in the area, several individuals also winter there each year; the Black Kite *(Milvus migrans)* is a regular nester and the Red Kite

Křivé jezero NNR represents a typical floodplain forest biotope of Southern Moravia – it is an important nesting site of many bird species and it hosts large colonies of Cormorants and tree-nesting White Storks

(M. milvus) is an irregular one. Pálava is the Czech Republic's most important breeding site of the Hoopoe *(Upupa epops)* and the only wintering site of the Wallcreeper *(Tichodroma muraria)*. The Milovický forest holds important populations of the Red-backed Shrike *(Lanius collurio)* and Barred Warbler *(Sylvia nisoria)*. These two species along with the Corn Bunting *(Miliaria calandra)* are also abundant at steppe localities with scattered bushes.

84

Criteria species		
White Stork	10–12 p.	B2
Honey Buzzard	5–8 p.	B3
Wryneck	200–300 p.	B2
Middle Spotted Woodpecker	70–150 p.	B3
Barred Warbler	350–600 p.	B3
Collared Flycatcher	1,000–2,000 p.	B3
Red-backed Shrike	1,000–1,300 p.	B2

The Barred Warbler often nests in open areas with scattered bushes

The Greylag Goose used to nest, in quite a unique way, on the heads of pollarded willows, which are a remarkable landscape phenomenon of the area

Flora and fauna

Because of various natural conditions within the area, the flora and fauna of Pálava is one of the most diverse in the Czech Republic. It hosts many typical steppe species (such as the African Sedge – *Salvia aethiops,* or the ground beetle *Carabus hungaricus),* typical floodplain species (such as the Summer Snowflake – *Leucojum aestivum* or the ground beetle *Carabus clathratus),* and species typical for Central Europe, but rare in other parts of the Czech Republic (such as the Broomrape – *Orobanche* sp. or Dwarf Iris – *Iris pumila).* Pálava is also one of the richest localities in the country where bats are concerned.

LEDNICKÉ PONDS

IBA code: 011
Criteria: B1i, B2, B3
Administrative region: Břeclav
Coordinates: 48°45' N 16°45' E
Area: 653 ha, 100% protected
Altitude: 161–175 m

Site description

The complex of four large ponds built in the 14th century (Nesyt – 320 ha, Hlohovecký – 104 ha, Prostřední – 48 ha, Mlýnský – 107 ha) is situated in a wide lowland part of southern Moravia between the towns of Sedlec u Mikulova and

Lednice. The ponds are filled with water from the Včelínk stream. The isolated Zámecký rybník pond (30 ha) in Lednice is filled from the Dyje river. The ponds are shallow and eutrophic with extensive reedbeds (they cover up to 50 ha of the total area). The Zámecký rybník pond is situated in a park with many old trees. In the pond there are also 15 islets with stands of oaks and other trees. Each of the other ponds, except for Nesyt, includes two small islets. The ponds are a part of the Lednice-Valtice Cultural Landscape, which was listed as an UNESCO World Heritage Site in 1996.

Two thirds of the Czech Republic's population of the Night Heron nest at the islets in Zámecký rybník pond

Partial summer drying of ponds, asserted by nature conservancy bodies, allows for the breeding of waders and existence of rare plant communities of bare pond bottom

The Collared Flycatcher is a common nesting species of the park in Lednice

Protection

National Nature Reserve Lednické rybníky ponds – since 1953 (653 ha);
Lednice fishponds Ramsar site – since 1990 (665 ha).

The area is covered by the proposal for the enlargement of the Pálava Protected Landscape Area and Biosphere Reserve.

Threats

The ponds are used for fishfarming, with carp as the primary fish species. The ponds are state-owned and the fisheries lease them, which allows for greater influence by the nature conservancy. Because of the negative impact the intensive fishpond management had on the numbers of birds, the nature conservancy authorities started setting limits for the quantity of fishstock in the ponds in 1994. Since then the numbers of many bird species have been rising. The partial summer drying of at least one of the ponds (Zámecký rybník is excluded from this measure) is also required, which has positive effect on birds. Recreation and tourism represent other forms of pond-use. Visitors often swim outside areas designed for this purpose and enter the bare bed of ponds that are being dried. This causes enormous disturbance to the birds. Since 2001 the parks surrounding the ponds have been reconstructed, which has included cutting and replanting many trees and bushes. This should not affect waterbirds nor birds of reedbeds. However, cutting large areas of reedbeds is also included in the park reconstruction plans, and such action would directly affect many bird species. It is still possible that the nature conservancy authorities will not allow reedbed cutting (or at least not to the planned extent).

Land use

Fisheries/aquaculture	90%
Tourism/recreation	+

Habitats

Wetland (saltmarsh, standing freshwater, water-fringe vegetation)	90%
Artificial landscape (urban parks/gardens)	10%

Ornithological Importance

As for breeding birds, the most important site is the mixed colony of Night Herons (*Nycticorax nycticorax*, about 250 pairs) and Grey Herons (*Ardea cinerea*, about 240 pairs) at three islets in Zámecký rybník pond.

Criteria species		
Night Heron	250–270 p.	B2
Greylag Goose (M)	2,000–4,000 ex.	B1i
Red-crested Pochard	20–30 p.	B2
Wryneck	10–20 p.	B2
Middle Spotted Woodpecker	10–15 p.	B3
Barred Warbler	10–20 p.	B3

Flora and fauna

The castle park is a home to hundreds of invertebrate species, including large populations of the Stag Beetle (*Lucanus cervus*) and a critically endangered ant *Liometopum microcephalum*. The area is also important for bats; altogether, 16 species have been recorded there including the largest colony of Geoffrey's Bat (*Myotis emarginatus*). From a botanical point of view, the halophyte communities of saltmarshes (at the western edge of the Nesyt pond) and the communities of bare pond floors are considered the most interesting ones.

A mixed colony of Night and Grey Herons at Zámecký rybník pond in Lednice

CONFLUENCE OF THE MORAVA AND DYJE RIVERS

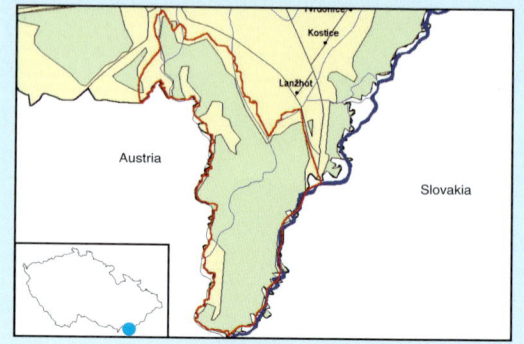

IBA code: 012
Criteria: B2, B3
Administrative region: Břeclav
Coordinates: 48°40' N 16°57' E
Area: 5,000 ha, 1% protected
Altitude: 148–157 m

Site description

The IBA includes the confluence of the Morava (March) and Dyje (Thaya) rivers south of Lanžhot. It is a complex of woods of various age, woodland clearings, and meadows with solitary oaks crossed by a network of canals, oxbows, streams, and swamps. The most common wood species of the drier areas are the Pedunculate Oak *(Quercus robur)*, the Narrow-leaved Ash *(Fraxinus angustifolia)*, and the European White Elm *(Ulmus laevis)*. At waterlogged areas the White Willow *(Salix alba)* and poplars *(Populus* sp.) prevail. Spring floods are a typical phenomenon of this area. The whole area serves as a deer park where red and fallow deer are bred.

Protection

National Nature Reserves – 2 (33 ha)
   Ranšpurk (19.2 ha), Cahnov-Soutok (13.3 ha);
The area is a part of the Floodplain of lower Dyje River Ramsar site (5,000 ha of the Ramsar Site's 11,500 ha) established in 1993.

The area is covered by the proposal for the enlargement of the Pálava Protected Landscape Area and

Floodplain forest during the spring floods

Biosphere Reserve. Three proposals for establishing new small-scale protected areas – Sekulská Morava, Krumpava, and Košárské louky – Pláky are being prepared.

Threats

Due to the uneven age composition of the woods (trees reaching cutting age in this or the next decade prevail) there is a risk of sudden loss of coherent (and extensive) old woods and consequently a loss of breeding opportunities for raptors, the Black Stork *(Ciconia nigra)*, and cavity-nesting bird species. The members of the caretaker group and officials from the Agency for Nature Conservation and Landscape Protection in Brno are keen on consulting during the work on the forest management plan. Due to the canalisation of the Morava and Dyje rivers, the balanced regime of regular spring floods was impaired. Since then, some localities are flooded artificially. Each year discussions among various specialists (ornithologists, ichthyologists, and botanists) concerning the regulated flooding of the southern part of the Košárské louky meadows are undertaken. A management plan for the proposed nature reserve is being prepared in order to reach an acceptable compromise between different interests concerning the flooding. The planned navigation canal Danube-Odra-Elbe represents a serious potential threat to the area.

Research

Research is aimed at monitoring breeding populations of all raptor species, the Black Stork *(Ciconia nigra)* and the White Stork *(C. ciconia)* and monitoring water and wetland birds in the area of the Košárské louky meadows with respect to the effects of artificial flooding and water regime. The breeding population of the Corncrake *(Crex crex)* is being monitored. There is also a long-term study of bird populations nesting in nest-boxes (small passerines, the Wryneck *Jynx torquilla,* the Long-eared Owl *Asio otus,* the Tawny Owl *Strix aluco,* the Kestrel *Falco tinnunculus* and others). In the winter and during the spring floods a regular trilateral (Austria, the Czech Republic, Slovakia) waterbird census is taken in the area.

Černá jezera lakes at Pohansko – a nesting colony of White Storks on centuries-old oaks

Young Imperial Eagles – the rarest nesting raptor species in the Czech Republic

Land use
Forestry	80%
Hunting	90%
Agriculture	5%

Habitats
Forest and woodland (alluvial/very wet forest)	80%
Grassland (humid grassland)	15%
Wetland (river/stream, fen/transition mire/spring, saltmarsh)	5%

Ornithological Importance
Altogether 205 bird species have been recorded in the area. For 125 of those breeding has been confirmed or suspected. The rest are birds wintering in the area or birds using it as a migration stopover or feeding grounds. The locality is important for the breeding of many raptor species, such as the Black Kite *(Milvus migrans)* and Red Kite *(M. milvus)*, the Goshawk *(Accipiter gentilis)*, the Hobby *(Falco subbuteo)*, the Saker *(Falco cherrug)*, and – since 1998 – also the Imperial Eagle *(Aquila heliaca)*.

Criteria species
White Stork	30–36 p.	B2
Wryneck	35–40 p.	B2
Middle Spotted Woodpecker	400 p.	B3
Collared Flycatcher	1,000–1,500 p.	B3

Flora and fauna
Unique communities of local flora and fauna include many endangered species. Invertebrates of temporary water pools are typical for the area. A large number of insect species also inhabit old trees and swamp margins. Endangered and protected species of the area include 11 amphibian species, such as the Moor Frog *(Rana arvalis)*, the Danube Crested Newt *(Triturus dobrogicus)*, and the Spade-foot Toad *(Pelobates fuscus)* plus many fish species such as the Sterlet *(Acipenser ruthenus)*, the Danubian Roach *(Rutilus pigus)*, the Nase *(Chondrostoma nasus)*, and the Wild Carp *Cyprinus carpio carpio)*. A rare freshwater mollusc *Theodoxus danubialis* considered extinct in the Czech Republic for the past 40 years was recently recorded in the area. Small crustaceans inhabiting still waters represent an important food source for waders, ducks, and other waterbirds. The primary species of branchiopods include the Tadpole Shrimp *(Lepidurus apus)* and the Fairy Shrimp *(Siphonophanes grubii)*. As for mammals, the Otter *(Lutra lutra)* has been found here permanently since 1999; the European Suslik *(Spermophilus citellus)* appeared temporarily after the floods in 1997.

BESKYDY MOUNTAINS

IBA code: 013
Criteria: A1, B2, B3
Administrative regions: Nový Jičín,
Frýdek-Místek, Vsetín
Coordinates: 49°26' N 18°22' E
Area: 116,000 ha, 100% protected
Altitude: 350–1,324 m

Slovakia

Site description

An area including three mountain ranges stretching from north-west to south-east: the Moravskoslezské Beskydy mountains, the Vsetínské vrchy hills, and Javorníky mountains, all of them with steep slopes, rounded summits, and valleys up to 700 m deep. At some places karstic formations are found, both under and above ground. About 70% of the area is covered by forests, mainly secondary spruce monocultures. Primary broadleaved forests have been preserved in relatively large areas. They are herb-rich beech forests, to some degree also acidophilous beech forests and remains of scree-woods. Only at the highest peaks and on their slopes have the primeval spruce

forest been preserved. The majority of the most important primeval forests and other typical covers are protected in nature reserves. Farmland (mainly meadows and pastures) covers approximately 25% of the area. Important habitats of the southern part of the area include rich flowering meadows with orchids. Human settlements, streams, and four water reservoirs cover the remaining part of the area. Part of the area was colonised in the 16th and 17th centuries, and this is when the management of the area, which included clear-cutting, dramatically changed the look of the mountains,

The Kněhyně summit with remaining primeval spruce stands in Kněhyně – Čertův mlýn NNR

Mountain beech forest at Čertův mlýn in Kněhyně – Čertův mlýn NNR

especially the Vsetínské vrchy hills, and the Javorníky mountains. The nature conservancy authorities control the principal economic activities of the area: forestry and farming. The area is very important for the management of water supplies, and it is an important recreational area, especially for the inhabitants of the large industrial Ostrava agglomeration. The forests have been seriously affected by air pollution.

Protection

Protected Landscape Area Beskydy – established in 1973 (116,000 ha);
National Nature Reserves – 7 (690 ha);
  Kněhyně – Čertův mlýn (195.0 ha), Mazák (61.6 ha), Mionší (171.1 ha), Pulčín – Hradisko (72.7 ha), Radhošť (144.9 ha), Razula (23.2 ha), Salajka (21.8 ha);

National Natural Monument Valašské muzeum v přírodě (66.1 ha);
Nature Reserves – 15 (702 ha)
  Černovina (61.3 ha), Galovské lúky (2 ha), Huštýn (11.9 ha), Klíny (58.1 ha), Kutaný (14.9 ha), Mazácký Grúnik (47.4 ha), Noříčí (52.4 ha), Poledňana (15.9 ha), Smrk (161.3 ha), Travný (154.9 ha), Trávný potok (20.3 ha), Trojačka (9.8 ha), Velký Polom (73.7 ha), Velký kámen (3.7 ha), V Podolánkách (32.1 ha).
Natural Monuments – 20 (138 ha)
  Brodská (3.9 ha), Byčinec (0.9 ha), Kladnatá – Grapy (62.8 ha), Kněhyňská jeskyně (1.0 ha), Kudlačena (5.5 ha), Kyčmol (0.1 ha), Lišková (2.5 ha), Motyčanka (0.2 ha), Obidová (7.3 ha), Ondrášovy díry (4.5 ha), Pod Juráškou (1.0 ha),

A bushy slope in Nový Hrozenkov hosts the Barred Warbler and the Red-backed Shrike

Pod Lukšincem (0.1 ha), Podgrúň (2.1 ha), Poskla (2.5 ha), Rákosina ve Stříteži nad Bečvou (1.8 ha), Skálí (9.3 ha), Smradlavá (9.3 ha), Stříbrník (14.5 ha), Vachalka (8.3 ha), Zubří (0.1 ha).

Threats

The main threat is the use of the area for recreational purposes, which includes building recreational houses in open places and building sporting facilities (mainly ski tows and funiculars). Cars and motorbikes often enter forbidden areas and disturb the wildlife. Air pollution is a serious threat to the primeval spruce forests at top elevations. Coal-mining and consequent landscape changes might represent a serious threat in the near future in the vicinity of Frenštát pod Radhoštěm. A survey of natural gas reserves was approved in 2001, so natural gas extraction represents another potential threat. Unsuitable forest management between 1970–1990 damaged the state of the forests and their flora and fauna. Illegal logging is one of the negative factors in the area as well.

Research

The Corncrake *(Crex crex)* and the Quail *(Coturnix coturnix)* are intensively researched in the area. Other monitored species include the Barred Warbler *(Sylvia nisoria)*, the Wryneck *(Jynx torquilla)*, and the Red-breasted Flycatcher *(Ficedula parva)*. Since 1995, counts on three point transects under the Atlas Work umbrella have been carried out.

Land use

Forestry	71%
Hunting	+
Agriculture	22%
Tourism/recreation	+
Urban/industrial/transport	+

Habitats

Forest and woodland (broadleaved deciduous forest, native coniferous forest, mixed forest)	71%
Grassland (humid grassland, mesophile grassland)	16%
Wetland (standing freshwater, river/stream, fen/transition mire/spring)	1%
Artificial landscape (arable land, perennial crops/orchards/groves, urban parks/gardens, other urban/industrial areas)	12%

Ornithological Importance

The Beskydy mountains are important for bird species that prefer nesting in native primeval forests with a high proportion of beech. The area hosts the country's only native population of the Ural Owl *(Strix uralensis)*. The Tengmalm's Owl *(Aegolius funereus)*, and the Pygmy Owl *(Glaucidium passerinum)* nest there as well. Treeless areas host significant populations of the Corncrake *(Crex crex)* and the Red-backed Shrike *(Lanius collurio)*. The area holds the Czech Republic's biggest populations of the White-backed Woodpecker

(*Dendrocopos leucotos*), and the Red-breasted Flycatcher *(Ficedula parva)*. At migration time and in the winter, it is possible to encounter large flocks of the Brambling *(Fringilla montifrigilla)* and the Waxwing *(Bombycilla garrulus)*.

Criteria species		
Black Stork	20–25 p.	B2
Corncrake	150–250 males	A1
Stock Dove	150–250 p.	B3
Kingfisher	5–20 p.	B2
Wryneck	25–40 p.	B2
Grey-headed Woodpecker	50–100 p.	B2
Green Woodpecker	60–100 p.	B2
Three-toed Woodpecker	60–120 p.	B2
Redstart	300–500 p.	B2
Ring Ouzel	500–800 p.	B3
Barred Warbler	30–40 p.	B3
Firecrest	1,500–3,000 p.	B3
Red-backed Shrike	1,000–1,500 p.	B2

Flora and fauna

The Pale Orchid *(Orchis pallens)*, the Dark-winged Orchid *(Orchis ustulata)*, the Blue Sow-thistle *(Mulgedium alpinum)*, the Meadow Gladiolus *(Gladiolus imbricatus)*, the Round-leaved Sundew *(Drosera rotundifolia)*, the Chickweed Wintergreen *(Trientalis europaeus)*, a local subspecies of the Stiff Monk's Hood *(Aconitum firmum* ssp. *moravicum)*, and the Currant *(Ribes petraeum)* are important plant species of the area. As for invertebrates, the rare mollusc *Bielzia coerulans,* the ground beetle *Carabus variolosus,* the Large Blue Butterfly *(Maculinea arion)*, and the Purse Web Spider *(Atypus piceus)* are worth mentioning. Important vertebrates include the Spirlin *(Alburnoides bipunctatus),* the Siberian Bullhead *(Cottus poecilopus)*, the Smooth Snake *(Coronella austriaca)*, the Adder *(Vipera berus)*, the Carpathian Newt *(Triturus montandoni)*, the Alpine Shrew *(Sorex alpinus),* and the Northern Birch Mouse *(Sicista betulina).* The area also hosts some large carnivores – the Lynx *(Lynx lynx)* breeds there, the Brown Bear *(Ursus arctos)* regularly crosses the border from Slovakia, and since 1995 even the Wolf *(Canis lupus)* appears irregularly.

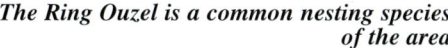

The Ring Ouzel is a common nesting species of the area

POODŘÍ

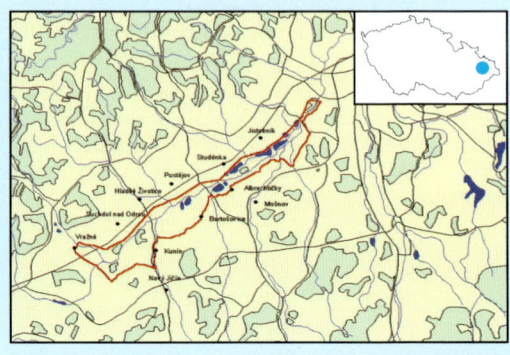

IBA code: 014
Criteria: A4iii, B2, B3
Administrative regions: Nový Jičín, Ostrava,
Frýdek-Místek
Coordinates: 49°42' N 18°03' E
Area: 8,150 ha, 100% protected
Altitude: 214–289 m

Site description

A floodplain of the Odra river with adjoining terraces between the town of Jeseník nad Odrou and the city of Ostrava. It is mainly a flat landscape with arable land, wet meadows, mainly broad-leaved forests and ponds crossed by the Odra river and its side streams, drainage canals, and mill races. The river in most of the area naturally meanders and creates oxbows. Meadows and forests near the river are flooded regularly in the spring

The Odra river at Jistebník

An old part of the Odra river at Jistebník

and irregularly during other seasons after long periods of rain. Floodplain forests with willows, poplars, aspens, and alders give way to lime-maple and oak-hornbeam woods at the river terraces. Meadows with scattered greenery and numerous solitary oaks make the landscape look like a park. Farming is the main economic activity of the area. The ponds are used for fish farming, yet some of the less-intensively used ones look like natural water bodies, due to plant succesion.

Protection

Protected Landscape Area Poodří – established in 1991 (8,150 ha);
Poodří Ramsar site – since 1993 (5,450 ha);
National Nature Reserve Polanská Niva (122.3 ha);
Přírodní rezervace – 3 (178 ha);
Polanský les (59,2 ha), Kotvice (105,5 ha), Koryta (12.9 ha);
Natural Monuments – 2 (27 ha) Pusté nivy (0.7 ha), Meandry Staré Odry (25.8 ha).
A proposal for establishing two small-scale protected areas – Bartošovický luh and Oderský luh Nature Reserves – has been prepared.

Threats

The main threats to the area include intensive management at some of the ponds, farming (especially the application of slurry and urine), and tree cutting. Hunting is not a negligible threat either. There is a pheasantry at Bartšovice and deer parks between Kunín and Suchdol nad Odrou. There have been several cases of rare bird shootings, such as the case of Great White Egret *(Egretta alba)* in 2000. The planned highway and the upgrade of a railway corridor (both situated on or close to the border of the area) represent potential threats to the nature of Poodří. If approved, the development of a distribution centre for the Mošnov airport would damage one of the most important sites of Poodří, the Kotvice nature reserve, by changing its hydrogeological regime. From the long-term perspective, the construction of the Danube-Odra-Elbe navigation canal is threatening to severely damage the whole IBA. The same applies to a proposed nuclear power plant in Blahutovice (the southern border of the PLA) and follow-up developments (such as the pumped-storage plant in Spálov) potentially influencing the water regime of the Odra river.

Research

Since 1992, the avifauna of the ponds has been monitored as a part of national and international

Ornithological Importance

Poodří is important mainly for water and wetland birds during both the breeding season and the migration time. The Bittern *(Botaurus stellaris)* is found at several localities, the Goldeneye *(Bucephala clangula)* and other rare duck species nest there. Since the late 1990's breeding species of the area have included the Greylag Goose *(Anser anser)* and the Cormorant *(Phalacrocorax carbo)*. The Red-crested Pochard *(Netta rufina)* first bred there in 2000. The area also hosts a nesting colony of the Black-headed Gull *(Larus ridibundus)*. Large quantities of waders (with Lapwing *Vanellus vanellus* being a dominant species), ducks, and gulls are found there during migration.

Criteria species		
Black Stork	12–15 p.	B2
Gadwall	180–200 p.	B2
Pochard	200–220 p.	B3
Kingfisher	15–25 p.	B2
River Warbler	120–140 p.	B3

Flora and fauna:

Typical representatives of local flora are the Lesser Naiad *(Caulinia minor)*, the Water Chesnut *(Trapa natans)*, the Floating Fern *(Salvinia natans)*, the Water-lily *(Nymphaea candida)*, the Fringed Water-lily *(Nymphoides pellata)*, the European Yellow Pond-lily *(Nuphar lutea)*, and the Elbe-river Helleborine *(Epipactis albensis)*. Important animal species include the Flat Pond Mussel *(Anodonta complanata)*, the Fairy Shrimp *(Siphonophanes grubii)*, the Large Marsh Grasshopper *(Stethophyma grossum)*, the Spirlin *(Alburnoides bipunctatus)*, the Marsh Frog *(Rana ridibunda)*, the Moor Frog *(R. arvalis)* the Agile Frog *(R. dalmatina)*, the Great Crested Newt *(Triturus cristatus)*, and the Otter *(Lutra lutra)*.

monitoring programs (Monitoring of Breeding Water Birds, International Waterbird Census). The Corncrake *(Crex crex)* has been monitored in most of the region since 1997. A regular bird census is carried out at two transects. With sponsoring and methodical help from the Royal Society for the Protection of Birds and involvement of the local caretaker group members an agri-environmental scheme for the SAPARD program is being prepared. The caretaker group also cooperated in the Odra River Floodplain Atlas project of 1999.

Land use	
Agriculture	65%
Forestry	10%
Hunting	5%
Fisheries/aquaculture	8%
Urban/industrial/transport	16%

Habitats	
Forest and woodland (broadleaved deciduous forest, alluvial/very wet forest)	10%
Grassland (humid grassland)	30%
Wetland (standing freshwater, river/stream, water-fringe vegetation)	15%
Artificial landscape (highly improved reseeded grassland, arable land, perennial crops/orchards/groves, urban parks/gardens, other urban/industrial areas)	45%

Little Crake is a rare nesting species of the area

Horní bartošovický rybník pond at Bartošovice   *White Stork*

HEŘMANSKÝ STAV POND-STRUŽKA WETLANDS

IBA code: 015
Criteria: B2
Administrative regions: Karviná, Ostrava
Coordinates: 49°52' N 18°20' E
Area: 3,000 ha, 1% protected
Altitude: 195–230 m

Site description

The area is situated in the north-eastern part of Czech Silesia on the border with Poland. Geomorphologically it belongs to the Ostravská plateau. It is a network of wetland localities in a flat landscape of the densely inhabited Ostrava and Karviná administrative regions. The IBA includes the remains of floodplain forests along the Odra river and its branches - Stružka and Olše, although the most important part of the area is the complex of four large ponds (Heřmanský stav, Lesník, Nový Stav, and Záblatský rybník) with adjoining wetlands. The total area of reedbeds in the locality (100 ha) represents the largest coherent reedbed cover in Moravia and Silesia. The whole area is significantly affected by coal mining. There are several complexes of small fishponds at Rychvaldská Stružka between the towns of Rychvald and Orlová. Apart from ponds, streams, oxbows, wet meadows, and swamps, there are also several reservoirs in former gravel pits around the Odra river.

Heřmanský stav pond

Protection
Nature Reserve rybník Skučák pond (30 ha) established in 1969.

Threats
The wetlands in the core of the area are threatened by recultivation activities: the wetlands are filled and mine waste is deposed there. Roads for easier access by trucks are being built in valuable reedbed stands. Waste dumps appear in woods, Odra river oxbows and around the streams. Sites important for valuable species of amphibians are filled with mine waste. Intensive fish-farming at the complex of ponds between Orlová and Rychvald led to a decrease in the numbers of important wetland plant species. The hunters' shooting-range at Heřmanský stav pond causes a lot of disturbance to breeding birds, such as the Greylag Goose *(Anser anser)*, the Redshank *(Tringa totanus)*, and the Lapwing *(Vanellus vanellus)*. As entry to the area is not restricted, disturbance to nesting birds caused by visitors is a problem in many parts of it. In the long term, the area around the Odra river is threatened by the proposed construction of the Danube-Odra-Elbe navigation canal.

Research
The research activities are not yet completely harmonised. Several local ornithologists and visitors from elsewhere monitor the area. The caretaker group still has only three members meeting irregularly. Many findings are recorded during random visits and stay unpublished. Important data was collected during a successful bird-ringing action called **Acrocephalus,** which took place between the late 1970's and early 1990's at the Heřmanský stav pond.

Meadows at the Heřmanský stav pond
are the nesting site of the Redshank

Land use

Forestry	5%
Agriculture	20%
Fisheries/aquaculture	10%
Tourism/recreation	5%
Urban/industrial/transport	10%
Not utilised (recultivation included)	20%

Habitats

Forest and woodland (broadleaved deciduous forest, mixed forest, alluvial/very wet forest)	15%
Grassland (humid grassland)	5%
Wetland (standing freshwater, river/stream, water-fringe vegetation)	30%
Artificial landscape (arable land, perennial crops/orchards/groves, other urban/industrial areas, ruderal land)	50%

Ornithological Importance
Where waterbirds and their protection are concerned, the most important part of the area is comprised of the four largest ponds. The Bittern *(Botaurus stellaris),* which even winters there, is a typical species of the area. For the past five years the Little Bittern *(Ixobrychus minutus)* has became more and more common, the number of breeding pairs of the Greylag Goose *(Anser anser)* has risen significantly, the Common Crane *(Grus grus)* has been recorded several times, and several breeding pairs of the Redshank *(Tringa totanus)* have regularly nested there. The Mediterranean Gull *(Larus melanocephalus)* and the Goosander *(Mergus merganser)* are two newly recorded breeding species. As for quantity and diversity of waders, it is one of the most important wader migration stopovers in the Czech Republic. One or two White-tailed Eagles *(Halliaetus albicilla)* winter at the Odra river each year and the numbers of wintering Goosanders *(Mergus merganser)* reach up to one hundred.

Criteria species		
White Stork	3 p.	B2
Gadwall	> 30 p.	B2
Kingfisher	> 10 p.	B2

Flora and fauna
Ten out of Czech Republic's 17 amphibian species have been recorded in the area – they include endangered species, such as the Smooth Newt *(Triturus vulgaris),* the Great Crested Newt *(T. cristatus),* the Fire-bellied Frog *(Bombina bombina*), the Tree Frog *(Hyla arborea),* and the Marsh Frog *(Rana ridibunda).* Numerous rare and endangered water and wetland polant species are found there as well. They include the Fringed Water-lily *(Nymphoides peltata),* the Floating Fern *(Salvinia natans)* – creating extensive covers at some localities, the Water Violet *(Hottonia palustris),* the Lesser Naiad *(Caulinia minor),* and the Bladderwort *(Utricularia australis).*

JESENÍKY MOUNTAINS

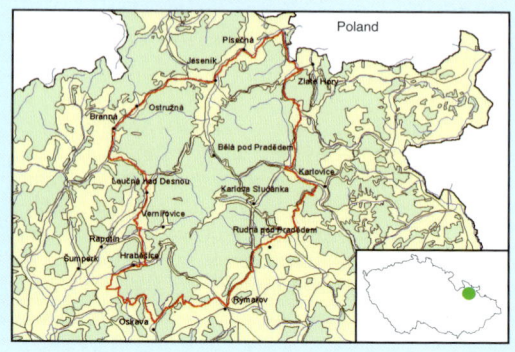

IBA code: 016
Criteria: A1, B2, B3
Administrative regions: Bruntál, Jeseník, Šumperk
Coordinates: 50°12' N 17°13' E
Area: 74,391 ha, 100% protected
Altitude: 330–1,492 m

Site description

A mountainous region of the Hrubý Jeseník massif with deep valleys and the highest peak, Praděd (1,492 m a. s. l.), in northern Moravia. Acidic rocks with low nutrient content prevail in the geological composition of the mountains. Almost 80% of the area is covered with forest. Secondary spruce monocultures dominate, while primary spruce and fir-spruce forests have been preserved only at some sites. Above the treeline (altitude of about 1,300 m), there are, from a natural history point of view, extremely valuable treeless areas – alpine grasslands with geological formations that document glaciation of the area in the past. The mountain pine *(Pinus mugo)* is not a native species there, and thus some areas in the alpine zone have remained extremely rich in other plant species. The Velká kotlina basin hosts about 450 species of higher plants, which makes it the most botanically rich locality in the Czech Republic. The climate of the area is cold and humid. The main economic activity of the area is forestry. Farmland, mainly meadows and pastures, covers 16% of the area. The Jeseníky are an important outdoor recreation area, both in the winter and in the summer.

Protection

Protected Landscape Area Jeseníky – established in 1969 (74,000 ha);
National Nature Reserves – 4 (3,763 ha)
   Praděd (2,031.4 ha), Rašeliniště Skřítek (166.7 ha), Rejvíz (390.5 ha), Šerák-Keprník (1,174.4 ha);
Nature Reserves – 14 (1,397 ha)
   Bučina (26.4 ha), Jelení bučina (25.6 ha), Františkov (13.3 ha), Suchý vrch (49.6 ha), Borek u Domašova (12.7 ha), Pod Slunečnou strání (15.0 ha), Rabštejn (20.0 ha), Filipovické louky (2.1 ha), Vysoký vodopád (137.1 ha), Pstruží potok (22.1 ha), Pod Jelení Studánkou

Praděd national nature reserve, the Velká kotlina basin with the remains of snowfields

(946.5 ha), Sněžná kotlina (107.9 ha), Šumárník (0.9 ha), Franz-Franz (18.8 ha);
Natural Monuments – 4 (89 ha)
Smrčina (1.0 ha), Zadní hutisko (0.9 ha), Pasák (2.5 ha), Štola pod Jelení cestou (84.2 ha).

Threats

Air pollution and acid rain represent the biggest threats to the forests. Small-scale damage caused by winds is recorded every year, calamities occur once in every 10 to 30 years. Many trees are damaged by snow and frosts. Other problems include superabundant populations of red deer and introduced chamois, which prevent the natural restoration of damaged forests in the upper parts of

Deforestation of the upper areas of mountain ranges in the Jeseníky Mountains is caused by air pollution

Hrubý Jeseník and endanger rare plant communities at rocky biotopes. The recreational use of the area, including the most valuable parts of Praděd and surroundings, causes ever growing pressure on the nature there. The extensive reconstruction of stream channels in the inhabited parts of the PLA as well as on the lower parts of the streams outside the PLA after the floods in 1997 led to significant decrease in biodiversity of these streams. Enduring problems are caused by water abstraction, mainly for small hydroelectric plants. A growing number of domestic and feral cats in the area is considered another threat to birds. A management plan to regulate the impact of human activities in the area is currently being prepared. The landscape protection programs of the Ministry of the Environment helped to implement some nature conservancy measures that have led to the improvement of the state of the environment.

Research

The PLA administration carries out long term research and documentation in the area. Many individual species of plants and animals are targeted and the effect of recreational use is being surveyed in order to find sustainable solutions. Many research institutes, universities, and individuals are involved in research activities. Long-term research of ants around the Alfrédka cottage is being carried out. Other projects are focused on monitoring the Water Pipit in the upper parts of the mountain range, monitoring surface waters and peat-bogs, etc. Research projects surveyed the effects of large hooved mammals on the area, spatial activity of the Chamois or the changes in water ecosystems in the Jeseníky Mountains.

Land use	
Forestry	80%
Hunting	95%
Agriculture	16%
Fisheries/aquaculture	15%
Tourism/recreation	90%

Interior of the nature reserve Skalní potok –
a stream with a rocky bottom hosts the River Trout
and the Siberian Bullhead, and is an important
feeding ground of the Black Stork

Habitats	
Forest and woodland (broadleaved deciduous forest, native coniferous forest, mixed forest, treeline ecotone)	80%
Scrub	+
Grassland (alpine/subalpine/boreal grassland, humid grassland, mesophile grassland)	1%
Wetland (standing freshwater, river/stream, raised bog, fen/transition mire/spring)	1%
Rocky areas (inland cliff)	+
Artificial landscape (highly improved reseeded grassland, arable land, perennial crops/orchards/groves, urban parks/gardens, other urban/industrial areas)	18%

The Water Pipit

Ornithological Importance

The area is important for the bird species of forests and alpine grasslands as well as for species of valley meadows. Species of otherwise limited distribution in the Czech Republic, such as the Alpine Accentor (*Prunella collaris*) and the Water Pipit (*Anthus spinoletta*), are found there. The situation with the Capercaillie *(Tetrao urogallus)* is quite critical – only several individuals still survive. The numbers of the Black Grouse *(Tetrao tetrix)* are swiftly declining as well. On the other hand, the Peregrine Falcon (*Falco peregrinus*) is expected to start breeding in the area soon. Isolated recordings of the Dotterel (*Charadrius morinellus*) and the Red-spotted Bluethroat (*Luscinia svecica svecica*) deserve special attention. Alarming is the decline in the number of breeding pairs of the Water Pipit in the mountain ranges of the area impacted by air pollution, acidification and human intervention.

Criteria species		
Black Stork	5 p.	B2
Corncrake	100–200 p.	A1
Stock Dove	10–30 p.	B3
Ring Ouzel	10–20 p.	B3

Flora and fauna

The extremely rich fauna of the area includes the Northern Birch Mouse *(Sicista betulina)* in the subalpine zone and the Hazel Dormouse *(Muscardinus avellanarius)* at lower altitudes. The Red Deer (Cervus elaphus), the Roe Deer (Capreolus capreolus) and the introduced Chamois (Rupicapra rupicapra) are abundant in the Jeseníky Mountains. Streams host the River Trout *(Salmo trutta* m. *fario),* the Grayling *(Thymallus thymallus),* the Siberian Bullhead *(Cottus poecilopus),* and, in marginal areas also the Brook Lamprey *(Lampetra planeri).* The Lynx *(Lynx lynx)* is rare there and the Brown Bear *(Ursus arctos)* appears occasionally. Many bat species are found there and the area holds also some of their important wintering sites. The Carpathian Newt *(Triturus montandoni)* and infrequently even the Great Crested Newt *(T. cristatus)* are found there. Around the Alfrédka cottage, about 2,000 nests of the Hairy Wood Ant *(Formica lugubris)* have been recorded. The area hosts an endemic species of ringlet *Erebia sudetica sudetica,* the stonefly *Perla grandis* has been recorded in water streams, and a capricorn beetle *Cornumutila quadrivittata* inhabits the highest parts of the mountain range. Other arcto-alpine relics of the area include a species of fruitworm *Sparganothis rubicundana* and dung beetle *Aphodius limbolarius.* From the botanical viewpoint, the most important locality of the area is the glacial cirque of the Velká kotlina basin, which is one of the most species-rich localities in central Europe. It hosts, for example, the Dark Hedysarum *(Hedysarum hedysaroides),* the Siberian Hawk's Beard *(Crepis sibirica),* several species of the Alpine Hawkweed *(Hieracium alpinum, H. pilo-* *sum,* and *H. silesiacum),* the Siberian Milk-Parsley *(Conioselinum tataricum),* the Harebell *(Campanula rotundifolia sudetica),* the Alpine Aster *(Aster alpinus),* a local endemite of a Plantain *(Plantago atra sudetica)* and the Sudeten-Mountains Carthusian Pink *(Dianthus carthusianorum sudeticus).* Other endemites of the Jeseníky Mountains include the Ash-mountains Meadow-grass *(Poa riphaca)* and the Jeseník Mountain Bohemian Bellflower *(Campanula gelida)* growing at the rocky peak of Petrovy kameny cliff.

The Alpine Accentor is a rare nesting species of several sites in the subalpine zone of Hrubý Jeseník

A view of the main range from Nová Ves – from left to right: the Malá kotlina basin, Jelení žleb valley, and Velká kotlina basin

Tables

Tables 15–30 show the numbers of selected bird species in all the 16 Czech IBAs. Birds are selected based on inclusion in Annex I of the Birds Directive or legal protection in the Czech Republic. For nesting species minimal estimates are given (**p.** – pairs, **males, females**). **B** (breeding) indicates a nesting species if an estimate is unknown. If there is no exact estimate **B-rare**, **B-sporadic**, and **B-common** indicate the status of the species. For the Šumava mountains exact estimates are not available and so the figures given are in tens, hundreds and thousands. **B-possible** indicates probable but unproven nesting. Figures given as **0–1 p.** or **0–2 p.** mean irregular nesting of one or two pairs. Migrating species are indicated by **M**, wintering species by **W**, **F** indicates species using the site as a feeding ground, and **I** indicates incidental occurrence. The last column shows the protection categories in the Czech Republic (**CE** – critically endangered, **SE** – severely endangered, **E** – endangered).

Table 31 shows the total numbers for IBAs in the Czech Republic. Minimum estimates as published by Šťastný et al. (1997) were used where there was not more recent data from published or unpublished sources. Areas with possible and irregular breeding are included in the total number of IBAs where a species nests. The third figure shows the size of the Czech breeding population nesting in all of the IBAs as a percentage of the minimal estimate for the country.

Table 15: **Populations of selected bird species at Krkonoše mountains IBA**

Common name	Scientific name	Population estimate	Annex I	Protection in the CR
Black Stork	*Ciconia nigra*	12–16 p.	+	SE
White Stork	*Ciconia ciconia*	1–2 p.	+	E
Honey Buzzard	*Pernis apivorus*	3–5 p.	+	SE
Black Kite	*Milvus migrans*	1–2 p.	+	CE
Red Kite	*Milvus milvus*	1 p.	+	CE
Hen Harrier	*Circus cyaneus*	1–4 p.	+	SE
Goshawk	*Accipiter gentilis*	20–25 p.		E
Sparrowhawk	*Accipiter nisus*	50–65 p.		SE
Lesser Spotted Eagle	*Aquila pomarina*	0–1 p.	+	CE
Kestrel	*Falco tinnunculus*	110–140 p.		
Merlin	*Falco columbarius*	0–1 p.	+	SE
Hobby	*Falco subbuteo*	12–17 p.		SE
Peregrine	*Falco peregrinus*	1–2 p.	+	CE
Hazel Grouse	*Bonasa bonasia*	0–1 p.	+	SE
Black Grouse	*Tetrao tetrix*	100–120 males	+	SE
Capercaillie	*Tetrao urogallus*	10 males	+	CE
Partridge	*Perdix perdix*	15–20 p.		E
Quail	*Coturnix coturnix*	30–40 p.		SE
Corncrake	*Crex crex*	>120 males	+	SE
Dotterel	*Charadrius morinellus*	1 p.	+	CE
Snipe	*Gallinago gallinago*	3–5 p.		SE
Woodcock	*Scolopax rusticola*	15–30 p.		E
Common Sandpiper	*Actitis hypoleucos*	2–4 p.		SE
Stock Dove	*Columba oenas*	90 p.		SE
Eagle Owl	*Bubo bubo*	8–10 p.	+	E
Pygmy Owl	*Glaucidium passerinum*	7–10 p.	+	SE
Tengmalm's Owl	*Aegolius funereus*	90 p.	+	SE
Nightjar	*Caprimulgus europaeus*	0–2 p.	+	SE
Swift	*Apus apus*	600 p.		E

Common name	Scientific name	Population estimate	Annex I	Protection in the CR
Kingfisher	*Alcedo atthis*	7–9 p.	+	SE
Hoopoe	*Upupa epops*	0–1 p.		SE
Wryneck	*Jynx torquilla*	11–16 p.		SE
Grey-headed Woodpecker	*Picus canus*	15–20 p.	+	
Middle Spotted Woodpecker	*Dendrocopos medius*	0–1 p.	+	E
Woodlark	*Lullula arborea*	0–1 p.	+	SE
Swallow	*Hirundo rustica*	700 p.		E
Water Pipit	*Anthus spinoletta*	80–100 p.		SE
Yellow Wagtail	*Motacilla flava*	0–3 p.		SE
Alpine Accentor	*Prunella collaris*	9–14 p.		SE
Red-spotted Bluethroat	*Luscinia svecica svecica*	25–30 p.	+	CE
Redstart	*Phoenicurus phoenicurus*	700 p.		
Whinchat	*Saxicola rubetra*	800 p.		E
Stonechat	*Saxicola torquata*	5–10 p.		E
Wheatear	*Oenanthe oenanthe*	20–25 p.		SE
Ring Ouzel	*Turdus torquatus*	240 p.		SE
Barred Warbler	*Sylvia nisoria*	0–1 p.	+	SE
Red-breasted Flycatcher	*Ficedula parva*	80 p.	+	SE
Golden Oriole	*Oriolus oriolus*	4–8 p.		SE
Red-backed Shrike	*Lanius collurio*	1,200 p.	+	E
Great Grey Shrike	*Lanius excubitor*	1–2 p.		E
Nutcracker	*Nucifraga caryocatactes*	60–80 p.		E
Jackdaw	*Corvus monedula*	15–20 p.		SE
Raven	*Corvus corax*	15–25 p.		E
Scarlet Rosefinch	*Carpodacus erythrinus*	290 p.		E
Ortolan Bunting	*Emberiza hortulana*	0–2 p.	+	CE

Table 16: **Populations of selected bird species at Žehuňský rybník pond IBA**

Common name	Scientific name	Population estimate	Annex I	Protection in the CR
Little Grebe	*Tachybaptus ruficollis*	3–5 p., M, W		E
Great Crested Grebe	*Podiceps cristatus*	11–26 p., M		E
Red-necked Grebe	*Podiceps grisegena*	I		SO
Black-necked Grebe	*Podiceps nigricollis*	0–2 p., M		E
Cormorant	*Phalacrocorax carbo*	M, P, W		E
Bittern	*Botaurus stellaris*	1–2 p., M, W	+	CE
Little Bittern	*Ixobrychus minutus*	1–3 p.	+	CE
Night Heron	*Nycticorax nycticorax*	I	+	SO
Little Egret	*Egretta garzetta*	I	+	SO
Great White Egret	*Egretta alba*	W, P	+	SO
Purple Heron	*Ardea purpurea*	0–1 p., I	+	CE
Black Stork	*Ciconia nigra*	M, P	+	SO
White Stork	*Ciconia ciconia*	P	+	E
Spoonbill	*Platalea leucorodia*	I	+	CE
Gadwall	*Anas strepera*	14 p., M		E
Pintail	*Anas acuta*	M, W		CE
Teal	*Anas crecca*	M, W		E
Garganey	*Anas querquedula*	1–5 p., M		SO
Shoveler	*Anas clypeata*	1–3 p., M		SO
Red-crested Pochard	*Netta rufina*	M		SO
Ferruginous Duck	*Aythya nyroca*	W, I	+	CE
Goldeneye	*Bucephala clangula*	M		SO
Goosander	*Mergus merganser*	M, W		CE

Common name	Scientific name	Population estimate	Annex I	Protection in the CR
Honey Buzzard	*Pernis apivorus*	1–2 p., M	+	SO
Red Kite	*Milvus milvus*	1p., M, P	+	CE
White-tailed Eagle	*Haliaeetus albicilla*	1 p. (in 2000), W	+	CE
Marsh Harrier	*Circus aeruginosus*	4–6 p., M	+	E
Hen Harrier	*Circus cyaneus*	0–1 p., M, W	+	SO
Montagu's Harrier	*Circus pygargus*	I	+	SO
Goshawk	*Accipiter gentilis*	1 p.		E
Sparrowhawk	*Accipiter nisus*	3–5 p., W		SO
Lesser Spotted Eagle	*Aquila pomarina*	I	+	CE
Golden Eagle	*Aquila chrysaetos*	I	+	CE
Osprey	*Pandion haliaeetus*	M	+	CE
Red-footed Falcon	*Falco vespertinus*	I		CE
Merlin	*Falco columbarius*	I	+	SO
Hobby	*Falco subbuteo*	1 p., M		SO
Peregrine	*Falco peregrinus*	M	+	CE
Partridge	*Perdix perdix*	1–3 p.		E
Quail	*Coturnix coturnix*	2–4 p., M		SO
Water Rail	*Rallus aquaticus*	15–20 p., W		SO
Spotted Crake	*Porzana porzana*	1–2 p., M	+	SO
Little Crake	*Porzana parva*	1–2 p.	+	CE
Corncrake	*Crex crex*	2 p., M	+	SO
Crane	*Grus grus*	M	+	CE
Avocet	*Recurvirostra avosetta*	I	+	CE
Snipe	*Gallinago gallinago*	1–2 p.		SO
Great Snipe	*Gallinago media*	M	+	E
Woodcock	*Scolopax rusticola*	B - possible, M		E
Black-tailed Godwit	*Limosa limosa*	I		CE
Curlew	*Numenius arquata*	M		CE
Redshank	*Tringa totanus*	M		CE
Green Sandpiper	*Tringa ochropus*	B - possible, M		SO
Common Sandpiper	*Actitis hypoleucos*	M		SO
Mediterranean Gull	*Larus melanocephalus*	0–1 p.	+	SO
Common Tern	*Sterna hirundo*	M	+	SO
Black Tern	*Chlidonias niger*	M	+	CE
Stock Dove	*Columba oenas*	2–3 p.		SO
Barn Owl	*Tyto alba*	0–1 p.		SO
Little Owl	*Athene noctua*	1 p.		SO
Short-eared Owl	*Asio flammeus*	0–1 p.	+	SO
Nightjar	*Caprimulgus europaeus*	1 p., M	+	SO
Swift	*Apus apus*	20–40 p., M		E
Kingfisher	*Alcedo atthis*	3 p.	+	SO
Hoopoe	*Upupa epops*	0–1 p., M		SO
Wryneck	*Jynx torquilla*	3–7 p.		SO
Grey-headed Woodpecker	*Picus canus*	1–2 p.	+	
Black Woodpecker	*Dryocopus martius*	2–5 p.	+	
Middle Spotted Woodpecker	*Dendrocopos medius*	5 p.	+	E
Woodlark	*Lullula arborea*	M, I	+	SO
Sand Martin	*Riparia riparia*	M		E
Swallow	*Hirundo rustica*	40–50 p.		E
Tawny Pipit	*Anthus campestris*	I	+	SO
Water Pipit	*Anthus spinoletta*	I, M		SO
Yellow Wagtail	*Motacilla flava*	1–12 p., M		SO

Common name	Scientific name	Population estimate	Annex I	Protection in the CR
Waxwing	*Bombycilla garrulus*	W, M		E
Thrush Nightingale	*Luscinia luscinia*	M, N		SO
Nightingale	*Luscinia megarhynchos*	6–15 p.		E
White-spotted Bluethroat	*Luscinia svecica cyanecula*	1 p., M	+	SO
Whinchat	*Saxicola rubetra*	1–2 p.		E
Stonechat	*Saxicola torquata*	0–1 p.		E
Redwing	*Turdus iliacus*	M		SO
Savi's Warbler	*Locustella luscinioides*	5–10 p.		E
Great Reed Warbler	*Acrocephalus arundinaceus*	12–20 p.		SO
Barred Warbler	*Sylvia nisoria*	15 p.	+	SO
Spotted Flycatcher	*Muscicapa striata*	10 p., M		E
Collared Flycatcher	*Ficedula albicollis*	15 p.	+	
Bearded Tit	*Panurus biarmicus*	4–10 p., M, W		SO
Penduline Tit	*Remiz pendulinus*	8–15 p., M, W		E
Golden Oriole	*Oriolus oriolus*	5–10 p.		SO
Red-backed Shrike	*Lanius collurio*	20 p.	+	E
Great Grey Shrike	*Lanius excubitor*	2–4 p.		E
Nutcracker	*Nucifraga caryocatactes*	M, W		E
Jackdaw	*Corvus monedula*	W		SO
Raven	*Corvus corax*	1–2 p.		E
Scarlet Rosefinch	*Carpodacus erythrinus*	N		E
Corn Bunting	*Miliaria calandra*	15 p., W		CE
Ortolan Bunting	*Emberiza hortulana*	1 M, M	+	CE

Table 17: **Populations of selected bird species at Křivoklátsko IBA**

Common name	Scientific name	Population estimate	Annex I	Protection in the CR
Little Grebe	*Tachybaptus ruficollis*	5–10 p.		E
Great Crested Grebe	*Podiceps cristatus*	0–1 p.		E
Black-necked Grebe	*Podiceps nigricollis*	M		E
Cormorant	*Phalacrocorax carbo*	M, W		E
Great White Egret	*Egretta alba*	N	+	SE
Black Stork	*Ciconia nigra*	4–8 p	+	SE
White Stork	*Ciconia ciconia*	M, P	+	E
Gadwall	*Anas strepera*	M		E
Pintail	*Anas acuta*	M		CE
Teal	*Anas crecca*	M		E
Garganey	*Anas querquedula*	M		SE
Shoveler	*Anas clypeata*	M		SE
Goldeneye	*Bucephala clangula*	M, W		SE
Goosander	*Mergus merganser*	M, W		CE
Honey Buzzard	*Pernis apivorus*	5–15 p.	+	SE
Black Kite	*Milvus migrans*	B - possible, M	+	CE
Red Kite	*Milvus milvus*	0–3 p.	+	CE
White-tailed Eagle	*Haliaeetus albicilla*	W	+	CE
Marsh Harrier	*Circus aeruginosus*	6–12 p.	+	E
Hen Harrier	*Circus cyaneus*	B - possible, W,M	+	SE
Montagu's Harrier	*Circus pygargus*	M	+	SE
Goshawk	*Accipiter gentilis*	H		E
Sparrowhawk	*Accipiter nisus*	40–80 p.		SE

Common name	Scientific name	Population estimate	Annex I	Protection in the CR
Lesser Spotted Eagle	*Aquila pomarina*	M	+	CE
Osprey	*Pandion haliaeetus*	M	+	CE
Hobby	*Falco subbuteo*	M		SE
Hazel Grouse	*Bonasa bonasia*	N	+	SE
Black Grouse	*Tetrao tetrix*	N	+	SE
Partridge	*Perdix perdix*	120–240 p.		E
Quail	*Coturnix coturnix*	300–500 p.		SE
Water Rail	*Rallus aquaticus*	N		SE
Corncrake	*Crex crex*	H	+	SE
Crane	*Grus grus*	N	+	CE
Snipe	*Gallinago gallinago*	M		SE
Woodcock	*Scolopax rusticola*	120–220 p.		E
Curlew	*Numenius arquata*	N		CE
Redshank	*Tringa totanus*	M		CE
Green Sandpiper	*Tringa ochropus*	M, P		SE
Common Sandpiper	*Actitis hypoleucos*	B - possible, M		SE
Stock Dove	*Columba oenas*	150–250 p.		SE
Barn Owl	*Tyto alba*	4–8 p.		SE
Eagle Owl	*Bubo bubo*	15–20 p.	+	E
Pygmy Owl	*Glaucidium passerinum*	40–80 p.	+	SE
Little Owl	*Athene noctua*	H		SE
Tengmalm's Owl	*Aegolius funereus*	H	+	SE
Nightjar	*Caprimulgus europaeus*	H	+	SE
Swift	*Apus apus*	250–500 p.		E
Kingfisher	*Alcedo atthis*	16–28 p.	+	SE
Hoopoe	*Upupa epops*	M		SE
Wryneck	*Jynx torquilla*	60–100 p.		SE
Grey-headed Woodpecker	*Picus canus*	45–90 p.	+	
Black Woodpecker	*Dryocopus martius*	90–130 p.	+	
Middle Spotted Woodpecker	*Dendrocopos medius*	120–250 p.	+	E
Crested Lark	*Galerida cristata*	0–2 p.		E
Woodlark	*Lullula arborea*	H	+	SE
Sand Martin	*Riparia riparia*	0–10 p.		E
Swallow	*Hirundo rustica*	1,500–3,000 p.		E
Yellow Wagtail	*Motacilla flava*	B - possible, M		SE
Waxwing	*Bombycilla garrulus*	M, W		E
Nightingale	*Luscinia megarhynchos*	0–10 p.		E
Whinchat	*Saxicola rubetra*	20–40 p.		E
Wheatear	*Oenanthe oenanthe*	B - possible, M		SE
Redwing	*Turdus iliacus*	M, W		SE
Barred Warbler	*Sylvia nisoria*	60–90 p.	+	SE
Spotted Flycatcher	*Muscicapa striata*	400–800 p.		E
Red-breasted Flycatcher	*Ficedula parva*	40–60 p.	+	SE
Collared Flycatcher	*Ficedula albicollis*	4,000–6,000 p.	+	
Wallcreeper	*Tichodroma muraria*	N		CE
Penduline Tit	*Remiz pendulinus*	N		E
Golden Oriole	*Oriolus oriolus*	30–50 p.		SE
Red-backed Shrike	*Lanius collurio*	400–700 p.	+	E
Great Grey Shrike	*Lanius excubitor*	10–20 p.		E
Nutcracker	*Nucifraga caryocatactes*	H		E
Jackdaw	*Corvus monedula*	M		SE
Raven	*Corvus corax*	15–20 p.		E
Corn Bunting	*Miliaria calandra*	N		CE

Table 18: **Populations of selected bird species at Doupov hills IBA**

Common name	Scientific name	Population estimate	Annex I	Protection in the CR
Little Grebe	*Tachybaptus ruficollis*	50–70 p.		E
Great Crested Grebe	*Podiceps cristatus*	40–60 p.		E
Red-necked Grebe	*Podiceps grisegena*	I		SE
Black-necked Grebe	*Podiceps nigricollis*	20–30 p.		E
Cormorant	*Phalacrocorax carbo*	F, W		E
Bittern	*Botaurus stellaris*	2–3 p.	+	CE
Great White Egret	*Egretta alba*	I	+	SE
Black Stork	*Ciconia nigra*	10–12 p.	+	SE
White Stork	*Ciconia ciconia*	I, F	+	E
Gadwall	*Anas strepera*	20–40 p.		E
Pintail	*Anas acuta*	W		CE
Teal	*Anas crecca*	10–20 p.		E
Garganey	*Anas querquedula*	25–50 p.		SE
Shoveler	*Anas clypeata*	15–20 p.		SE
Ferruginous Duck	*Aythya nyroca*	W	+	CE
Goldeneye	*Bucephala clangula*	W		SE
Goosander	*Mergus merganser*	W		CE
Honey Buzzard	*Pernis apivorus*	10–15 p.	+	SE
Black Kite	*Milvus migrans*	I, F	+	CE
Red Kite	*Milvus milvus*	2–4 p.	+	CE
White-tailed Eagle	*Haliaeetus albicilla*	I, W	+	CE
Marsh Harrier	*Circus aeruginosus*	35–45 p.	+	E
Hen Harrier	*Circus cyaneus*	3–5 p.	+	SE
Montagu's Harrier	*Circus pygargus*	2–3 p.	+	SE
Goshawk	*Accipiter gentilis*	20–30 p.		E
Sparrowhawk	*Accipiter nisus*	30–50 p.		SE
Lesser Spotted Eagle	*Aquila pomarina*	I	+	CE
Osprey	*Pandion haliaeetus*	F	+	CE
Merlin	*Falco columbarius*	W	+	SE
Hobby	*Falco subbuteo*	5–8 p.		SE
Peregrine	*Falco peregrinus*	I, F	+	CE
Black Grouse	*Tetrao tetrix*	20–25 males	+	SE
Partridge	*Perdix perdix*	30–50 p.		E
Quail	*Coturnix coturnix*	80–120 p.		SE
Water Rail	*Rallus aquaticus*	10–15 p.		SE
Spotted Crake	*Porzana porzana*	3–5 p.	+	SE
Corncrake	*Crex crex*	40–60 males	+	SE
Crane	*Grus grus*	I	+	CE
Avocet	*Recurvirostra avosetta*	I	+	CE
Snipe	*Gallinago gallinago*	30–40 p.		SE
Woodcock	*Scolopax rusticola*	40–60 p.		E
Black-tailed Godwit	*Limosa limosa*	I		CE
Curlew	*Numenius arquata*	I		CE
Redshank	*Tringa totanus*	I		CE
Green Sandpiper	*Tringa ochropus*	5–10 p.		SE
Common Sandpiper	*Actitis hypoleucos*	10–15 p.		SE
Common Tern	*Sterna hirundo*	M	+	SE
Black Tern	*Chlidonias niger*	M	+	CE
Stock Dove	*Columba oenas*	300–500 p.		SE
Barn Owl	*Tyto alba*	5–8 p.		SE

Common name	Scientific name	Population estimate	Annex I	Protection in the CR
Eagle Owl	Bubo bubo	15–25 p.	+	E
Pygmy Owl	Glaucidium passerinum	6–10 p.	+	SE
Little Owl	Athene noctua	8–10 p.		SE
Short-eared Owl	Asio flammeus	W	+	SE
Tengmalm's Owl	Aegolius funereus	5–10 p.	+	SE
Nightjar	Caprimulgus europaeus	10–20 p.	+	SE
Swift	Apus apus	80–100 p.		E
Kingfisher	Alcedo atthis	10–15 p.	+	SE
Hoopoe	Upupa epops	1–3 p.		SE
Wryneck	Jynx torquilla	80–100 p.		SE
Grey-headed Woodpecker	Picus canus	30–50 p.	+	
Black Woodpecker	Dryocopus martius	70–95 p.	+	
Middle Spotted Woodpecker	Dendrocopos medius	10–15 p.	+	E
Three-toed Woodpecker	Picoides tridactylus	I	+	SE
Crested Lark	Galerida cristata	10–15 p.		E
Woodlark	Lullula arborea	25–35 p.	+	SE
Sand Martin	Riparia riparia	30–40 p.		E
Swallow	Hirundo rustica	500–600 p.		E
Tawny Pipit	Anthus campestris	1–3 p.	+	SE
Yellow Wagtail	Motacilla flava	40–50 p.		SE
Waxwing	Bombycilla garrulus	M, W		E
Nightingale	Luscinia megarhynchos	50–70 p.		E
White-spotted Bluethroat	Luscinia svecica cyanecula	5–10 p.	+	SE
Whinchat	Saxicola rubetra	150–200 p.		E
Stonechat	Saxicola torquata	10–20 p.		E
Wheatear	Oenanthe oenanthe	3–5 p.		SE
Ring Ouzel	Turdus torquatus	1–2 p.		SE
Redwing	Turdus iliacus	M		SE
Savi's Warbler	Locustella luscinioides	2–3 p.		E
Great Reed Warbler	Acrocephalus arundinaceus	20–25 p.		SE
Barred Warbler	Sylvia nisoria	150–200 p.	+	SE
Spotted Flycatcher	Muscicapa striata	30–50 p.		E
Red-breasted Flycatcher	Ficedula parva	50–75 p.	+	SE
Collared Flycatcher	Ficedula albicollis	30–55 p.	+	
Bearded Tit	Panurus biarmicus	W		SE
Penduline Tit	Remiz pendulinus	10–20 p.		E
Golden Oriole	Oriolus oriolus	30–40 p.		SE
Red-backed Shrike	Lanius collurio	400–500 p.	+	E
Great Grey Shrike	Lanius excubitor	15–18 p.		E
Woodchat Shrike	Lanius senator	1–2 p.		SE
Nutcracker	Nucifraga caryocatactes	30–50 p.		E
Raven	Corvus corax	10–15 p.		E
Scarlet Rosefinch	Carpodacus erythrinus	10–15 p.		E
Corn Bunting	Miliaria calandra	100–150 p.		CE
Ortolan Bunting	Emberiza hortulana	2–3 p.	+	CE

Table 19: **Populations of selected bird species at Šumava mountains IBA**

Common name	Scientific name	Population estimate	Annex I	Protection in the CR
Little Grebe	*Tachybaptus ruficollis*	10 p.		E
Great Crested Grebe	*Podiceps cristatus*	B - tens of p.		E
Black Stork	*Ciconia nigra*	5 p.	+	SE
White Stork	*Ciconia ciconia*	4 p.	+	E
Gadwall	*Anas strepera*	B - sporadic		E
Teal	*Anas crecca*	B - rare		E
Honey Buzzard	*Pernis apivorus*	10–20 p.	+	SE
Marsh Harrier	*Circus aeruginosus*	B - sporadic	+	E
Hen Harrier	*Circus cyaneus*	2–4 p.	+	SE
Goshawk	*Accipiter gentilis*	B - tens of p.		E
Sparrowhawk	*Accipiter nisus*	B - tens of p.		SE
Lesser Spotted Eagle	*Aquila pomarina*	0–2 p.	+	CE
Hobby	*Falco subbuteo*	10–20 p.		SE
Peregrine	*Falco peregrinus*	2 p.	+	CE
Hazel Grouse	*Bonasa bonasia*	1,000 p.	+	SE
Black Grouse	*Tetrao tetrix*	150 males	+	SE
Capercaillie	*Tetrao urogallus*	50 males	+	CE
Partridge	*Perdix perdix*	B - rare		E
Quail	*Coturnix coturnix*	B - tens of p.		SE
Water Rail	*Rallus aquaticus*	B - sporadic		SE
Spotted Crake	*Porzana porzana*	1–2 p.	+	SE
Corncrake	*Crex crex*	100–200 males	+	SE
Snipe	*Gallinago gallinago*	B - hundreds of p.		SE
Woodcock	*Scolopax rusticola*	B - tens of p.		E
Green Sandpiper	*Tringa ochropus*	B - sporadic		SE
Common Sandpiper	*Actitis hypoleucos*	B - rare		SE
Common Tern	*Sterna hirundo*	10 p.	+	SE
Stock Dove	*Columba oenas*	B - tens of p.		SE
Barn Owl	*Tyto alba*	B - sporadic		SE
Eagle Owl	*Bubo bubo*	10 p.	+	E
Pygmy Owl	*Glaucidium passerinum*	250 p.	+	SE
Little Owl	*Athene noctua*	B - sporadic		SE
Ural Owl	*Strix uralensis*	2 p.	+	CE
Tengmalm's Owl	*Aegolius funereus*	200 p.	+	SE
Nightjar	*Caprimulgus europaeus*	B - sporadic	+	SE
Swift	*Apus apus*	H - běžně		E
Kingfisher	*Alcedo atthis*	B - sporadic	+	SE
Hoopoe	*Upupa epops*	B - sporadic		SE
Wryneck	*Jynx torquilla*	B - tens to hundreds of p.		SE
Grey-headed Woodpecker	*Picus canus*	B - tens of p.	+	
Black Woodpecker	*Dryocopus martius*	B - hundreds of p.	+	
White-backed Woodpecker	*Dendrocopos leucotos*	10–20 p.	+	SE
Three-toed Woodpecker	*Picoides tridactylus*	B - hundreds of p.	+	SE
Crested Lark	*Galerida cristata*	B - sporadic		E
Swallow	*Hirundo rustica*	H - běžně		E
Yellow Wagtail	*Motacilla flava*	B - sporadic		SE
White-spotted Bluethroat	*Luscinia svecica cyanecula*	5 p.	+	SE
Whinchat	*Saxicola rubetra*	H - běžně		E
Ring Ouzel	*Turdus torquatus*	450 p.		SE
Redwing	*Turdus iliacus*	B - sporadic		SE

Common name	Scientific name	Population estimate	Annex I	Protection in the CR
Barred Warbler	*Sylvia nisoria*	B - tens of p.	+	SE
Spotted Flycatcher	*Muscicapa striata*	B - hundreds of p.		E
Red-breasted Flycatcher	*Ficedula parva*	B - tens of p.	+	SE
Golden Oriole	*Oriolus oriolus*	B - sporadic		SE
Red-backed Shrike	*Lanius collurio*	B - hundreds of p.	+	E
Great Grey Shrike	*Lanius excubitor*	B - tens of p.		E
Nutcracker	*Nucifraga caryocatactes*	B - tens to hundreds of p.		E
Jackdaw	*Corvus monedula*	B - sporadic		SE
Raven	*Corvus corax*	B - tens of p.		E
Scarlet Rosefinch	*Carpodacus erythrinus*	370 p.		E
Corn Bunting	*Miliaria calandra*	B - sporadic		CE

Table 20: **Populations of selected bird species at Řežabinec pond IBA**

Common name	Scientific name	Population estimate	Annex I	Protection in the CR
Little Grebe	*Tachybaptus ruficollis*	5 p.		E
Great Crested Grebe	*Podiceps cristatus*	2 p.		E
Red-necked Grebe	*Podiceps grisegena*	M		SE
Black-necked Grebe	*Podiceps nigricollis*	30–40 p.		E
Cormorant	*Phalacrocorax carbo*	M		E
Bittern	*Botaurus stellaris*	M	+	CE
Little Bittern	*Ixobrychus minutus*	M	+	CE
Night Heron	*Nycticorax nycticorax*	M	+	SE
Little Egret	*Egretta garzetta*	M	+	SE
Great White Egret	*Egretta alba*	M	+	SE
Purple Heron	*Ardea purpurea*	M	+	CE
Black Stork	*Ciconia nigra*	M	+	SE
White Stork	*Ciconia ciconia*	M	+	E
Gadwall	*Anas strepera*	30–40 p.		E
Pintail	*Anas acuta*	M		CE
Teal	*Anas crecca*	5–10 p.		E
Garganey	*Anas querquedula*	1–3 p.		SE
Shoveler	*Anas clypeata*	M		SE
Red-crested Pochard	*Netta rufina*	M		SE
Goldeneye	*Bucephala clangula*	M		SE
White-tailed Eagle	*Haliaeetus albicilla*	W	+	CE
Marsh Harrier	*Circus aeruginosus*	3 p.	+	E
Hen Harrier	*Circus cyaneus*	M	+	SE
Montagu's Harrier	*Circus pygargus*	M	+	SE
Goshawk	*Accipiter gentilis*	M		E
Sparrowhawk	*Accipiter nisus*	M		SE
Osprey	*Pandion haliaeetus*	W	+	CE
Merlin	*Falco columbarius*	M	+	SE
Hobby	*Falco subbuteo*	M		SE
Partridge	*Perdix perdix*	2 p.		E
Quail	*Coturnix coturnix*	2 p.		SE
Water Rail	*Rallus aquaticus*	5 p.		SE
Spotted Crake	*Porzana porzana*	1 p.	+	SE
Little Crake	*Porzana parva*	1 p.	+	CE

Common name	Scientific name	Population estimate	Annex I	Protection in the CR
Crane	*Grus grus*	M	+	CE
Snipe	*Gallinago gallinago*	M		SE
Black-tailed Godwit	*Limosa limosa*	M		CE
Curlew	*Numenius arquata*	M		CE
Redshank	*Tringa totanus*	M		CE
Green Sandpiper	*Tringa ochropus*	M		SE
Common Sandpiper	*Actitis hypoleucos*	M		SE
Mediterranean Gull	*Larus melanocephalus*	M	+	SE
Common Tern	*Sterna hirundo*	10–15 p.	+	SE
Black Tern	*Chlidonias niger*	3–5 p.	+	CE
Stock Dove	*Columba oenas*	M		SE
Eagle Owl	*Bubo bubo*	M	+	E
Short-eared Owl	*Asio flammeus*	M	+	SE
Swift	*Apus apus*	F		E
Kingfisher	*Alcedo atthis*	F	+	SE
Grey-headed Woodpecker	*Picus canus*	1 p.	+	
Black Woodpecker	*Dryocopus martius*	M	+	
Sand Martin	*Riparia riparia*	F		E
Swallow	*Hirundo rustica*	F		E
Thrush Nightingale	*Luscinia luscinia*	M		SE
Nightingale	*Luscinia megarhynchos*	2–3 p.		E
White-spotted Bluethroat	*Luscinia svecica cyanecula*	3–5 p.	+	SE
Savi's Warbler	*Locustella luscinioides*	3 p.		E
Great Reed Warbler	*Acrocephalus arundinaceus*	3 p.		SE
Spotted Flycatcher	*Muscicapa striata*	2 p.		E
Bearded Tit	*Panurus biarmicus*	2–5 p.		SE
Penduline Tit	*Remiz pendulinus*	2 p.		E
Golden Oriole	*Oriolus oriolus*	2–4 p.		SE
Red-backed Shrike	*Lanius collurio*	5 p.	+	E
Great Grey Shrike	*Lanius excubitor*	1 p.		E
Jackdaw	*Corvus monedula*	M		SE
Raven	*Corvus corax*	M		E

Table 21: **Populations of selected bird species at Dehtář pond IBA**

Common name	Scientific name	Population estimate	Annex I	Protection in the CR
Little Grebe	*Tachybaptus ruficollis*	M		E
Great Crested Grebe	*Podiceps cristatus*	5–10 p.		E
Red-necked Grebe	*Podiceps grisegena*	M		SE
Black-necked Grebe	*Podiceps nigricollis*	0–5 p.		E
Cormorant	*Phalacrocorax carbo*	M		E
Great White Egret	*Egretta alba*	0–1 p.	+	SE
Black Stork	*Ciconia nigra*	F	+	SE
White Stork	*Ciconia ciconia*	1 p.	+	E
Spoonbill	*Platalea leucorodia*	F	+	CE
Gadwall	*Anas strepera*	0–5 p.		E
Pintail	*Anas acuta*	M		CE
Teal	*Anas crecca*	M		E
Garganey	*Anas querquedula*	M		SE

Common name	Scientific name	Population estimate	Annex I	Protection in the CR
Shoveler	*Anas clypeata*	M		SE
Red-crested Pochard	*Netta rufina*	M		SE
Ferruginous Duck	*Aythya nyroca*	M	+	CE
Goldeneye	*Bucephala clangula*	M, W		SE
Goosander	*Mergus merganser*	M		CE
Black Kite	*Milvus migrans*	M	+	CE
Red Kite	*Milvus milvus*	M	+	CE
White-tailed Eagle	*Haliaeetus albicilla*	M, W	+	CE
Marsh Harrier	*Circus aeruginosus*	1–3 p.	+	E
Hen Harrier	*Circus cyaneus*	W	+	SE
Montagu's Harrier	*Circus pygargus*	0–1 p.	+	SE
Goshawk	*Accipiter gentilis*	B		E
Montagu's Harrier	*Circus pygargus*	0–1 p.	+	SE
Sparrowhawk	*Accipiter nisus*	F		SE
Osprey	*Pandion haliaeetus*	M	+	CE
Peregrine	*Falco peregrinus*	F	+	CE
Partridge	*Perdix perdix*	0–10 p.		E
Quail	*Coturnix coturnix*	0–3 p.		SE
Water Rail	*Rallus aquaticus*	M		SE
Spotted Crake	*Porzana porzana*	M	+	SE
Crane	*Grus grus*	M	+	CE
Black-winged Stilt	*Himantopus himantopus*	M	+	
Avocet	*Recurvirostra avosetta*	M	+	CE
Snipe	*Gallinago gallinago*	0–3 p.		SE
Black-tailed Godwit	*Limosa limosa*	M		CE
Curlew	*Numenius arquata*	M		CE
Redshank	*Tringa totanus*	0–2 p.		CE
Green Sandpiper	*Tringa ochropus*	M		SE
Common Sandpiper	*Actitis hypoleucos*	M		SE
Common Tern	*Sterna hirundo*	10–100 p.	+	SE
Black Tern	*Chlidonias niger*	M	+	CE
Stock Dove	*Columba oenas*	B		SE
Swift	*Apus apus*	F		E
Kingfisher	*Alcedo atthis*	M, B-possible	+	SE
Sand Martin	*Riparia riparia*	F		E
Swallow	*Hirundo rustica*	F		E
Yellow Wagtail	*Motacilla flava*	0–3 p.		SE
Nightingale	*Luscinia megarhynchos*	0–3 p.		E
Whinchat	*Saxicola rubetra*	0–3 p.		E
Wheatear	*Oenanthe oenanthe*	M		SE
Spotted Flycatcher	*Muscicapa striata*	M		E
Collared Flycatcher	*Ficedula albicollis*	5–10 p.	+	
Penduline Tit	*Remiz pendulinus*	1–5 p.		E
Golden Oriole	*Oriolus oriolus*	1–3 p.		SE
Red-backed Shrike	*Lanius collurio*	1–3 p.	+	E
Great Grey Shrike	*Lanius excubitor*	0–1 p.		E
Jackdaw	*Corvus monedula*	M		SE

Table 22: **Populations of selected bird species at Třeboňsko IBA**

Common name	Scientific name	Population estimate	Annex I	Protection in the CR
Little Grebe	*Tachybaptus ruficollis*	150–250 p.		E
Great Crested Grebe	*Podiceps cristatus*	250–350 p.		E
Red-necked Grebe	*Podiceps grisegena*	I		SE
Black-necked Grebe	*Podiceps nigricollis*	30–50 p.		E
Cormorant	*Phalacrocorax carbo*	50–100 p.		E
Bittern	*Botaurus stellaris*	1–3 p.	+	CE
Little Bittern	*Ixobrychus minutus*	1–5 p.	+	CE
Night Heron	*Nycticorax nycticorax*	50–120 p.	+	SE
Little Egret	*Egretta garzetta*	0–2 p.	+	SE
Great White Egret	*Egretta alba*	0–3 p., M	+	SE
Purple Heron	*Ardea purpurea*	0–2 p.	+	CE
Black Stork	*Ciconia nigra*	10–15 p.	+	SE
White Stork	*Ciconia ciconia*	10–15 p.	+	E
Spoonbill	*Platalea leucorodia*	I	+	CE
Gadwall	*Anas strepera*	500–700 p.		E
Pintail	*Anas acuta*	0–1 p., M		CE
Teal	*Anas crecca*	1–5 p., M		E
Garganey	*Anas querquedula*	0–5 p., M		SE
Shoveler	*Anas clypeata*	0–5 p., M		SE
Red-crested Pochard	*Netta rufina*	25–35 p.		SE
Ferruginous Duck	*Aythya nyroca*	M	+	CE
Goldeneye	*Bucephala clangula*	30–60 p.		SE
Goosander	*Mergus merganser*	M		CE
Honey Buzzard	*Pernis apivorus*	10–20 p.	+	SE
Black Kite	*Milvus migrans*	1–2 p.	+	CE
Red Kite	*Milvus milvus*	1–2 p.	+	CE
White-tailed Eagle	*Haliaeetus albicilla*	10–13 p., W	+	CE
Marsh Harrier	*Circus aeruginosus*	40–60 p.	+	E
Hen Harrier	*Circus cyaneus*	0–3 p., W	+	SE
Montagu's Harrier	*Circus pygargus*	0–2 p.	+	SE
Goshawk	*Accipiter gentilis*	15–20 p.		E
Sparrowhawk	*Accipiter nisus*	20–50 p.		SE
Lesser Spotted Eagle	*Aquila pomarina*	I	+	CE
Imperial Eagle	*Aquila heliaca*	I	+	
Golden Eagle	*Aquila chrysaetos*	I	+	CE
Osprey	*Pandion haliaeetus*	M	+	CE
Red-footed Falcon	*Falco vespertinus*	I		CE
Merlin	*Falco columbarius*	W	+	SE
Hobby	*Falco subbuteo*	5–10 p.		SE
Peregrine	*Falco peregrinus*	I	+	CE
Hazel Grouse	*Bonasa bonasia*	6–10 p.	+	SE
Black Grouse	*Tetrao tetrix*	I	+	SE
Partridge	*Perdix perdix*	30–80 p.		E
Quail	*Coturnix coturnix*	30–50 p.		SE
Water Rail	*Rallus aquaticus*	100–150 p.		SE
Spotted Crake	*Porzana porzana*	5–10 p.	+	SE
Little Crake	*Porzana parva*	0–5 p.	+	CE
Corncrake	*Crex crex*	0–10 p.	+	SE
Crane	*Grus grus*	I	+	CE
Avocet	*Recurvirostra avosetta*	0–2 p.	+	CE
Snipe	*Gallinago gallinago*	30–50 p.		SE

Common name	Scientific name	Population estimate	Annex I	Protection in the CR
Great Snipe	*Gallinago media*	I	+	E
Woodcock	*Scolopax rusticola*	10–50 p.		E
Black-tailed Godwit	*Limosa limosa*	1–3 p.		CE
Curlew	*Numenius arquata*	M		CE
Redshank	*Tringa totanus*	2–5 p.		CE
Green Sandpiper	*Tringa ochropus*	15–30 p.		SE
Common Sandpiper	*Actitis hypoleucos*	M		SE
Mediterranean Gull	*Larus melanocephalus*	0–2 p.	+	SE
Common Tern	*Sterna hirundo*	50–100 p.	+	SE
Black Tern	*Chlidonias niger*	5–10 p.	+	CE
Stock Dove	*Columba oenas*	10–20 p.		SE
Barn Owl	*Tyto alba*	5–10 p.		SE
Eagle Owl	*Bubo bubo*	10–15 p.	+	E
Pygmy Owl	*Glaucidium passerinum*	100–150 p.	+	SE
Little Owl	*Athene noctua*	5–10 p.		SE
Short-eared Owl	*Asio flammeus*	W	+	SE
Tengmalm's Owl	*Aegolius funereus*	30–50 p.	+	SE
Nightjar	*Caprimulgus europaeus*	20–40 p.	+	SE
Swift	*Apus apus*	300–400 p.		E
Kingfisher	*Alcedo atthis*	10–20 p.	+	SE
Hoopoe	*Upupa epops*	3–5 p.		SE
Wryneck	*Jynx torquilla*	20–50 p.		SE
Grey-headed Woodpecker	*Picus canus*	50–100 p.	+	
Black Woodpecker	*Dryocopus martius*	50–100 p.	+	
Middle Spotted Woodpecker	*Dendrocopos medius*	50–70 p.	+	E
Crested Lark	*Galerida cristata*	0–2 p.		E
Woodlark	*Lullula arborea*	20–40 p.	+	SE
Sand Martin	*Riparia riparia*	1,000–2,000 p.		E
Swallow	*Hirundo rustica*	1,000–1,500 p.		E
Water Pipit	*Anthus spinoletta*	M		SE
Yellow Wagtail	*Motacilla flava*	10–20 p.		SE
Waxwing	*Bombycilla garrulus*	M, W		E
Thrush Nightingale	*Luscinia luscinia*	0–2 p.		SE
Nightingale	*Luscinia megarhynchos*	10–30 p.		E
White-spotted Bluethroat	*Luscinia svecica cyanecula*	150–250 p.	+	SE
Whinchat	*Saxicola rubetra*	50–100 p.		E
Stonechat	*Saxicola torquata*	0–5 p.		E
Wheatear	*Oenanthe oenanthe*	I		SE
Redwing	*Turdus iliacus*	M		SE
Savi's Warbler	*Locustella luscinioides*	10–20 p.		E
Great Reed Warbler	*Acrocephalus arundinaceus*	10–15 p.		SE
Barred Warbler	*Sylvia nisoria*	0–3 p.	+	SE
Spotted Flycatcher	*Muscicapa striata*	300–500 p.		E
Red-breasted Flycatcher	*Ficedula parva*	0–5 p.	+	SE
Collared Flycatcher	*Ficedula albicollis*	100–200 p.	+	
Bearded Tit	*Panurus biarmicus*	0–5 p.		SE
Penduline Tit	*Remiz pendulinus*	100–250 p.		E
Golden Oriole	*Oriolus oriolus*	300–500 p.		SE
Red-backed Shrike	*Lanius collurio*	200–400 p.	+	E
Great Grey Shrike	*Lanius excubitor*	10–20 p.		E
Nutcracker	*Nucifraga caryocatactes*	5–10 p.		E
Jackdaw	*Corvus monedula*	50–100 p.		SE
Raven	*Corvus corax*	10–20 p.		E

Common name	Scientific name	Population estimate	Annex I	Protection in the CR
Scarlet Rosefinch	*Carpodacus erythrinus*	0–5 p.		E
Corn Bunting	*Miliaria calandra*	0–5 p.		CE
Ortolan Bunting	*Emberiza hortulana*	I	+	CE

Table 23: **Populations of selected bird species at Nové Mlýny middle reservoir IBA**

Common name	Scientific name	Population estimate	Annex I	Protection in the CR
Little Grebe	*Tachybaptus ruficollis*	2–5 p.		E
Great Crested Grebe	*Podiceps cristatus*	M		E
Red-necked Grebe	*Podiceps grisegena*	M		SE
Cormorant	*Phalacrocorax carbo*	M, W		E
Great White Egret	*Egretta alba*	M, W	+	SE
Gadwall	*Anas strepera*	20–30 p.		E
Pintail	*Anas acuta*	M		CE
Teal	*Anas crecca*	M		E
Garganey	*Anas querquedula*	M		SE
Shoveler	*Anas clypeata*	M		SE
Red-crested Pochard	*Netta rufina*	30–40 p.		SE
Goldeneye	*Bucephala clangula*	W		SE
Goosander	*Mergus merganser*	W		CE
White-tailed Eagle	*Haliaeetus albicilla*	M, W	+	CE
Marsh Harrier	*Circus aeruginosus*	1–3 p.	+	E
Hen Harrier	*Circus cyaneus*	M	+	SE
Osprey	*Pandion haliaeetus*	M	+	CE
Water Rail	*Rallus aquaticus*	2–5 p.		SE
Spotted Crake	*Porzana porzana*	M	+	SE
Snipe	*Gallinago gallinago*	M		SE
Black-tailed Godwit	*Limosa limosa*	M		CE
Curlew	*Numenius arquata*	M		CE
Redshank	*Tringa totanus*	0–2 p.		CE
Green Sandpiper	*Tringa ochropus*	M, W		SE
Common Sandpiper	*Actitis hypoleucos*	M		SE
Mediterranean Gull	*Larus melanocephalus*	5–15 p.	+	SE
Common Tern	*Sterna hirundo*	230–270 p.	+	SE
Black Tern	*Chlidonias niger*	M	+	CE
Kingfisher	*Alcedo atthis*	M	+	SE
Wryneck	*Jynx torquilla*	2–5 p.		SE
Sand Martin	*Riparia riparia*	M		E
Swallow	*Hirundo rustica*	M		E
Yellow Wagtail	*Motacilla flava*	15–30 p.		SE
Nightingale	*Luscinia megarhynchos*	2–5 p.		E
White-spotted Bluethroat	*Luscinia svecica cyanecula*	M	+	SE
Savi's Warbler	*Locustella luscinioides*	1–3 p.		E
Great Reed Warbler	*Acrocephalus arundinaceus*	1–5 p.		SE
Spotted Flycatcher	*Muscicapa striata*	5–10 p.		E
Bearded Tit	*Panurus biarmicus*	M		SE
Penduline Tit	*Remiz pendulinus*	10–20 p.		E
Golden Oriole	*Oriolus oriolus*	5–10 p.		SE
Red-backed Shrike	*Lanius collurio*	1–5 p.	+	E
Jackdaw	*Corvus monedula*	1–3 p.		SE

Table 24: **Populations of selected bird species at Pálava IBA**

Common name	Scientific name	Population estimate	Annex I	Protection in the CR
Little Grebe	*Tachybaptus ruficollis*	5–10 p.		E
Great Crested Grebe	*Podiceps cristatus*	8–10 p.		E
Cormorant	*Phalacrocorax carbo*	60–80 p.		E
Little Bittern	*Ixobrychus minutus*	0–3 p.	+	CE
Night Heron	*Nycticorax nycticorax*	M	+	SE
Great White Egret	*Egretta alba*	M, W	+	SE
Black Stokr	*Ciconia nigra*	1–2 p.	+	SE
White Stork	*Ciconia ciconia*	10–12 p.	+	E
Gadwall	*Anas strepera*	10–15 p.		E
Teal	*Anas crecca*	M		E
Garganey	*Anas querquedula*	M		SE
Shoveler	*Anas clypeata*	M		SE
Red-crested Pochard	*Netta rufina*	5–10 p.		SE
Goldeneye	*Bucephala clangula*	M		SE
Goosander	*Mergus merganser*	M		CE
Honey Buzzard	*Pernis apivorus*	5–8 p.	+	SE
Black Kite	*Milvus migrans*	1–2 p.	+	CE
Red Kite	*Milvus milvus*	0–1 p., M	+	CE
White-tailed Eagle	*Haliaeetus albicilla*	0–1 p., M, W	+	CE
Marsh Harrier	*Circus aeruginosus*	6–8 p.	+	E
Hen Harrier	*Circus cyaneus*	M	+	SE
Montagu's Harrier	*Circus pygargus*	M	+	SE
Goshawk	*Accipiter gentilis*	4–7 p.		E
Sparrowhawk	*Accipiter nisus*	3–5 p.		SE
Imperial Eagle	*Aquila heliaca*	M	+	
Osprey	*Pandion haliaeetus*	M	+	CE
Merlin	*Falco columbarius*	M	+	SE
Hobby	*Falco subbuteo*	0–3 p., M		SE
Saker	*Falco cherrug*	0–1 p.		CE
Peregrine	*Falco peregrinus*	M	+	CE
Partridge	*Perdix perdix*	20–30 p.		E
Quail	*Coturnix coturnix*	15–25 p.		SE
Water Rail	*Rallus aquaticus*	10–15 p.		SE
Little Crake	*Porzana parva*	0–1 p.	+	CE
Snipe	*Gallinago gallinago*	M		SE
Woodcock	*Scolopax rusticola*	M		E
Green Sandpiper	*Tringa ochropus*	M		SE
Common Sandpiper	*Actitis hypoleucos*	0–1 p., M		SE
Common Tern	*Sterna hirundo*	M	+	SE
Black Tern	*Chlidonias niger*	M	+	CE
Stock Dove	*Columba oenas*	5–10 p.		SE
Barn Owl	*Tyto alba*	0–2 p.		SE
Eagle Owl	*Bubo bubo*	4–5 p.	+	E
Little Owl	*Athene noctua*	0–1 p.		SE
Swift	*Apus apus*	30–50 p.		E
Kingfisher	*Alcedo atthis*	3–5 p.	+	SE
Bee-eater	*Merops apiaster*	1–3 p.		SE
Hoopoe	*Upupa epops*	7–10 p.		SE
Wryneck	*Jynx torquilla*	200–300 p.		SE
Grey-headed Woodpecker	*Picus canus*	8–16 p.	+	
Black Woodpecker	*Dryocopus martius*	20–25 p.	+	

Common name	Scientific name	Population estimate	Annex I	Protection in the CR
Syrian Woodpecker	*Dendrocopos syriacus*	60 p.	+	SE
Middle Spotted Woodpecker	*Dendrocopos medius*	70–150 p.	+	E
Crested Lark	*Galerida cristata*	2–3 p.		E
Woodlark	*Lullula arborea*	M	+	SE
Sand Martin	*Riparia riparia*	100–300 p.		E
Swallow	*Hirundo rustica*	200–400 p.		E
Yellow Wagtail	*Motacilla flava*	10–20 p.		SE
Waxwing	*Bombycilla garrulus*	M		E
Nightingale	*Luscinia megarhynchos*	20–40 p.		E
White-spotted Bluethroat	*Luscinia svecica cyanecula*	M	+	SE
Whinchat	*Saxicola rubetra*	M		E
Stonechat	*Saxicola torquata*	500–1,000 p.		E
Wheatear	*Oenanthe oenanthe*	0–2 p.		SE
Redwing	*Turdus iliacus*	M		SE
Savi's Warbler	*Locustella luscinioides*	10–15 p.		E
Great Reed Warbler	*Acrocephalus arundinaceus*	15–25 p.		SE
Barred Warbler	*Sylvia nisoria*	350–600 p.	+	SE
Spotted Flycatcher	*Muscicapa striata*	2,000–3,000 p.		E
Collared Flycatcher	*Ficedula albicollis*	1,000–2,000 p.	+	
Bearded Tit	*Panurus biarmicus*	5–15 p.		SE
Wallcreeper	*Tichodroma muraria*	M, W		CE
Penduline Tit	*Remiz pendulinus*	25–35 p.		E
Golden Oriole	*Oriolus oriolus*	200–300 p.		SE
Red-backed Shrike	*Lanius collurio*	1,000–1,300 p.	+	E
Great Grey Shrike	*Lanius excubitor*	0–2 p., W		E
Jackdaw	*Corvus monedula*	20–30 p.		SE
Raven	*Corvus corax*	1–2 p.		E
Corn Bunting	*Miliaria calandra*	300–400 p.		CE

Table 25: **Populations of selected bird species at Lednické rybníky ponds IBA**

Common name	Scientific name	Population estimate	Annex I	Protection in the CR
Little Grebe	*Tachybaptus ruficollis*	5–10 p.		O
Great Crested Grebe	*Podiceps cristatus*	10–30 p.		O
Red-necked Grebe	*Podiceps grisegena*	M		SE
Black-necked Grebe	*Podiceps nigricollis*	0–5 p.		O
Cormorant	*Phalacrocorax carbo*	M, W		O
Bittern	*Botaurus stellaris*	M	+	CE
Little Bittern	*Ixobrychus minutus*	0–5 p.	+	CE
Night Heron	*Nycticorax nycticorax*	250–270 p.	+	SE
Little Egret	*Egretta garzetta*	0–1 p.	+	SE
Great White Egret	*Egretta alba*	M, W	+	SE
Purple Heron	*Ardea purpurea*	0–1 p.	+	CE
Black Stork	*Ciconia nigra*	M	+	SE
White Stork	*Ciconia ciconia*	1–3 p.	+	O
Spoonbill	*Platalea leucorodia*	M	+	CE
Gadwall	*Anas strepera*	10–15 p.		O
Pintail	*Anas acuta*	M		CE
Teal	*Anas crecca*	M		O
Garganey	*Anas querquedula*	M		SE

Common name	Scientific name	Population estimate	Annex I	Protection in the CR
Shoveler	*Anas clypeata*	M		SE
Red-crested Pochard	*Netta rufina*	20–30 p.		SE
Goldeneye	*Bucephala clangula*	W		SE
Goosander	*Mergus merganser*	W		CE
White-tailed Eagle	*Haliaeetus albicilla*	W	+	CE
Marsh Harrier	*Circus aeruginosus*	5–10 p.	+	E
Osprey	*Pandion haliaeetus*	M	+	CE
Hobby	*Falco subbuteo*	0–1 p.		SE
Partridge	*Perdix perdix*	1–3 p.		E
Quail	*Coturnix coturnix*	1–2 p.		SE
Water Rail	*Rallus aquaticus*	10–15 p.		SE
Spotted Crake	*Porzana porzana*	M	+	SE
Little Crake	*Porzana parva*	0–3 p.	+	CE
Avocet	*Recurvirostra avosetta*	M	+	CE
Snipe	*Gallinago gallinago*	M		SE
Black-tailed Godwit	*Limosa limosa*	M		CE
Curlew	*Numenius arquata*	M		CE
Redshank	*Tringa totanus*	0–1 p.		CE
Green Sandpiper	*Tringa ochropus*	M		SE
Common Sandpiper	*Actitis hypoleucos*	M		SE
Common Tern	*Sterna hirundo*	M	+	SE
Black Tern	*Chlidonias niger*	M	+	CE
Stock Dove	*Columba oenas*	0–2 p.		SE
Kingfisher	*Alcedo atthis*	1–2 p.	+	SE
Hoopoe	*Upupa epops*	0–1 p.		SE
Wryneck	*Jynx torquilla*	10–20 p.		SE
Grey-headed Woodpecker	*Picus canus*	1–2 p.	+	
Black Woodpecker	*Dryocopus martius*	2–5 p.	+	
Syrian Woodpecker	*Dendrocopos syriacus*	5–10 p.	+	SE
Middle Spotted Woodpecker	*Dendrocopos medius*	10–15 p.	+	E
Sand Martin	*Riparia riparia*	M		E
Yellow Wagtail	*Motacilla flava*	0–5 p.		SE
Waxwing	*Bombycilla garrulus*	M, W		E
Nightingale	*Luscinia megarhynchos*	30–50 p.		E
White-spotted Bluethroat	*Luscinia svecica cyanecula*	5–10 p.	+	SE
Stonechat	*Saxicola torquata*	2–5 p.		E
Redwing	*Turdus iliacus*	M		SE
Savi's Warbler	*Locustella luscinioides*	20–30 p.		E
Great Reed Warbler	*Acrocephalus arundinaceus*	50–80 p.		SE
Barred Warbler	*Sylvia nisoria*	10–20 p.	+	SE
Spotted Flycatcher	*Muscicapa striata*	30–50 p.		E
Collared Flycatcher	*Ficedula albicollis*	30–50 p.	+	
Bearded Tit	*Panurus biarmicus*	30–50 p.		SE
Penduline Tit	*Remiz pendulinus*	15–30 p.		E
Golden Oriole	*Oriolus oriolus*	20–30 p.		SE
Red-backed Shrike	*Lanius collurio*	20–30 p.	+	E
Great Grey Shrike	*Lanius excubitor*	W		E
Jackdaw	*Corvus monedula*	5–10 p.		SE
Corn Bunting	*Miliaria calandra*	5–10 p.		CE

Table 26: Populations of selected bird species at the Confluence of the Morava and Dyje rivers IBA

Common name	Scientific name	Population estimate	Annex I	Protection in the CR
Little Grebe	*Tachybaptus ruficollis*	15 p., M, W		E
Great Crested Grebe	*Podiceps cristatus*	M		E
Red-necked Grebe	*Podiceps grisegena*	M		SE
Black-necked Grebe	*Podiceps nigricollis*	0–1 p., M		E
Cormorant	*Phalacrocorax carbo*	M, W		E
Bittern	*Botaurus stellaris*	M, I	+	CE
Night Heron	*Nycticorax nycticorax*	M, F	+	SE
Little Egret	*Egretta garzetta*	M, F	+	SE
Great White Egret	*Egretta alba*	M, W, F	+	SE
Purple Heron	*Ardea purpurea*	M, F	+	CE
Black Stork	*Ciconia nigra*	4–5 p., M	+	SE
White Stork	*Ciconia ciconia*	30–36 p.	+	E
Spoonbill	*Platalea leucorodia*	M	+	CE
Gadwall	*Anas strepera*	1 p.		E
Pintail	*Anas acuta*	M		CE
Teal	*Anas crecca*	M, W		E
Garganey	*Anas querquedula*	5 p., M		SE
Shoveler	*Anas clypeata*	0–1 p, M		SE
Red-crested Pochard	*Netta rufina*	M		SE
Ferruginous Duck	*Aythya nyroca*	M	+	CE
Goldeneye	*Bucephala clangula*	M, W		SE
Goosander	*Mergus merganser*	M, W		CE
Honey Buzzard	*Pernis apivorus*	4–10 p	+	SE
Black Kite	*Milvus migrans*	8–10 p, M	+	CE
Red Kite	*Milvus milvus*	4–8 p, M, W	+	CE
White-tailed Eagle	*Haliaeetus albicilla*	M, W	+	CE
Marsh Harrier	*Circus aeruginosus*	0–1 p, M, F	+	E
Hen Harrier	*Circus cyaneus*	M, W	+	SE
Montagu's Harrier	*Circus pygargus*	M	+	SE
Goshawk	*Accipiter gentilis*	3–4 p		O
Sparrowhawk	*Accipiter nisus*	1 p. (since 2000)		SE
Lesser Spotted Eagle	*Aquila pomarina*	M	+	CE
Imperial Eagle	*Aquila heliaca*	1 p.	+	
Golden Eagle	*Aquila chrysaetos*	I	+	CE
Osprey	*Pandion haliaeetus*	M	+	CE
Red-footed Falcon	*Falco vespertinus*	M		CE
Merlin	*Falco columbarius*	M, W	+	SE
Hobby	*Falco subbuteo*	2–5 p.		SE
Saker	*Falco cherrug*	0–2 p., W		CE
Peregrine	*Falco peregrinus*	M, W	+	CE
Quail	*Coturnix coturnix*	2–6 males		SE
Water Rail	*Rallus aquaticus*	1–7 p.		SE
Spotted Crake	*Porzana porzana*	1–8 males, M	+	SE
Little Crake	*Porzana parva*	0–2 males	+	CE
Corncrake	*Crex crex*	10–23 males	+	SE
Crane	*Grus grus*	M	+	CE
Snipe	*Gallinago gallinago*	0–5 p., M		SE
Woodcock	*Scolopax rusticola*	M		E
Black-tailed Godwit	*Limosa limosa*	M		CE
Curlew	*Numenius arquata*	M		CE
Redshank	*Tringa totanus*	0–1 p., M, F		CE

Common name	Scientific name	Population estimate	Annex I	Protection in the CR
Green Sandpiper	*Tringa ochropus*	B - possible, M, W, F		SE
Common Sandpiper	*Actitis hypoleucos*	4–5 p.		SE
Common Tern	*Sterna hirundo*	M, F	+	SE
Stock Dove	*Columba oenas*	> 15 p.		SE
Eagle Owl	*Bubo bubo*	I	+	E
Short-eared Owl	*Asio flammeus*	M, W	+	SE
Nightjar	*Caprimulgus europaeus*	0–1 p.	+	SE
Swift	*Apus apus*	M, F		E
Kingfisher	*Alcedo atthis*	< 10 p.	+	SE
Bee-eater	*Merops apiaster*	M		SE
Roller	*Coracias garrulus*	M	+	CE
Hoopoe	*Upupa epops*	0–3 p.		SE
Wryneck	*Jynx torquilla*	35–40 p.		SE
Grey-headed Woodpecker	*Picus canus*	> 10–15 p.	+	
Black Woodpecker	*Dryocopus martius*	10–15 p.	+	
Syrian Woodpecker	*Dendrocopos syriacus*	0–5 p.	+	SE
Middle Spotted Woodpecker	*Dendrocopos medius*	400 p.	+	E
Woodlark	*Lullula arborea*	M	+	SE
Sand Martin	*Riparia riparia*	30–100 p.		E
Swallow	*Hirundo rustica*	H		E
Yellow Wagtail	*Motacilla flava*	> 1–5 p., M		SE
Waxwing	*Bombycilla garrulus*	M, W		E
Nightingale	*Luscinia megarhynchos*	H		E
White-spotted Bluethroat	*Luscinia svecica cyanecula*	M	+	SE
Whinchat	*Saxicola rubetra*	0–2 p.; M		E
Stonechat	*Saxicola torquata*	30–35 p.		E
Wheatear	*Oenanthe oenanthe*	M		SE
Redwing	*Turdus iliacus*	M, W		SE
Savi's Warbler	*Locustella luscinioides*	< 10 p.		E
Great Reed Warbler	*Acrocephalus arundinaceus*	1–5 p.		SE
Barred Warbler	*Sylvia nisoria*	10–20 p.	+	SE
Spotted Flycatcher	*Muscicapa striata*	H		E
Collared Flycatcher	*Ficedula albicollis*	1,000–1,500 p.	+	
Penduline Tit	*Remiz pendulinus*	0–5 p.		E
Golden Oriole	*Oriolus oriolus*	H		SE
Red-backed Shrike	*Lanius collurio*	100–200 p.	+	E
Great Grey Shrike	*Lanius excubitor*	1–7 p.		E
Woodchat Shrike	*Lanius senator*	M, I		SE
Jackdaw	*Corvus monedula*	M, W		SE
Raven	*Corvus corax*	0–1 p.		E
Corn Bunting	*Miliaria calandra*	4–10 males, M		CE
Ortolan Bunting	*Emberiza hortulana*	M, I	+	CE

Table 27: **Populations of selected bird species at Beskydy mountains IBA**

Common name	Scientific name	Population estimate	Annex I	Protection in the CR
Black Stork	*Ciconia nigra*	20–25 p.	+	SE
White Stork	*Ciconia ciconia*	3–5 p.	+	O
Honey Buzzard	*Pernis apivorus*	15–25 p.	+	SE
Goshawk	*Accipiter gentilis*	25–40 p.		O

Common name	Scientific name	Population estimate	Annex I	Protection in the CR
Sparrowhawk	*Accipiter nisus*	100–200 p.		SE
Lesser Spotted Eagle	*Aquila pomarina*	0–1 p., M	+	CE
Imperial Eagle	*Aquila heliaca*	M	+	
Golden Eagle	*Aquila chrysaetos*	M	+	CE
Osprey	*Pandion haliaeetus*	M	+	CE
Merlin	*Falco columbarius*	W	+	SE
Hobby	*Falco subbuteo*	10–15 p.		SE
Peregrine	*Falco peregrinus*	M	+	CE
Hazel Grouse	*Bonasa bonasia*	100–150 p.	+	SE
Capercaillie	*Tetrao urogallus*	5–10 F.	+	CE
Partridge	*Perdix perdix*	10–20 p.		E
Quail	*Coturnix coturnix*	10–30 p.		SE
Water Rail	*Rallus aquaticus*	1–2 p.		SE
Corncrake	*Crex crex*	150–250 males	+	SE
Woodcock	*Scolopax rusticola*	100–200 p.		E
Common Sandpiper	*Actitis hypoleucos*	5–10 p.		SE
Stock Dove	*Columba oenas*	150–250 p.		SE
Eagle Owl	*Bubo bubo*	1–3 p.	+	E
Pygmy Owl	*Glaucidium passerinum*	30–60 p.	+	SE
Ural Owl	*Strix uralensis*	4–8 p.	+	CE
Tengmalm's Owl	*Aegolius funereus*	30–60 p.	+	SE
Swift	*Apus apus*	60–120 p.		E
Kingfisher	*Alcedo atthis*	5–20 p.	+	SE
Hoopoe	*Upupa epops*	0–1 p., M		SE
Wryneck	*Jynx torquilla*	25–40 p.		SE
Grey-headed Woodpecker	*Picus canus*	50–100 p.	+	
Black Woodpecker	*Dryocopus martius*	80–150 p.	+	
Middle Spotted Woodpecker	*Dendrocopos medius*	2–3 p.	+	E
White-backed Woodpecker	*Dendrocopos leucotos*	60–120 p.	+	SE
Three-toed Woodpecker	*Picoides tridactylus*	50–100 p.	+	SE
Woodlark	*Lullula arborea*	M	+	SE
Sand Martin	*Riparia riparia*	M		E
Swallow	*Hirundo rustica*	250–500 p.		E
Yellow Wagtail	*Motacilla flava*	M		SE
Waxwing	*Bombycilla garrulus*	M, W		E
Thrush Nightingale	*Luscinia luscinia*	M		SE
Whinchat	*Saxicola rubetra*	80–150 p.		E
Stonechat	*Saxicola torquata*	50–100 p.		E
Wheatear	*Oenanthe oenanthe*	M		SE
Ring Ouzel	*Turdus torquatus*	400–600 p.		SE
Redwing	*Turdus iliacus*	M, W		SE
Great Reed Warbler	*Acrocephalus arundinaceus*	0–1 p., M		SE
Barred Warbler	*Sylvia nisoria*	30–40 p.	+	SE
Spotted Flycatcher	*Muscicapa striata*	300–500 p.		E
Red-breasted Flycatcher	*Ficedula parva*	250–500 p.	+	SE
Collared Flycatcher	*Ficedula albicollis*	250–500 p.	+	
Golden Oriole	*Oriolus oriolus*	2–4 p.		SE
Red-backed Shrike	*Lanius collurio*	1,000–1,500 p.	+	E
Great Grey Shrike	*Lanius excubitor*	0–2 p., W		E
Nutcracker	*Nucifraga caryocatactes*	60–120 p.		E
Raven	*Corvus corax*	60–90 p.		E
Scarlet Rosefinch	*Carpodacus erythrinus*	10–20 p.		E
Corn Bunting	*Miliaria calandra*	1–3 p.		CE

Table 28: **Populations of selected bird species at Poodří IBA**

Common name	Scientific name	Population estimate	Annex I	Protection in the CR
Little Grebe	*Tachybaptus ruficollis*	25–35 p., M, W		E
Great Crested Grebe	*Podiceps cristatus*	110–130 p., M, W		E
Red-necked Grebe	*Podiceps grisegena*	0–1 p., M		SE
Black-necked Grebe	*Podiceps nigricollis*	70–80 p., M		E
Cormorant	*Phalacrocorax carbo*	2–5 p., M, W		E
Bittern	*Botaurus stellaris*	3–5 p., M, W	+	CE
Little Bittern	*Ixobrychus minutus*	1–3 p., W	+	CE
Night Heron	*Nycticorax nycticorax*	0–1 p., M, p	+	SE
Little Egret	*Egretta garzetta*	I	+	SE
Great White Egret	*Egretta alba*	M, W	+	SE
Purple Heron	*Ardea purpurea*	M	+	CE
Black Stork	*Ciconia nigra*	0–2 p., M	+	SE
White Stork	*Ciconia ciconia*	12–15 p., M	+	E
Spoonbill	*Platalea leucorodia*	I	+	CE
Gadwall	*Anas strepera*	180–200 p., M		E
Teal	*Anas crecca*	2–5 p., M, W		E
Garganey	*Anas querquedula*	10–15 p., M		SE
Shoveler	*Anas clypeata*	5–10 p., M		SE
Red-crested Pochard	*Netta rufina*	2 p., M		SE
Ferruginous Duck	*Aythya nyroca*	0–1 p., M	+	CE
Goldeneye	*Bucephala clangula*	7–10 p., M, W		SE
Goosander	*Mergus merganser*	M, W		CE
Honey Buzzard	*Pernis apivorus*	1–3 p., M	+	SE
Black Kite	*Milvus migrans*	1 p., M	+	CE
Red Kite	*Milvus milvus*	1 p., M	+	CE
White-tailed Eagle	*Haliaeetus albicilla*	0–1 p., M, W, F	+	CE
Marsh Harrier	*Circus aeruginosus*	5–45 p., M	+	E
Hen Harrier	*Circus cyaneus*	M, W	+	SE
Montagu's Harrier	*Circus pygargus*	M	+	SE
Goshawk	*Accipiter gentilis*	1–3 p., W		E
Sparrowhawk	*Accipiter nisus*	5–10 p., W		SE
Lesser Spotted Eagle	*Aquila pomarina*	M	+	CE
Imperial Eagle	*Aquila heliaca*	I	+	
Golden Eagle	*Aquila chrysaetos*	M	+	CE
Osprey	*Pandion haliaeetus*	M	+	CE
Red-footed Falcon	*Falco vespertinus*	M		CE
Merlin	*Falco columbarius*	M, W	+	SE
Hobby	*Falco subbuteo*	0–2 p., M		SE
Saker	*Falco cherrug*	0–1 p.		CE
Peregrine	*Falco peregrinus*	M	+	CE
Partridge	*Perdix perdix*	10–20 p.		E
Quail	*Coturnix coturnix*	5–10 p., M		SE
Water Rail	*Rallus aquaticus*	15–25 p., M, W		SE
Spotted Crake	*Porzana porzana*	2–5 p., M	+	SE
Little Crake	*Porzana parva*	1–3 p., M	+	CE
Corncrake	*Crex crex*	10–15 p., M	+	SE
Crane	*Grus grus*	0–1 p., M	+	CE
Avocet	*Recurvirostra avosetta*	I	+	CE
Snipe	*Gallinago gallinago*	1–3 p., M		SE
Great Snipe	*Gallinago media*	M	+	E

Common name	Scientific name	Population	Annex I estimate	Protection in the CR
Woodcock	*Scolopax rusticola*	M		E
Black-tailed Godwit	*Limosa limosa*	1–5 p., M		CE
Curlew	*Numenius arquata*	0–1 p., M, F		CE
Redshank	*Tringa totanus*	1–3 p., M		CE
Green Sandpiper	*Tringa ochropus*	0–3 p., M, W		SE
Common Sandpiper	*Actitis hypoleucos*	10–15 p., M		SE
Mediterranean Gull	*Larus melanocephalus*	0–1 p., M	+	SE
Common Tern	*Sterna hirundo*	5–10 p., M	+	SE
Black Tern	*Chlidonias niger*	1 p., M	+	CE
Stock Dove	*Columba oenas*	M		SE
Barn Owl	*Tyto alba*	5–8 p., W		SE
Little Owl	*Athene noctua*	0–1 p.		SE
Short-eared Owl	*Asio flammeus*	M, W	+	SE
Nightjar	*Caprimulgus europaeus*	1–3 p., M	+	SE
Swift	*Apus apus*	B - common, M		E
Kingfisher	*Alcedo atthis*	15–25 p., M, W	+	SE
Bee-eater	*Merops apiaster*	I		SE
Hoopoe	*Upupa epops*	M		SE
Wryneck	*Jynx torquilla*	H, M		SE
Grey-headed Woodpecker	*Picus canus*	10–20 p., W	+	
Black Woodpecker	*Dryocopus martius*	0–2 p., W, F	+	
Middle Spotted Woodpecker	*Dendrocopos medius*	5–10 p., W	+	E
Sand Martin	*Riparia riparia*	50–100 p., M, F		E
Swallow	*Hirundo rustica*	H, M, F		E
Water Pipit	*Anthus spinoletta*	M		SE
Yellow Wagtail	*Motacilla flava*	1–5 p., M, F		SE
Waxwing	*Bombycilla garrulus*	M, F, W		E
Thrush Nightingale	*Luscinia luscinia*	M		SE
Nightingale	*Luscinia megarhynchos*	20–30 p., M		E
White-spotted Bluethroat	*Luscinia svecica cyanecula*	B - possible, M	+	SE
Whinchat	*Saxicola rubetra*	10–20 p., M		E
Stonechat	*Saxicola torquata*	10–20 p., M		E
Wheatear	*Oenanthe oenanthe*	M		SE
Ring Ouzel	*Turdus torquatus*	M		SE
Redwing	*Turdus iliacus*	M, W		SE
Savi's Warbler	*Locustella luscinioides*	5–20 p., M, F		E
Great Reed Warbler	*Acrocephalus arundinaceus*	10–15 p., M, F		SE
Spotted Flycatcher	*Muscicapa striata*	20–30 p., M		E
Collared Flycatcher	*Ficedula albicollis*	50–70 p., M	+	
Bearded Tit	*Panurus biarmicus*	M, W		SE
Penduline Tit	*Remiz pendulinus*	0–50 p., M, F		E
Golden Oriole	*Oriolus oriolus*	20–30 p., M		SE
Red-backed Shrike	*Lanius collurio*	20–30 p., M	+	E
Great Grey Shrike	*Lanius excubitor*	5–10 p., M, W		E
Nutcracker	*Nucifraga caryocatactes*	M, F		E
Jackdaw	*Corvus monedula*	30–50 p., M, W		SE
Raven	*Corvus corax*	3–10 p., W, F		E
Scarlet Rosefinch	*Carpodacus erythrinus*	1–5 p., M		E
Corn Bunting	*Miliaria calandra*	0–1 p., M		CE

Table 29: Populations of selected bird species at Heřmanský stav pond-Stružka wetlands IBA

Common name	Scientific name	Population estimate	Annex I	Protection in the CR
Little Grebe	*Tachybaptus ruficollis*	12 p., M, W		E
Great Crested Grebe	*Podiceps cristatus*	25 p., M, W		E
Red-necked Grebe	*Podiceps grisegena*	0–1 p., M		SE
Black-necked Grebe	*Podiceps nigricollis*	15 p., M		E
Cormorant	*Phalacrocorax carbo*	M, W		E
Bittern	*Botaurus stellaris*	1–5 p., M, W	+	CE
Little Bittern	*Ixobrychus minutus*	4 p., M	+	CE
Night Heron	*Nycticorax nycticorax*	0–2 p., M	+	SE
Great White Egret	*Egretta alba*	M	+	SE
Black Stork	*Ciconia nigra*	0–2 p., M	+	SE
White Stork	*Ciconia ciconia*	3–6 p., M	+	E
Gadwall	*Anas strepera*	25 p., M		E
Pintail	*Anas acuta*	0–1 p., M		CE
Teal	*Anas crecca*	3 p., M, W		E
Garganey	*Anas querquedula*	4 p., M		SE
Shoveler	*Anas clypeata*	4 p., M		SE
Goldeneye	*Bucephala clangula*	M, W		SE
Goosander	*Mergus merganser*	1–2 p., M, W		CE
Honey Buzzard	*Pernis apivorus*	1 p., M	+	SE
Black Kite	*Milvus migrans*	M, I	+	CE
Red Kite	*Milvus milvus*	M, I	+	CE
White-tailed Eagle	*Haliaeetus albicilla*	M, W	+	CE
Marsh Harrier	*Circus aeruginosus*	10–20 p., M	+	O
Hen Harrier	*Circus cyaneus*	M, W	+	SE
Montagu's Harrier	*Circus pygargus*	M	+	SE
Goshawk	*Accipiter gentilis*	M, W		E
Sparrowhawk	*Accipiter nisus*	3 p., M, W		SE
Lesser Spotted Eagle	*Aquila pomarina*	M	+	CE
Osprey	*Pandion haliaeetus*	M	+	CE
Merlin	*Falco columbarius*	M	+	SE
Hobby	*Falco subbuteo*	0–1 p., M		SE
Saker	*Falco cherrug*	0–1 p., M		CE
Partridge	*Perdix perdix*	4 p., M, W		E
Quail	*Coturnix coturnix*	M, I		SE
Water Rail	*Rallus aquaticus*	10 p., M		SE
Spotted Crake	*Porzana porzana*	0–2 p., M	+	SE
Corncrake	*Crex crex*	M, I	+	SE
Crane	*Grus grus*	0–1 p., M	+	CE
Snipe	*Gallinago gallinago*	0–2 p., M		SE
Woodcock	*Scolopax rusticola*	M, I		E
Black-tailed Godwit	*Limosa limosa*	0–1 p., M		CE
Curlew	*Numenius arquata*	M		CE
Redshank	*Tringa totanus*	5–13 p., M		CE
Green Sandpiper	*Tringa ochropus*	B - possible, M, W		SE
Common Sandpiper	*Actitis hypoleucos*	8 p., M		SE
Mediterranean Gull	*Larus melanocephalus*	1–2 p., M	+	SE
Common Tern	*Sterna hirundo*	1–3 p., M	+	SE
Black Tern	*Chlidonias niger*	M	+	CE
Stock Dove	*Columba oenas*	M		SE
Little Owl	*Athene noctua*	0–1 p.		SE

Common name	Scientific name	Population estimate	Annex I	Protection in the CR
Nightjar	*Caprimulgus europaeus*	B - possible	+	SE
Swift	*Apus apus*	H, M		E
Kingfisher	*Alcedo atthis*	10 p.	+	SE
Hoopoe	*Upupa epops*	M		SE
Wryneck	*Jynx torquilla*	M		SE
Grey-headed Woodpecker	*Picus canus*	7–15 p., W	+	
Black Woodpecker	*Dryocopus martius*	0–3 p., M, W	+	
Crested Lark	*Galerida cristata*	M		E
Sand Martin	*Riparia riparia*	10 p., M		E
Swallow	*Hirundo rustica*	40 p., M		E
Water Pipit	*Anthus spinoletta*	M, W		SE
Yellow Wagtail	*Motacilla flava*	8 p., M		SE
Waxwing	*Bombycilla garrulus*	M, W		E
Thrush Nightingale	*Luscinia luscinia*	M		SE
Nightingale	*Luscinia megarhynchos*	11 p., M		E
White-spotted Bluethroat	*Luscinia svecica cyanecula*	10–25 p., M	+	SE
Whinchat	*Saxicola rubetra*	2 p., M		E
Stonechat	*Saxicola torquata*	6 p., M		E
Wheatear	*Oenanthe oenanthe*	5 p., M		SE
Redwing	*Turdus iliacus*	M		SE
Savi's Warbler	*Locustella luscinioides*	5 p., M		E
Great Reed Warbler	*Acrocephalus arundinaceus*	10 p., M		SE
Barred Warbler	*Sylvia nisoria*	M	+	SE
Spotted Flycatcher	*Muscicapa striata*	25 p., M		E
Collared Flycatcher	*Ficedula albicollis*	10 p., M	+	
Bearded Tit	*Panurus biarmicus*	10 p., M, W		SE
Penduline Tit	*Remiz pendulinus*	10 p., M		E
Golden Oriole	*Oriolus oriolus*	15 p., M		SE
Red-backed Shrike	*Lanius collurio*	13 p., M	+	E
Great Grey Shrike	*Lanius excubitor*	M, W, F		E
Jackdaw	*Corvus monedula*	5 p., M, W		SE
Raven	*Corvus corax*	1–2 p., M, W		E
Scarlet Rosefinch	*Carpodacus erythrinus*	9 p., M		E
Corn Bunting	*Miliaria calandra*	2–4 p.		CE

Table 30: **Populations of selected bird species at Jeseníky mountains IBA**

Common name	Scientific name	Population estimate	Annex I	Protection in the CR
Little Grebe	*Tachybaptus ruficollis*	1–2 p.		E
Black Stork	*Ciconia nigra*	5 p.	+	SE
White Stork	*Ciconia ciconia*	6 p.	+	E
Honey Buzzard	*Pernis apivorus*	3 p.	+	SE
Hen Harrier	*Circus cyaneus*	2 p.	+	SE
Goshawk	*Accipiter gentilis*	10 p.		E
Sparrowhawk	*Accipiter nisus*	20 p.		SE
Hobby	*Falco subbuteo*	5 p.		SE
Hazel Grouse	*Bonasa bonasia*	80 p.	+	SE
Black Grouse	*Tetrao tetrix*	10 ex.	+	SE
Capercaillie	*Tetrao urogallus*	1–6 ex.	+	CE

Common name	Scientific name	Population estimate	Annex I	Protection in the CR
Partridge	*Perdix perdix*	B - common		E
Quail	*Coturnix coturnix*	B - common		SE
Corncrake	*Crex crex*	200 p.	+	SE
Dotterel	*Charadrius morinellus*	I	+	CE
Woodcock	*Scolopax rusticola*	40–50 p.		E
Common Sandpiper	*Actitis hypoleucos*	2–3 p.		SE
Stock Dove	*Columba oenas*	20–30 p.		SE
Barn Owl	*Tyto alba*	1–2 p.		SE
Eagle Owl	*Bubo bubo*	6 p.	+	E
Pygmy Owl	*Glaucidium passerinum*	2 p.	+	SE
Little Owl	*Athene noctua*	2 p.		SE
Tengmalm's Owl	*Aegolius funereus*	30 p.	+	SE
Nightjar	*Caprimulgus europaeus*	1–2 p.	+	SE
Swift	*Apus apus*	150–200 p.		E
Kingfisher	*Alcedo atthis*	1–2 p.	+	SE
Wryneck	*Jynx torquilla*	5–8 p.		SE
Grey-headed Woodpecker	*Picus canus*	10 p.	+	
Black Woodpecker	*Dryocopus martius*	50 p.	+	
Middle Spotted Woodpecker	*Dendrocopos medius*	10 p.	+	E
Swallow	*Hirundo rustica*	600 p.		E
Water Pipit	*Anthus spinoletta*	30–50 p.		SE
Alpine Accentor	*Prunella collaris*	2–4 p.		SE
Whinchat	*Saxicola rubetra*	120 p.		E
Stonechat	*Saxicola torquata*	5–10 p.		O
Wheatear	*Oenanthe oenanthe*	5–10 p.		SE
Ring Ouzel	*Turdus torquatus*	30–40 p.		SE
Barred Warbler	*Sylvia nisoria*	20 p.	+	SE
Spotted Flycatcher	*Muscicapa striata*	80–100 p.		E
Red-breasted Flycatcher	*Ficedula parva*	30–50 p.	+	SE
Collared Flycatcher	*Ficedula albicollis*	B - possible	+	
Red-backed Shrike	*Lanius collurio*	80–120 p.	+	E
Nutcracker	*Nucifraga caryocatactes*	40–60 p.		E
Jackdaw	*Corvus monedula*	20 p.		SE
Raven	*Corvus corax*	30–40 p.		O
Scarlet Rosefinch	*Carpodacus erythrinus*	60 p.		O

Table 31: **Selected bird species with breeding populations at IBAs in the Czech Republic**

Common name	Scientific name	Minimum national breeding population	Number of IBAs where the species breed	Proportion (%) of national population breeding at all IBAs
Cormorant	*Phalacrocorax carbo*	150 p.	3	75
Bittern	*Botaurus stellaris*	20 p.	5	40
Little Bittern	*Ixobrychus minutus*	50 p.	6	14
Night Heron	*Nycticorax nycticorax*	450 p.	5	67
Little Egret	*Egretta garzetta*	1 p.	2	100
Purple Heron	*Ardea purpurea*	2 p.	3	100
Black Stork	*Ciconia nigra*	200 p.	11	34
White Stork	*Ciconia ciconia*	930 p.	11	9
Gadwall	*Anas strepera*	1,500 p.	11	cca 50
Teal	*Anas crecca*	50 p.	6	50

Common name	Scientific name	Minimum national breeding population	Number of IBAs where the species breed	Proportion (%) of national population breeding at all IBAs
Garganey	Anas querquedula	50 p.	7	> 90
Shoveler	Anas clypeata	40 p.	7	65
Red-crested Pochard	Netta rufina	160 p.	5	> 50
Goldeneye	Bucephala clangula	50 p.	2	74
Honey Buzzard	Pernis apivorus	600 p.	12	12
Black Kite	Milvus migrans	30 p.	6	53
Red Kite	Milvus milvus	30 p.	8	37
White-tailed Eagle	Haliaeetus albicilla	25 p.	5	68
Marsh Harrier	Circus aeruginosus	900 p.	12	< 15
Hen Harrier	Circus cyaneus	50 p.	7	20
Montagu's Harrier	Circus pygargus	20 p.	3	10
Lesser Spotted Eagle	Aquila pomarina	0–3 p.	3	100
Imperial Eagle	Aquila heliaca	1 p.	1	100
Saker	Falco cherrug	5 p.	4	cca 50
Peregrine	Falco peregrinus	10 p.	2	30
Black Grouse	Tetrao tetrix	800 p.	4	34
Capercaillie	Tetrao urogallus	150 ex.	3	cca 100
Spotted Crake	Porzana porzana	20 p.	8	80
Little Crake	Porzana parva	8 p.	7	50
Corncrake	Crex crex	1,500 males	8	43
Black-tailed Godwit	Limosa limosa	30 p.	3	7
Redshank	Tringa totanus	40 p.	7	20
Mediterranean Gull	Larus melanocephalus	25 p.	5	28
Common Tern	Sterna hirundo	350 p.	7	90
Black Tern	Chlidonias niger	15 p.	3	100
Eagle Owl	Bubo bubo	600 p.	8	11
Pygmy Owl	Glaucidium passerinum	900 p.	7	48
Ural Owl	Strix uralensis	6 p.	22	100
Tengmalm's Owl	Aegolius funereus	550 p.	5	70
Nightjar	Caprimulgus europaeus	600 p.	9	< 10
Kingfisher	Alcedo atthis	400 p.	12	< 25
Hoopoe	Upupa epops	60 p.	8	< 25
Grey-headed Woodpecker	Picus canus	3,000 p.	14	< 35
Black Woodpecker	Dryocopus martius	3,000 p.	12	< 50
Syrian Woodpecker	Dendrocopos syriacus	300 p.	3	22
Middle Spotted Woodpecker	Dendrocopos medius	3,000 p.	11	23
White-backed Woodpecker	Dendrocopos leucotos	150 p.	2	> 50
Three-toed Woodpecker	Picoides tridactylus	300 p.	2	100
Woodlark	Lullula arborea	600 p.	3	8
Tawny Pipit	Anthus campestris	40 p.	1	25
Water Pipit	Anthus spinolleta	130 p.	2	85
Alpine Accentor	Prunella collaris	11 p.	2	100
White-spotted Bluethroat	Luscinia svecica cyanecula	300 p.	7	58
Red-spotted Bluethroat	Luscinia svecica svecica	25 p.	1	100
Barred Warbler	Sylvia nisoria	1,500 p.	10	< 45
Red-breasted Flycatcher	Ficedula parva	800 p.	6	< 65
Collared Flycatcher	Ficedula albicollis	25,000 p.	11	10
Red-backed Shrike	Lanius collurio	25,000 p.	15	< 25
Scarlet Rosefinch	Carpodacus erythrinus	1,440 p.	8	52
Ortolan Bunting	Emberiza hortulana	200 p.	2	1

References

BirdLife International, 1995: IBA criteria. Categories and thresholds. *BirdLife International, Cambridge, UK (unpublished report).*

Bufka L., Málková P., 1999: [Re-introduction of Capercaillie in the Šumava Mts.] *Zpravodaj IB A, prosinec 1999: 6 (in Czech only).*

Bureš J., 1999: [The release of semi-wild mallards reaches a catastrophic scale in the Třeboňsko PLA.] *Zpravodaj IBA, červenec 1999: 3 (in Czech only).*

Bureš J., 2000: [Restriction of ducks and geese hunting in the Třeboňsko area.] *Zpravodaj IBA, prosinec 2000: 2 (in Czech only).*

Bureš S., 1996: [Jeseníky Mts.] *Zpravodaj IBA, listopad 1996: 5 (in Czech only).*

Bürger P., 1995: [Conference of Šumava Mts. Biodiversity.] *Zpravodaj IBA, listopad 1995: 6 (in Czech only).*

Bürger P., Pykal J., Hora J., 1997: [Corncrake in the Šumava Mts.] *Zpravodaj IBA, 1997: 3 (in Czech only).*

Cepák J., Ševčík J., 1998: (The first breeding of Yellow-legged Gull, *Larus cachinnans*, in Bohemia.) *Sylvia 34: 149–152 (in Czech with an English summary).*

Chytil J., 1996a: [Lednice fishponds.] *Zpravodaj IBA, listopad 1996: 3 (in Czech only).*

Chytil J., 1996b: [Nové Mlýny middle reservoir.] *Zpravodaj IBA, listopad 1996: 4 (in Czech only).*

Chytil J., 1996c: [Confluence of Morava and Dyje rivers.] *Zpravodaj IBA, listopad 1996: 4 (in Czech only).*

Chytil J., 1996: [Pálava IBA.] *Zpravodaj IBA, listopad 1996: 5 (in Czech only).*

Chytil J., 1997: (The report of the Czech Rarities Committee for the period 1995–1996.) *Zprávy ČSO 45: 18–21 (in Czech with an English summary).*

Chytil J, 1998: [Restriction of hunting on the Věstonice Reservoir.] *Ptačí svět V/4: 7 (in Czech only).*

Chytil J., Hakrová P., Hudec K., Husák Š., Jandová J., Pellantová J. (eds.), 1999: [Wetlands of the Czech Republic – the list of wetlands of the Czech Republic.] *Český ramsarský výbor, Mikulov, 327 pp. (in Czech, English version in 2001).*

Chytil J., Macháček P., 1997: [South-moravian Important Bird Areas.] *Zpravodaj IBA, 1997: 6 (in Czech only).*

Chytil J., Macháček P., 1998: [From south-moravian Important Bird Areas.] *Zpravodaj IBA, 1998: 5 (in Czech only).*

Chytil J., Macháček P., 1999: [Autumn/winter in south-moravian IBAs.] *Zpravodaj IBA, prosinec 1999: 2 (in Czech only).*

Chytil J., Macháček P., 2000: (Nové Mlýny middle reservoir.) *Sylvia 36/1 – Aktuální problémy ochrany ptáků a jejich prostředí v ČR: 15–20 (in Czech with an English summary).*

Collar N. J., Crosby M. J., Stattersfield A. J., 1994: Birds to watch 2. The world list of threatened birds. *BirdLife International, Cambridge, UK (Conservation Series No. 4), 407 pp.*

Damohorský M., Stejskal V., 1998: [Bird protection in the Czech legislation.] *In: Hora J. (ed.), 1998: Legislativa EU a ochrana přírody. ČSO, Praha: 17–32 (in Czech only).*.

Flousek J., 1999: [Important bird area (IBA) Krkonoše.] *Zpravodaj IBA 8/99: 4 (in Czech only).*

Grimmet R. F. A., Gammell A. B., 1989: Inventory of Important Bird areas in the European Community. (Unpublished report prepared for the Directorate-General for the Environment, Consumer Protection and Nuclear Safety of the European Community, study contract B6610-54–88). *ICBP, Cambridge, UK.*

Grimmet R. F. A., Jones T. A., 1989: Important Bird Areas in Europe. *ICBP, Cambridge (Tech. Publ. No. 9), 888 pp.*

Hajný L., Baláž P., 1999: [About activities in the IBA Jeseníky Mts.] *Zpravodaj IBA, červenec 1999: 4 (in Czech only).*

Heath M. F., Evans M. I. (eds.), 2000: Important Bird Areas in Europe: Priority sites for conservation. 2 Volumes. *BirdLife International, Cambridge, UK (BirdLife Conservation Series No. 8), 866 + 791 pp.*

Heredia B., Rose L., Painter M. (eds.), 1996: Globally threatened birds in Europe: action plans. *Council of Europe, Strasbourg, France, 408 pp.*

Hora J., 1992a: (Progress report on results of the IBA Programme in the Czech Republic.) *In: Hora J. et al., 1992: Významná ptačí území v České a Slovenské republice. Proc. of sem. Čsl. sekce ICBP. Třeboň 1992. Čsl. sekce ICBP, Praha: 7–12 (in Czech with an English summary).*

Hora J., 1992b: Ornithological Importance of Czechoslovakia. *In: Hora J., Kaňuch P. et al., 1992: Important Bird Areas in Europe. Czechoslovakia. Čsl. sekce ICBP, Praha: 46–47 (in Czech and in English).*

Hora J., 1994a: [Introduction.] *Zpravodaj IBA, listopad 1994: 1 (in Czech only).*

Hora J., 1994b: [XXIth World Conference of BirdLife International "Global Partnership for Conservation" Rosenheim (Germany), August 1994.] *Zprávy ČSO 39: 48–49 (in Czech only).*

Hora J., 1994c: [XXIth World Conference of BirdLife International.] *Ptačí svět I/3: 5 (in Czech only).*

Hora J., 1995a: (Results of the IBA Programme in the Czech Republic in 1992–1994.) *In: Hora J. et al., 1995: Významná ptačí území v České republice. Proc. of sem., Kostelec n. Č. l. 1995. ČSO, Praha: 7–12 (in Czech only).*

Hora J., 1995b: [Revision of IBAs list was opened.] *Zpravodaj IBA, červen 1995: 1 (in Czech only).*

Hora J., 1996a: [IBA Inventory Review Workshop.] *Zpravodaj IBA, červen 1996: 3 (in Czech only).*

Hora J., 1996b: [IBA Inventory Review Workshop II. (close).] *Zpravodaj IBA, listopad 1996: 6 (in Czech only) .*

Hora J., 1998: [From workshop in Jordan.] *Zpravodaj IBA, 1998: 6–7 (in Czech only).*

Hora J., 1999: [From workshop in Taiwan.]. *Zpravodaj IBA, červenec 1999: 7 (in Czech only).*

Hora J. Kaňuch P. et al., 1992: Important Bird Areas in Europe. Czechoslovakia. *Čsl. sekce ICBP, Praha, 115 pp (in Czech and in English).*

Hora J., Kaňuch, P., Thorn M., Safranek W., Pojer F., Přibylová D., Hajný L. (eds.), 1992: (Important bird areas in the Czech and Slovak Republic.) *Proc. of sem. Čsl. sekce ICBP. Třeboň 1992. Čsl. sekce ICBP, Praha, 175 pp. (in Czech with an English summary).*

Hora J., Málková P., 1999: [Important Bird Areas in the European programme of BirdLife International 2000–2004.] *Zpravodaj IBA, prosinec 1999: 2 (in Czech only).*

Hora J., Málková P., 2000: (Results of the IBA programme in the Czech Republic in 1995–1999.) *In: Málková P., Jandová J. (eds.), 2000: Významná ptačí území na konci tisíciletí. Proc. of sem. IBA, Mikulov 1999. ČSO, Praha: 5–11 (in Czech with an English summary).*

Hora J., Plesník J., 1996: [Sikalathi – important bird area of Finland.] *Zpravodaj IBA, červen 1996: 4 (in Czech only).*

Hora J., Plesník J., Jandová J. (eds.), 1995: (Important bird areas in the Czech Republic.) *Proc. of sem., Kostelec n. Č. l. 1995. ČSO, Praha, 95 pp. (in Czech with an English summary).*

Hudec K., Chytil J., Šťastný K., Bejček V., 1995: (The Birds of the Czech Republic.) *Sylvia 31: 97–149 (in Czech with an English summary).*

Hudec K., Šťastný K., Bejček V., 2000: (Results of the long-term studies of avifauna.) *Sylvia 36/1 – Aktuální problémy ochrany ptáků a jejich prostředí v ČR: 2–5 (in Czech with an English summary).*

Hůrka L., 1987 (ed.): [List of bird species recorded in the western part of Czechoslovakia.] *Sbor. Západoč. muz. v Plzni, Přír. 62: 1–59 (in Czech with a German summary).*

IUCN, 1994: Guidelines for protected area management categories. *Gland, Switzerland: IUCN – The World Conservation Union.*

IUCN Commission on National Parks and Protected Areas, 1994: Parks for Life: Action for Protected Areas in Europe. *IUCN, Gland, Switzerland and Cambridge, UK, 154 pp.*

Kondělka D., 1996: The first case of the breeding of the Little Tern *(Sterna albifrons)* in Czechia. *Čas. Slez. muz., Opava 45/1: 87–88.*

Kloubec B., 1998: [Adjustments in NNR Velký a Malý Tisý.] *Zpravodaj IBA, 1998: 3 (in Czech only).*

Kloubec B., 1999a: [The Ural Owl again in the Šumava Mts.] *Zpravodaj IBA, červenec 1999: 5 (in Czech only).*

Kloubec B., 1999b: [Continuation of project in NNR Velký a Malý Tisý.] *Zpravodaj IBA, listopad 1999: 7 (in Czech only).*

Kloubec B., Pykal J., 1996: [Dehtář pond.] *Zpravodaj IBA, 1996: 3 (in Czech only).*

Košťál J., 1997: [Exhibition Poodří – landscape and people.] *Zpravodaj IBA, 1997: 5 (in Czech only).*

Lemberk V., 1997: [Nature of the Pardubice region in the past and today.] *Východočes. muz. v Pardubicích. Pardubice, 100 pp.*

Málková P., 2000: (Results of the national Black Grouse *(Tetrao tetrix)* spring count in 2000.) *Zprávy ČSO 51: 26 (in Czech with an English summary).*

Málková P., Jandová J. (eds.), 2000: (Important bird areas at the end of the Millenium.) *Proc. of sem. IBA, Mikulov 1999. ČSO, Praha, 107 pp. (in Czech with an English summary).*

Martincová R., Musil P., Cepák J., 2000: (Great Cormorant, *Phalacrocorax carbo sinensis.) Sylvia 36/1 – Aktuální problémy ochrany ptáků a jejich prostředí v České republice: 39–42 (in Czech with English summary).*

Mlčoch S., Hošek J., Pelc F. (eds.), 1998: State nature conservation and landscape protection programme of the Czech Republic. *Ministry of Environment of the Czech Republic, Prague, 21 pp. + xxi (in Czech and in English).*

Osieck E. R., 1999: IBA review and the EU Birds Directive. *Internal Report; 6th and final draft. 18 April 1998. BirdLife International,Cambridge, UK.*

Osieck E. R., Mörzer Bruyns M. F., 1981 Important bird areas in the European community. *ICBP, Cambridge, UK.*

Pavelčík P., 2000: (First breeding record of the European Scops Owl, *Otus scops*, in the Czech Republic, history and present of occurrence in the Moravia.) *Buteo 11: 149–156 (in Czech with an English summary).*

Pavelka J., 1995: [From IBA Beskydy Mts.] *Zpravodaj IBA, listopad 1995: 6 (in Czech only).*

Pavelka J., 1996: [Beskydy Mts.] *Zpravodaj IBA, listopad 1996: 5 (in Czech only).*

Pavelka J., 1997: [Beskydy Mts.] *Zpravodaj IBA, 1997: 3 (in Czech only).*

Pavelka J., 2000a: [IBA Beskydy Mts. in 2000.] *Zpravodaj IBA, prosinec 2000: 2 (in Czech only).*

Pavelka J., 2000b: [Lethal glass.] *Ptačí svět VII/1: 2 (in Czech only).*

Pavelka K., 1996: : [Poodří IBA.] *Zpravodaj IBA, listopad 1996: 4. (in Czech only)*

Pavelka K., 1997: : [Poodří IBA.] *Zpravodaj IBA, 1997: 5 (in Czech only).*

Pavelka K., 1998: : [Poodří IBA.] *Zpravodaj IBA, 1998: 5 (in Czech only).*

Pavelka K., Košťál J., Pospíšil J., 2000: [IBA Poodří – news in 2000.] *Zpravodaj IBA, srpen 2000: 3 (in Czech only).*

Pecl K., 1996: [Řežabinec pond.] *Zpravodaj IBA, listopad 1996: 3 (in Czech only).*

Pecl K., 1997: [Řežabinec pond.] *Zpravodaj IBA, 1997: 2 (in Czech only)*.

Pecl K., 1999: [Fifty years of the existence of the Řežabinec ornithological reserve.] *Zpravodaj IBA, červenec 1999: 6 (in Czech only)*.

Plesník J., 1995: (Proposal of new IUCN Red List categories for assessing extinction threats in species.) *In: Hora J. et al., 1995: Významná ptačí území v České republice. Proc. of sem., Kostelec n. Č. l. 1995. ČSO, Praha: 85–95 (in Czech with an English sumary)*.

Plesník J., 1998: [Birds and Habitats Directives: fundamental EU legislation in nature conservancy.] *In: Hora, J. (ed.), 1998: Legislativa EU a ochrana přírody. ČSO, Praha: 33–44 (in Czech only)*.

Plesník J., 2000: [Agrienvironmental programs in the EU from the nature management view-point.] *Ochrana přírody 55: 268–270 (in Czech only)*.

Plesník J., Prchalová M. (eds.), in prep: National Biodiversity Conservsation Strategy and Action Plan in the Czech Republic. *Ministry of the Environment of the Czech Republic, Prague*.

Plesník J., Žáková G., 2000: [Nature management funding in the EU: current state and the outlook for the Czech Republic.] *Ochrana přírody 55: 276–277 (in Czech only)*.

Polčák J., 1997: (The first record of Blue-winged Teal *(Anas discors)* in the Czech Republic.) *Sylvia 33: 96–97 (in Czech with an English summary)*.

Procházka P., Musil P., 1999: (First documented breeding attempt of the Moustached Warbler *(Acrocephalus melanopogon)* in the Czech Republic.) *Sylvia 35: 101–105 (in Czech with an English summary)*.

Pykal J., 1995: [Workshop – Protection of the Corncrake in Europe. Gdaňsk (Poland), October 1994.] *Zprávy ČSO 40: 57–58 (in Czech only)*.

Pykal J., Kloubec B., 1998: [Dehtář pond was established as a by Temporary Protected Area.] *Zpravodaj IBA, 1998: 3 (in Czech only)*.

Rose P. M., Scott D. A., 1994: Waterfowl population estimates. *International Waterfowl and Wetland Research Bureau, UK (IWRB Publ. 29), 102 pp*.

Rose P. M., Scott D. A., 1997: Waterfowl population estimates. Second edition. *Wetlands International, Wageningen, Netherlands (Publ. No. 44), 106 pp*.

Scott D. A., Rose P. M., 1996: Atlas of Anatidae populations in Africa and Western Europe. *Wetlands International, Wageningen, Netherlands (Wetlands International Publ. No. 41), 336 pp*.

Sedláček K., Klescht V., 1992: Protection of Birds in Czechoslovakia. *In: Hora J., Kaňuch P et al., 1992: Important bird areas in Europe. Czechoslovakia. Čsl. sekce ICBP, Praha: 33–45 (in Czech and in English)*.

Schröpfer L., 2000: (The Little Owl, *Athene noctua*, in the Czech Republic – abundance and distribution in the years 1998–1999.) *Buteo 11: 161–174 (in Czech with an English summary)*.

Šafránek J., 1999: [Negative impact of transport on birdlife.] *Ptáci kolem nás 4: 2–8 (in Czech only)*.

Šálek M., Chytil J., 1994: [Site Management Planning for Conservation. Gdaňsk (Poland), April 1994.] *Zprávy ČSO 39: 46–48 (in Czech only)*.

Ševčík J., 1997: [Ornithological news from Třeboňsko.] *Zpravodaj IBA, 1997: 2 (in Czech only)*.

Ševčík J., Bureš J., 1996: [Building artificial istets in ponds in Třeboňsko PLA.] *Zpravodaj IBA, červen 1996: 2 (in Czech only)*.

Šimeček K., 1997: (The development of the population of European Bee-eater, *Merops apiaster,* in Moravia.) *Zpravodaj JMP ČSO 10: 7–15 (in Czech with an English summary)*.

Šimeček K., 1998a: (The first record of Purple Sandpiper, *Calidris maritima,* in the Czech Republic.) *Sylvia 34: 153–154 (in Czech with an English summary)*.

Šimeček K., 1998b: (Breeding of European Bee-eater, *Merops apiaster,* in South Moravia in 1997.) *Zpravodaj JMP ČSO 11: 16 (in Czech with an English summary)*.

Šimeček K., 1999: (Breeding of European Bee-eater, *Merops apiaster,* in South Moravia during 1998.) *Zpravodaj JMP ČSO 13: 23–25 (in Czech with an English summary)*.

Šťastný K., Bejček V., 1993: (Breeding bird populations sizes in the Czech Republic.) *Sylvia 29: 72–81 (in Czech with an English summary)*.

Šťastný K., Bejček V., in prep.: [Red list of birds in the Czech Republic.] *In: Plesník J., Hanzal V. (eds.): Červený seznam ohrožených druhů České republiky. Obratlovci (in Czech only)*.

Šťastný K., Bejček V., Hudec K., 1997: (The Atlas of breeding birds in the Czech Republic, 1985–1989.) *H&H, Praha, 457 pp. (in Czech with an English summary.)*

Šťastný K., Randík A., Hudec K., 1987: (The Atlas of breeding birds in Czechoslovakia, 1973–1977.) *Academia, Praha, 483 pp. (in Czech with an English summary)*.

Tejrovský V.,1996: [The Doupov Hills.] *Zpravodaj IBA, listopad 1996: 5 (in Czech only)*.

Tejrovský V.,1997: [The Doupov Hills.] *Zpravodaj IBA, listopad 1997: 4 (in Czech only)*.

Tejrovský V.,1998: [The Doupov Hills.] *Zpravodaj IBA, listopad 1998: 4 (in Czech only)*.

Tejrovský V.,1998/1999: (Avifauna of The Natural reserve – pond Vinařský rybník, Chomutov district: results from 1988–1998.) *Sbor. okr. muz. v Mostě, ř. přír., 20/21: 81–89 (in Czech with an English summary)*.

Tejrovský V., 1999a: [The Doupov Hills IBA – Vinařský rybník pond Nature reserve.] *Zpravodaj IBA, červenec 1999: 5–6 (in Czech only)*.

Tejrovský V., 1999b: [Records of rare and uncommon birds in The Doupov Hills IBA.] *Zpravodaj IBA, prosinec 1999: 7 (in Czech only).*

Tichai M., 1998: [Křivoklátsko.] *Zpravodaj IBA, 1998: 4 (in Czech only).*

Tucker G. M., Heath M. F., 1994: Birds in Europe: their conservation status. *BirdLife International, Cambridge, UK (Conservation Series No. 3), 600 pp.*

Tucker G. M., Evans M. I. (eds.), 1997: Habitats for birds in Europe: a conservation strategy for the wider environment. *BirdLife International, Cambridge, UK (Conservation Series No. 6), 464 pp.*

Urbánek L., 1996: [Žehuňský rybník pond.] *Zpravodaj IBA, listopad 1996: 2 (in Czech only).*

Urbánek L., 1997: [Žehunský rybník pond.] *Zpravodaj IBA, 1997: 2 (in Czech only).*

Urbánek L., 1998: [Žehuňský rybník pond.] *Zpravodaj IBA, 1998: 3 (in Czech only).*

Urbánek L., 2000: [Žehuňský rybník pond.] *Zpravodaj IBA, 2000: 3 (in Czech only).*

Voříšek P., Hora J., 1999: [World Conference of BirdLife International.] *Ptačí svět III/ 4: 8 (in Czech only).*

Vyhnálek V., Chytil J., Macháček P., Horal D., 1999: [The restriction of geese and ducks hunting in the district of Břeclav.] *Crex 14: 88–98 (in Czech only).*

001 – Krkonoše mountains (Giant mountains)

Buchar J. (ed.), 1983: (Results of the faunistic investigation of the Krkonoše -Giant Mountains 1.) *Opera Corcontica 20: 99–114 (in Czech with an English summary).*

Chutný B., 1991: (Study of Red-spotted bluethroat, *Luscinia svecica svecica*, population in the Krkonoše Mts.) *Panurus 3: 123–136 (in Czech with an English summary).*

Chutný B., 1992: (Problems in preserving the Red-spotted Bluethroat, *Luscinia svecica svecica*, in the Krkonoše Mountains.) *In: Hora J. et al., 1992: Významná ptačí území v České a Slovenské republice. Proc. of sem. Čsl. sekce ICBP. Třeboň 1992. Čsl. sekce ICBP, Praha: 18–21 (in Czech with an English summary).*

Fanta J. (ed.), 1969: [Nature of the Krkonoše National Park.] *SZN Praha: 1–221 (in Czech only).*

Fišera J., Grúz J., 1998: [Night mist-netting of birds, using light, in 1998.] *Prunella 24: 10–11 (in Czech only).*

Flousek J., 1988: Bird and mammal communities of the subarctic peatbog in the Krkonoše Mts. (Czechoslovakia). *Věst. čs. Společ. zool. 52: 7–21.*

Flousek J., 1989: Impact of industrial emissions on bird populations breeding in mountain spruce forests in Central Europe. *Ann. Zool. Fennici 26: 255–263.*

Flousek J., 1992: (Present status of and prospects for bird protection in the Krkonoše Mountains.) *In: Hora J. et al., 1992: Významná ptačí území v České a Slovenské republice. Proc. of sem. Čsl. sekce ICBP. Třeboň 1992. Čsl. sekce ICBP, Praha: 13–17 (in Czech with an English summary).*

Flousek J., 1994: Breeding bird communities and air pollution in the Krkonoše Mts. (Czech Republic) in 1983–1992. *In: Hagenmeijer E. J. M. & Verstrael T. J. (eds.): Bird numbers 1992. Distribution, monitoring and ecological aspects. Proc. 12th Int. Conf. IBCC/EOAC, Noordwijkerhout, The Netherlands: 233–238.*

Flousek J., 1994: Krkonoše/Karkonosze bilateral biosphere reserve. *In: Jeník J. & Price M. (eds.): Biosphere reserves on the crossroads of Central Europe. Czech Republic – Slovak Republic. Czech Nat. Comm. Unesco MAB Prague: 17–32.*

Flousek J., 1995: (Important bird area Krkonoše in 1992–1994.) *In: Hora J. et al., 1995: Významná ptačí území v České republice. Proc. of sem., Kostelec n. Č. l. 1995. ČSO, Praha: 13–15 (in Czech with an English summary).*

Flousek J., 1999: [Important bird area (IBA) Krkonoše.] *Zpravodaj IBA 8/99: 4 (in Czech only).*

Flousek J., 2000: (Birds in the valuable bird areas: Krkonoše.) *Sylvia 36: 26–30 (in Czech with an English summary).*

Flousek J., Gramsz B., 1999: (Atlas of breeding birds in the Krkonoše Mts., Czech Republic/Poland, in 1991–1994.) *Správa KRNAP Vrchlabí: 424 pp. (in Czech and Polish with an English summary).*

Flousek J., Hudec K., 1991: (Impact of industrial pollution and novel forest decline on breeding bird communities in Central Europe.) *Sylvia 28: 51–63 (in Czech with an English summary).*

Jahn A. (ed.), 1985: [The Polish Krkonoše Mts.] *PAN Wroclaw: 1–566 (in Polish).*

Jeník J., 1961: [Alpine Vegetation of the Krkonoše Mountains, Mt. Kralický Sněžník, and Mt. Hrubý Jeseník.] *NČAV Praha: 1–409 (in Czech with a German summary).*

Miles P., 1975: [The past and the present of ornithology in the Krkonoše Mts.] *Prunella 1: 1–13 (in Czech only).*

Miles P., 1986: (Ornithocenoses of the Krkonoše Mts. according to the results of the catch during the Operation Baltic. Operation Baltic – section Czechoslovakia, paper nr. 7.) *Opera Corcontica 23: 143–156 (in Czech with an English summary).*

Miles P., 1986: [Birds of the Krkonoše Mountains.] *Acta Univ. Carol., Biol. 1985: 1–101 (in German only).*

Miles P., 1991: (The investigation of population dynamism of birds in the Krkonoše Mts.) *Panurus 3: 113–121 (in Czech with an English summary).*

Pax F., 1925: [Vertebrates of Silesia.] *Verlag Gebrüder Borntraeger Berlin: 1–557 (in German only).*

Soukupová L., Kociánová M., Jeník J., Sekyra J. (eds.), 1995: Arctic-alpine tundra in the Krkonoše, the Sudetes. *Opera Corcontica 32: 5–88.*

Sýkora B. (ed.), 1983: (Krkonoše National Park.) *SZN Praha: 1–280 (in Czech with an English summary).*

Šourek J., 1969: [Flora of the Krkonoše Mountains.] *Academia Praha: 1–452 (in Czech with a German summary).*

002 – Žehuňský rybník pond

Čmejlová, J., Krátká, D., Pecina, P., Šachl, J., Ziegler, V., 1982: [The nature of the Nymburk district and its protection] *SPPOP Středočes. kr. a Polabské muz. v Poděbradech, 93 pp. (in Czech with German and Russian summaries).*

Jelínek M., 1996: (Results of ringing programme "Acrocephalus" in the National Nature Reserve Žehuňský rybník pond in 1993–95.) *Zprávy ČSO 42: 34–35 (in Czech with English summary).*

Jelínek M., 2000: (Occurrence of the Moustached Warbler (Acrocephalus melanopogon) in the Poděbrady region.) *Zprávy ČSO 51: 23–24 (in Czech with an English summary).*

Jelínek, M., Urbánek, L., 1993: (Results of Action "Acrocephalus" in the State Nature Reserve Žehuňský rybník pond.) *Zprávy ČSO 36: 17–19 (in Czech with an English summary).*

Pecina. P., Sedláček, K., 1978: (Notes to the vertebratofauna of the State Nature Reserve Žehuňský rybník pond.) *Čs. Ochrana přírody, 18: 39–57 (in Czech with English, German and Russian summaries).*

Souček Z., 1978: [30 years of the Žehuň game preserve State Nature Reserve.] *Vlastiv. Zpravodaj Polabí 18/1–2: 36–37 (in Czech only)*

Štěpánková R., 1974: [Birds of Žehuňský rybník pond and its surroundings.] *Postgrad. práce, Ped.fak. UK Praha, 107 pp., msc. (in Czech only).*

Tvrdíková L., 1984: [The history of fish-farming in Žehuň.] *Vlastivěd.zprav. Polabí, 24 (3–4): 67–72 (in Czech only).*

Urbánek L., 1980: (Interesting ornitological Observations in State Nature reserve Žehuňský rybník pond.) *Zprávy ČSO 21: 27–29 (in Czech with an English summary).*

Urbánek L., 1992: Important Bird Area Žehuňský rybník Pond.] *In Hora J. et al. IBA's in the Czech and Slovak Republic.] Proc. of sem. Čsl. Sekce ICBP. Třeboň 1992. Čsl. Sekce ICBP, Praha: 64–72 (in Czech with an English summary).*

Urbánek L., 1995: (Žehuňský rybník pond in 1992–1994.) *In Hora J. et al., 1995 Important Bird Areas in Czech Republic. Proc. of sem., Kostelec n. Č. l. 1995. ČSO, Praha: 36–38 (in Czech with English summary).*

Urbánek L., 1996: [Žehuňský rybník pond.] *Zpravodaj IBA, listopad 1996: 2 (in Czech only).*

Urbánek L., 1996: (IBA – Žehuňský rybník pond.) *Panurus 7: 5–56 (in Czech with an English summary).*

Urbánek L., 1997: [Žehunský rybník pond.] *Zpravodaj IBA 1997: 2 (in Czech only).*

Urbánek L., 1997: [50 years of the Nature Reserve Žehuňský rybník pond and 500 years since the foundation of Žehuňský rybník pond.] *Ptačí svět IV/2: 3 (in Czech only).*

Urbánek L., 1998: [Žehuňský rybník pond.] *Zpravodaj IBA, 1998: 3 (in Czech only).*

Urbánek L., 1999: (The Year 1999 in the IBA Žehuňský rybník pond.) *In: Málková A., Jandová J.,: Významná ptačí území na konci tisíciletí. Proc. of sem. IBA Mikulov, 19.–21. listopadu 1999. Praha 2000: 105–106 (in Czech with an English summary).*

Urbánek, L., Bártl, J., 1980: (The Waders of the Central Elbe-basin.) *Práce a studie-přír. Pardubice, 12: 123–132 (in Czech with an English summary).*

Urbánek, L., Jelínek, M., 1999: (Occurrence of the Gull-billed Tern, Gelochelidon nilotica, in the Poděbrady region – Central Bohemia.) *Zprávy ČSO, 49: 18–19 (in Czech with an English summary).*

003 – Křivoklátsko

Hůla P., Štěpánek P., Koreček T., Moucha P., Mutinský J., Pišvejc V., 1996: [Křivoklátsko biosphere reserve.] *In: Jeník J. et al., 1996: Biosférické rezervace České republiky. Příroda a lidé pod záštitou UNESCO. Empora, Praha: 65–88.*

Nedozrálová E., 2000: (Important bird area Křivoklátsko in 1986–2000.) *In: Málková P., Jandová J. (eds.), 2000: Významná ptačí území na konci tisíciletí. Proc. of sem. IBA, Mikulov 1999. ČSO, Praha: 62–65 (in Czech with an English summary).*

Pojer F., 1992: (Křivoklátsko Protected Landscape Area and Biosphere Reserve – important bird area.) *In: Hora J. et al., 1992: Významná ptačí území v České a Slovenské republice. Proc. of sem. Čsl. sekce ICBP. Třeboň 1992. Čsl. sekce ICBP, Praha: 13–17 (in Czech with an English summary).*

Pojer F., 1995: (Management plan for the Křivoklátsko Protected Landscape Area and Biosphere Reserve and bird protection.) *In: Hora et al., 1995: Významná ptačí území v České republice. Proc. of sem., Kostelec n. Č. l. 1995. ČSO, Praha: 64–69. (in Czech with an English summary).*

Šmaha J., 1983: [Avifauna of some biocenoses on the steep slopes in the Křivoklát surroundings.] *Bohemia Centralis, 12: 157–181 (in Czech with a German summary).*

Šmaha J., 1988: [Some examples of the dependence of anthropogenic changes in fauna on biotope characters in the Křivoklátsko Biosphere Reserve.] *Bohemia Centralis, 18: 275–291 (in Czech with a German summary).*

Šmaha J., 1989: [Diversity of birds and its causality in the Křivoklátsko Biosphere Reserve.] *Bohemia Centralis, 18: 275–291 (in Czech with a German summary).*

Šmaha J., 1990: [Report on the status of the orders Columbiformes to Piciformes in the Křivoklátsko Biosphere Reserve.] *In: Sitko J., Trpák P. (eds.), 1990: Proc. of conf., Přerov 1989: 43–53 (in Czech only).*

Tichai M., 1998: [Křivoklátsko.] *Zpravodaj IBA, 1998: 4 (in Czech only).*

004 – Doupov hills

Bušek O., Tejrovský V., Zavadil V., 1990: [The vertebrates of the Doupov Hills (Aves, Mammalia).] *Sborník Západočeského muzea, Plzeň, Příroda 76: 1–72 (in Czech with a German summary).*

Lorber J., Ondráček Č., Pitelová H., Táborský i. (ed.), Tejrovský V., Voženílek P., 1995: [The nature of the Chomutov district.] *RŽP OÚ v Chomutově, 52 pp. (in Czech only).*

Mackovičin P., (ed) 1999: [Protected Areas in Czech Republic I – Ústí nad Labem.] *AOPK ČR, Praha 351 pp. (in Czech only).*

Tejrovský V., 1995: (The Doupov Hills – an important bird area of the Czech Republic.) *In: Hora et al., 1995: Important birds areas in The Czech Republic. Proc. of sem., Kostelec n. Č. l. 1995. ČSO Praha: 70–72 (in Czech with an English summary).*

Tejrovský V., 1996: [The Doupov Hills.] *Zpravodaj IBA, listopad 1996: 5 (in Czech only).*

Tejrovský V., 1997: [The Doupov Hills.] *Zpravodaj IBA, listopad 1997: 4 (in Czech only).*

Tejrovský V., 1998: [The Doupov Hills.] *Zpravodaj IBA, listopad 1998: 4 (in Czech only).*

Tejrovský V., 1998/1999: (Avifauna of The Natural reserve – pond Vinařský rybník, Chomutov district -results from 1988–1998.) *Sbor. okr. muz. v Mostě, ř. přír., 20/21: 81–89 (in Czech with an English summary).*

Tejrovský V., 1999: [The IBA Doupov Hills – Natural reserve – pond Vinařský rybník.] *Zpravodaj IBA, červenec 1999: 5–6 (in Czech only).*

Tejrovský V., 1999: [Rare and uncommon records of bird in The IBA Doupov Hills.] *Zpravodaj IBA, prosinec 1999: 7 (in Czech only).*

Tejrovský V., 2000: (The Doupov Hills – present and future.) *In: Málková P., Jandová J. (eds), 2000: Významná ptačí území na konci tisíciletí. Proc. of sem. IBA, Mikulov 1999. ČSO, Praha: 101–104 (in Czech with an English summary).*

Tejrovský V., 2000: (Present Distribution of the Black Grouse in the Doupovské hory Mts.) *In: Málková P., (ed.), 2000: Proc. of intern. conf. Tetřevovití – Tetraonidae na přelomu tisíciletí. Č. Budějovice 2000: 110–113 (in Czech with an English summary).*

005 – Šumava mountains (Bohemian forest)

Andreska J., 1987: [Analysis of reasons of Capercaillie, Tetrao urogallus L, abundance decrease in the Šumava Mts.] *Proc. of conf. Avifauna jizních Čech a její změny, Č. Budějovice 1986: 16–21 (in Czech with a German summary).*

Bejček V., Šťastný K., Jarský V., 1999: [Changes of avifauna in damaged forest ecosystems of the Šumava National Park.] *In: Podrázský V., Vacek S., Ulbrochová I. (eds.), 1999: Proc. of conf. Monitoring, výzkum a management ekosystémů Národního parku Šumava. Kostelec n. Č. l. 1999: 17–23 (in Czech only).*

Bejček V., Šťastný K., Málková P., Svobodová J., 2000: [Influence of the spruce stands dieback caused by bark beetle disaster on bird communities in the Šumava National Park.] *In: Podrázský V., Ryšánková H. Vacek S., Ulbrochová I. (eds.), 1999: Proc. of conf. Monitoring, výzkum a management ekosystémů Národního parku Šumava. Kostelec n. Č. l. 2000: 21–27.*

Beneš J., 1996: The synantropic landscape history of the Šumava Mountains (Czech side). *Silva Gabreta 1: 237–241*

Bufka L., 2000: (Synopsis of the IBA Šumava Mts. Research Activities.) *In: Málková P., Jandová J. (eds.), 2000: Významná ptačí území na konci tisíciletí. Proc. of sem. IBA, Mikulov 1999. ČSO, Praha: 24–29 (in Czech with English summary).*

Bufka L., Červený J., Bürger P., 2000: (Development of Abundance of Capercailliie, *Tetrao urogallus,* in the Šumava Mts.) *In: Málková P. (ed.), 2000: Proc. of intern. conf. Tetřevovití – Tetraonidae na přelomu tisíciletí. Č. Budějovice 2000: 52–57 (in Czech with an English summary).*

Bufka L., Kloubec B., 1997: (Birds in secondary grasslands of military training areas and a former border zone in the Šumava Mts.) *Sylvia 33: 148–160 (in Czech with English abstract and summary).*

Bufka L., Kloubec B., 1998: The bird communities of the abandoned secondary grassland areas in the Šumava Mts. *Silva Gabreta 2: 277–294 (in English with Czech summary).*

Bufka L., Kloubec B., 1999: The history and current status of the ural owl *(Strix uralensis)* in Bohemian Forest (SW Czech Republic). *Buteo 1999, suppl.: 42–43.*

Bufka L., Málková P., 1999: [Re-introduction of the Capercaillie in the Šumava Mts.] *Zpravodaj IBA, prosinec 1999: 6 (in Czech only).*

Bufková I., Hladilin V., Bufka L., Gutzerová N., Hubený P., Urban F., Valenta M., 1996: [Šumava Biosphere Reserve.] *In: Jeník J. et al., 1996: Biosférické rezervace České republiky. Příroda a lidé pod záštitou UNESCO. Empora, Praha: 113–136 (in Czech only).*

Bürger P., 1987: [Inventory of the Boubín virgin forest State Nature Reserve– Birds.] *Záv. zpráva, depon. in Správa NP a CHKO Šumava, Kašp. Hory, msc. (in Czech only).*

Bürger P., 1987: [Inventory of the Trojmezná State Nature Reserve – birds of the climax spruce stands.] *Záv. zpráva, depon. in Správa NP a CHKO Šumava, Kašp. Hory, 10 pp., msc. (in Czech only).*

Bürger P., 1992: (Avifauna of the Šumava Mountains – its present status and prospects.) *In: Hora J. et al., 1992: Významná ptačí území v České a Slovenské republice. Proc. of sem. Čsl. sekce ICBP. Třeboň 1992. Čsl. sekce ICBP, Praha: 22–27 (in Czech with an English summary).*

Bürger P., 1995: [Conference on Šumava Mts. Biodiversity.] *Zpravodaj IBA, listopad 1995: 6 (in Czech only).*

Bürger P., Červený J., Bufka L., 2000: (Development of Abundance of Black Grouse, *Tetrao tetrix,* in the Šumava Mts.) *In: Málková P. (ed.), 2000: Proc. of internat. conf. Tetřevovití – Tetraonidae na přelomu tisíciletí. Č. Budějovice 2000: 82–89 (in Czech with an English summary).*

Bürger P., Hora J., Pykal J., 1995: (Current Results of Research on the Corncrake, *Crex crex*, in the Šumava Mountains, 1993–1994.) *In: Hora J. et al., 1995: Významná ptačí území v České republice. Proc. of sem., Kostelec n. Č. l. 1995. ČSO, Praha: 16–20 (in Czech with an English summary).*

Bürger P., Pykal J., Hora J., 1997: [Corncrake in the Šumava Mts.] *Zpravodaj IBA, 1997: 3 (in Czech).*

Chábera S. et al., 1987: [Nature of the Šumava Mts.] *Č. Budějovice, 181 pp. (in Czech with German and Russian sumarries).*

Červený J., Bufka L., Bürger P., 2000: (Development of Abundance of Hazel Grouse, *Bonasa bonasia*, in the Šumava Mts.) *In: Málková P. (ed.), 2000: Proc. of internat. conf. Tetřevovití – Tetraonidae na přelomu tisíciletí. Č. Budějovice 2000: 132–137 (in Czech with an English summary).*

Hanzák, J., 1987: [Changes of avifauna of the Šumava Mts. during the last 25 years.] *Sbor. před. Avifauna jižních Čech a její změny, Č. Budějovice 1986: 77–78 (in Czech with a German summary).*

Hanzák. J., 1980: [Basic ornithological research of reserves and protected areas I. Birds of the Mrtvý Luh and Stožec.] *Záv. zpr. resort. úkolu. Nár. muz. Praha, 32 pp., msc. (in Czech only).*

Havránek F., Červený J., Obuch J., 1996: [Distribution and diet analyse of the Eagle Owl in protected areas of the SW Bohemia.] *Záv. zpráva, depon. in Správa NP a CHKO Šumava, Kašp. Hory, 42 pp., msc. (in Czech only).*

Horal D., Hortl L., Kloubec B., 1998: (Confirmed breeding of the Ural Owl, *Strix uralensis*, in the Šumava Mts., Southern Bohemia in 1998.) *Buteo 10: 115–120 (in Czech with an English summary).*

Hruška J., 1983: (The possibilities of Grouse conservation in the Šumava – Bohemia Forest.) *Památky a příroda, 8/2: 105–108 (in Czech with English, German and Russian summaries).*

Janda J., 1989: [On the structure of the bird communities in an important area of the Šumava Mountains.] *Staphia 20: 101–118 (in German only).*

Janda J., Pykal J., 1987: [Structure of avifanna of selected biotopes of the Šumava Mts.] *Sbor. před. Avifauna jizních Čech a její změny, Č. Budějovice 1986: 97–115 (in Czech with a German summary).*

Janda J., Pykal J., Vozábal L, 1987: (Ornithofauna of Šuamava Peat-bogs.) *Zprávy MOS, 46: 97–114 (in Czech with an English summary).*

Klaus S., 1991: Effects of forestry on grouse population: Case studies from the Thuringian and Bohemian forests, Central Europe. *Ornis Scand. 22: 218–223.*

Klaus S., 1996: Hazel Grouse in the Bohemian Forest: Result of a 24-year-long study. *Silva Gabreta 1: 209–220.*

Klaus S., Sewitz A., 2000: Ecology and Conservation of Hazel Grouse *Bonasa bonasia* in the Bohemian Forest (Šumava, Czech Republic). *In: Málková P. (ed.), 2000: Proc. of internat. conf. Tetřevovití – Tetraonidae na přelomu tisíciletí. Č. Budějovice 2000: 138–146.*

Klíma M., 1959: (An analysis of avifauna in the primeval forest at Boubín.) *Zool. listy 8/3: 251–266 (in Czech with an English summary).*

Kloubec B., 1987: [Distribution, abundance and ecological reguirements of the Pygmy Owl (*Glaucidium passerinum* L.) in Southern Bohemia.] *Proc. of conf. Avifauna jižních Čech a její změny, Č. Budějovice, 1986: 116–136 (in Czech with German summary).*

Kloubec B., 1988: [Distribution, abundance and ecology claims of the Tengmalm's Owl *(Aegolius funereus)* in Southern Bohemia.] *Proc. of conf. Sovy 1986, Přerov 1986: 85–93 (in Czech with German summary).*

Kloubec B., 1995: (Project of the re-introduction of the Ural Owl, *Strix uralensis*, in the Šumava, Bohemian Forest, National Park.) *In: Plesník J. (ed.), 1995: Záchranné chovy živočichů v České republice. Příroda (Praha) 2: 48–54. (in Czech with an English summary).*

Kloubec B., 1997: (Results to date of the Ural Owl, *Strix uralensis*, re-introduction project in the Šumava National Park) *Buteo 9: 115–122 in Czech with English summary).*

Kloubec B., 1999: [The Ural Owl again in Šumava Mts.] *Zpravodaj IBA, červenec1999: 5 (in Czech.)*

Kloubec B., Bufka L., 1997: (Breeding bird communities in fir-spruce-beech virgin forests in the Šumava Mts., South Bohemia.) *Sylvia 33: 161–188 (in Czech with an English abstract and summary).*

Kučera L., 1970: Die Vögel des mittleren Böhmerwaldes (Šumava). *Orn. Mitt. 22: 223–242.*

Kučera L., 1972: [Birds of Šumava plains.] *Zprav. CHKOŠ 14: 19–29 (in Czech with a German summary).*

Kučera M., 2000: (Bird communities of mountain spruce forest damaged by bark beetle invasion.) *Silva Gabreta 5: 187–194 (in Czech with an English abstract).*

Mattas M., 1991: (Nesting distribution of the birds in western Bohemia, Czechoslovakia in 1985–1988.) *Sbor. Západoč. muz. v Plzni, Příroda 79: 1–111.*

Polák V., 1980: (The Peat-bogs of Southern Bohemia.) *Ochrana přírody 1: 147–170 (in Czech with English, German and Russian summaries).*

Pykal J., 1990: [Repeated inventory of the Mrtvý luh State Nature Reserve – Birds.] *KSSPPOP Č. Budějovice: 13 pp., msc. (in Czech only).*

Pykal J., 1991: [Inventory of the Velká niva State Nature Reserve – Birds.] *Záv. zpráva, depon. in Správa NP a CHKO Šumava, Kašp. Hory., 16 pp., msc.(in Czech only).*

Pykal J., Bürger P., Hora J., 1997: (Bird communities of non-forested landscape in the border area Nové Údolí.) *Sylvia 33: 141–147 (in Czech with an English summary).*

Pykal J., Bürger P., Hora J., 2000: (Corncrake study results not only in the IBA Šumava.) *In: Málková P., Jandová J. (eds.), 2000: Významná ptačí území na konci tisíciletí. Proc. of sem. IBA, Mikulov 1999. ČSO, Praha: 97–100 (in Czech with an English summary).*

Pykal J., Bürger P., Hora J., Janda J., 1991: (Birds of peatbogs in the Šumava mountains – a comparison periods 1979–1982 and 1989–1990.) *Sylvia 28: 65–75 (in Czech with an English summary).*

Pykal J., Kloubec B., 1994: Feeding ecology of Tengmalm's Owl *Aegolius funereus* in the Šumava National Park, Czechoslovakia. *In: Meyburg, B.-V., Chancellor R. D. (eds.): Raptor Conservation Today, WWGBP/The Pica Press: 537–541.*

Sewitz A., Klaus S., 1997: The Hazel Hen *(Bonasa bonasia)* colonisation of isolated wood patches at the foot of the Šumava Mountains. *Beiträge zur Jagd- und Wildforschung 22: 263–276.*

Soldán T., Papáček M., Novák K., Zelený J., 1996: The Šumava Mountains: an unique biocentre of aquatic insects *(Ephemeroptera, Odonata, Plecoptera, Megaloptera, Trichoptera* and *Heteroptera – Nepomorpha). Silva Gabreta1: 99–107 (in English).*

Soukupová L., 1996: Development diversity of peatlands in Bohemian Forest. *Silva Gabreta 1: 99–107 (in English).*

Vaněk M., 1991: [30 years in Boubín primeval forest.] *Šumava 32: 5–7 (in Czech only).*

006 – Řežabinec pond

Bureš J., Hlásek L., Pecl K., Šálek M., Všetečka R., 1995: [Birds of Písek Area.] *ZO ČSOP 18/08, Písek II, 171 pp. (in Czech only).*

Kolektiv, 1985: [Decree on protected natural features in the Písek administrative region]. *ONV Písek, 15 pp. (in Czech only).*

Pecl K., 1978: [Results of inventory ornithological research of the State Natural Reserve Řežabinec pond near Ražice.] *Sbor. ornitol. prací z jiz. Čech, Jihoč. ornitol. klub DK ROH, Č. Budějovice: 101–136 (in Czech with a German summary).*

Pecl K., 1984: [Ornithological research of the State Natural Reserve Řežabinec pond near Ražice, district Písek, in 1976–1984.] *Záv. práce postgrad. studia. PřFUK Praha: 183 pp., msc. (in Czech only).*

Pecl K., 1987: [Ornithological research of the State Natural Reserve Řežabinec in 1976–1984.] *Proc. of conf. Avifauna jižních Čech a její změny, Č. Budějovice 1986: 152–179 (in Czech with a German summary).*

Pecl K., 1989: [Informative report about results of the complex ornithological research of the Řežabinec State Nature Reserve in 1977–1989.] *Zpráva o činnosti za rok 1989, Okres. muz. Písek: 27–33 (in Czech only).*

Pecl K., 1992: (Waterfowl at the Řežabinec pond in 1984–1991.) *In: Hora J. et al., 1992: Významná ptačí území v České a Slovenské republice. Proc. of sem. Čsl. sekce ICBP. Třeboň 1992. Čsl. sekce ICBP, Praha: 52–60 (in Czech with an English summary).*

Pecl K., 1994: (Waterfowl occurence at Řežabinec National Nature Reserve in 1984–1991.) *Sylvia 30: 86–90 (in Czech with an English summary).*

Pecl K., 1996: [Řežabinec pond.] *Zpravodaj IBA, listopad 1996: 3 (in Czech only).*

Pecl K., 1997: [Řežabinec pond]. *Zpravodaj IBA, 1997: 2 (in Czech only).*

Pecl K., 1997: [Abundance of birds in the National Nature Reserve Řežabinec.] *AOPK ČR, Praha: 44 pp., msc. (in Czech only).*

Pecl K., 1999: [Fifty years of the existence of the Řežabinec ornithological reserve.] *Zpravodaj IBA, červenec 1999: 6 (in Czech only).*

Pecl K., 2000: (Combining complete ornitological research of the Řežabinec National Nature Reserve with its cultural-educational purpose.) *In: Málková P., Jandová J. (eds.), 2000: Významná ptačí území na konci tisíciletí. Proc. of sem. IBA, Mikulov 1999. ČSO, Praha: 92–96 (in Czech with an English summary).*

007 – Dehtář pond

Kloubec B., Pykal J., 1994 [IBA Dehtář pond in 1992–1994.] *Zpravodaj IBA, 1994: 5 (in Czech only).*

Kloubec B., Pykal J., 1996: [Dehtář pond.] *Zpravodaj IBA, 1996: 3 (in Czech only).*

Kloubec B., Pykal J., 2000: (Avifauna of the Dehtář pond in 1986–2000.) *In: Málková P., Jandová J. (eds.), 2000: Významná ptačí území na konci tisíciletí. Proc. of sem. IBA, Mikulov 1999. ČSO, Praha: 49–55 (in Czech with an English summary).*

Pykal J., Kloubec, B., 1995: (Recent changes in the IBA Dehtář pond in 1992–1994.) *In: Hora et al., 1995: Významná ptačí území v České republice. Proc. of sem., Kostelec n. Č. l. 1995. ČSO, Praha: 34–35 (in Czech with an English summary).*

Pykal J., Kloubec B., 1998: [Dehtář pond was established as a Temporary Protected Area.] *Zpravodaj IBA, 1998: 3 (in Czech only).*

Pykal J., Kloubec, B. Bureš J., Šálek M., 1992: (Waterfowl conservation problems at the Dehtář pond and their solution.) *In: Hora J. et al., 1992: Významná ptačí území v České a Slovenské republice. Proc. of sem. Čsl. Sekce ICBP. Třeboň 1992. Čsl. sekce ICBP, Praha: 47–51 (in Czech with an English summary).*

008 – Třeboňsko

Albrecht J., 1985: [Inventory research of the Ruda state nature reserve. Vegetation cover.] *KSSPPOP Č. Budějovice: 77 pp., msc. (in Czech only).*

Bejček V., Exnerová A., Musil P., Vašák P., Šimek L., Šťastný K., 1990: [Changes of abundance of water bird species at selected ponds in the Třeboň basin – comparison of the years 1981, 1982 and 1986, 1987.] *Proc. of conf. Ptáci v kulturní krajině, Č. Budějovice 1989: 17–24 (in Czech with a German summary).*

Bureš J., 1995: (A list of new nature reserves in the Třeboňsko PLA.) *In: Hora et al., 1995: Významná ptačí území v České republice. Proc. of sem., Kostelec n. Č. l. 1995. ČSO, Praha: 21–24 (in Czech with an English summary).*

Bureš J., 1999: [The release of semi-wild mallards reaches a catastrophic scale in the Třeboňsko PLA.] *Zpravodaj IBA, červenec 1999: 3 (in Czech only).*

Bureš J., 2000: [Restriction of ducks and geese hunting in Třeboň area.] *Zpravodaj IBA, prosinec 2000: 2 (in Czech only).*

Bureš J., Kloubec B., 2000: (PLA Třeboňsko Administration management of ponds in small-scale protected areas of Třeboň in 1996–2000.) *In: Málková P., Jandová J. (eds.), 2000: Významná ptačí území na konci tisíciletí. Proc. of sem. IBA, Mikulov 1999. ČSO, Praha: 30–33 (in Czech with an English summary).*

Cepák J., Musil P., 1996: (Changes in abundance of the Little Grebe, *Tachybaptus ruficollis,* in the Czech Republic in 1981–1996.) *Sylvia 32: 103–116 (in Czech with an English summary).*

Cepák J., Musil P., 2000: (Numbers of Waterbird breeding populations in the IBA Třeboňsko in 1994–1999.) *In: Málková P., Jandová J. (eds.), 2000: Významná ptačí území na konci tisíciletí. Proc. of sem. IBA, Mikulov 1999. ČSO, Praha: 34–45 (in Czech with an English summary).*

Cepák J., Ševčík J., 1998: (The first breeding of the Yellow-legged Gull, *Larus cachinnans,* in Bohemia.) *Sylvia 34: 149–152 (in Czech with an English summary).*

Dykyjová D., 2000: (Třeboňsko – Nature and People in the Country of the Five-Petalled Rose). *CARPIO, Třeboň, 111 pp. (in Czech with an English summary).*

Dykyjová D., Květ J. (eds.), 1978: Pond Littoral Ecosystems. *Ecological Studies, Vol. 28. Berlin-Heidelberg- New York, 464 pp.*

Finlayson M., 1992: Management and conservation of peat bogs, floodplains and fish ponds in Central and Eastern Europe. – In Finlayson M. (ed.): *Integrated Management and Conservation of Wetlands in Agricultural and Forested Landscapes. IWRB Special Publication, No. 22, Slimbridge, England, pp. 8898.*

Hátle M., 1994: The conservation in situ in the Czech biosphere reserves. In Cibien C., Lecuyer D., (eds.): *People and Protected areas. Proceeding of EUROMAB seminar in Florac, France (3.–8.10.1994): 31–35.*

Hátle M., Hlásek J., Ševčík J., Bureš J., Černá O., Janda J., Jandová J., Kučera S., Lukešová M., 1996: Třeboňsko Biosphere Reserve. *In: Jeník J. et al., 1996: Biosférické rezervace ČR. Příroda a lidé pod záštitou UNESCO. Empora, Praha: 138–160 (in Czech only).*

Hlásek J., 1987: [Abundance and distribution of raptors and owls in the Třeboň region.] *Proc. of conf. Avifauna jižních Čech a její změny, Č. Budějovice 1986: 89–96 (in Czech with a German summary).*

Hora J., 1974: [Ornithological observations from Horusický rybník pond and surroundings.] *Sbor. Jihoč. muz. v Č. Budějovicích, přír. vědy, Suppl. 2: 77–81 (in Czech with a German summary).*

Hora, J., 1982: [Interesting ornithological observations from the Třeboň region.] *Proc. of ornith. research, Jihoč. kr., Jihoč. muz. v Č. Budějovicích, přír. vědy: 81–93 81 (in Czech with a German summary).*

IUCN, 1996: (Importance of fishponds for the Central European landscape. Sustainable use of fishponds in the Třeboňsko Protected Landscape Area and Biosphere Reserve.) České koordinační středisko *IUCN-Světového svazu ochrany přírody Praha a IUCN Gland, Švýcarsko a Cambridge, Velká Británie: 23–38 (in Czech with English, German and Russian summaries).*

Janda J., 1987: [Velký and Malý Tisý ponds State Nature Reserve.] *Třeboňsko, Inf. zprav. Správy CHKO 5: 4–5 (in Czech only).*

Janda J., 1990: Investigational ornithological inventory of the Ruda peatbog State Nature Reserve.] *Správa CHKO Třeboňsko, 18 pp., msc. (in Czech only).*

Janda J., 1992: (Present status and conservation of important bird habitatsin the Třeboňsko region and factors involved in their management.) *In: Hora J. et al., 1992: Významná ptačí území v České a Slovenské republice. Proc. of sem. Čsl. sekce ICBP. Třeboň 1992. Čsl. sekce ICBP, Praha: 24–34 (in Czech with an English summary).*

Janda J., Macháček P., 1990: (Cormorant, *Phalacrocorax carbo,* in Bohemia and Moravia in 1982–1988.) *Sylvia, 27: 55–70 (in Czech with an English summary).*

Janda J., Ševčík J., 1990: [Changes of avifauna of Velký and Malý Tisý ponds State Nature Reserve in 1947–1988.] *Proc. of conf. Ptáci v kulturní krajině, Č. Budějovice 1989: 103–117 (in Czech with a German summary).*

Janda. J., Ševčík, J., 1990: Monitoring water-birds in the Třeboň Basin Biosphere Reserve: Methods and some preliminary results. *In: Šťastný K., Bejček V. (eds.): Bird Census and Atlas Studies. Proc. XIth Int. Conf. on Bird Census and Atlas Work, Praha 1989: 435–436.*

Kloubec B., 1995: (Bird species composition of reed stands in Southern Bohemia.) *Sylvia 31: 38–52 (in Czech with an English abstract and summary).*

Kloubec B., 1998: [Adjustments in NNR Velký a Malý Tisý.] *Zpravodaj IBA, 1998: 3 (in Czech only).*

Kloubec B., 1999: [Continuation of project in NNR Velký a Malý Tisý.] *Zpravodaj IBA, listopad 1999: 7 (in Czech only).*

Květ J., 1992: Wetlands of the Trebon Biosphere Reserve – an overview. *Proc. IWRB Workshop, Třeboň 1992. IWRB Spec. Publ. 22: 11–14.*

Musil P., 1995: (Changes in numbers of water and wetland birds on fishponds in the Třeboň basin in 1988–1995.) *In: Hora J. et al., 1995: Významná ptačí území v České republice. Proc. of sem., Kostelec n. Č. l. 1995. ČSO, Praha: 25–33 (in Czech with an English summary).*

Musil P., Šťastný K., Bejček V., 1992: (Abundance of particular water and wetland bird species on fishponds in the Třeboň Basin and changes over the last decade.) *In: Hora J. et al., 1992: Významná ptačí území v České a Slovenské republice. Proc. of sem. Čsl. sekce ICBP. Třeboň 1992. Čsl. sekce ICBP, Praha: 35–46 (in Czech with an English summary).*

Obstová M., 1989: [Reed stands of the Velký Tisý pond in PLA Třeboňsko.] *MSc. Thesis, PřF UK Praha, 114 pp., msc. (in Czech only).*

Obstová M., 1989: [Changes in littoral vegetation the Velký and Malý Tisý ponds State Nature Reserve.] *Třeboňsko, Inf. zprav. Správy CHKO 10: 16–17 (in Czech only).*

Prach K., Jeník J., Large A.R.G. (eds.), 1996: Floodplain ecology and management. The Lužnice River in the Třeboň Biosphere Reserve, Central Europe. *SPB Academic Publishing bv, Amsterdam, 285 pp.*

Pykal J., Janda J., 1994: (Relation between waterfowl numbers on South Bohemian ponds and fishponds management.) *Sylvia 30: 3–11 (in Czech with an English summary).*

Šálek M., 1996: (Changes in numbers and habitat choice of the Redshank, *Tringa totanus*, breeding population in South Bohemia, Czech Republic during the last fifty years.) *Sylvia 32: 117–135 (in Czech with an English summary).*

Ševčík J., 1986–89: [Birds of Třeboň region I–VIII.] *Třeboňsko, Inf. zprav. Správy CHKO, 3/86: 8–9, 4/86: 7–9, 5/87: 7–9, 6/87: 10–11, 7/88: 7–8, 8/88: 7–9, 9/89: 10–11, 10/89: 10–12 (in Czech only).*

Ševčík. J., 1987: [White-tailed Eagle in the Třeboň region – its wintering and breeding.] *Proc. of conf. Dravci 1985, Přerov: 229–234 (in Czech only).*

Ševčík J., 1990: [Investigational inventory of vertebrates of the Horusická Blata peatbog State Nature Reserve.] *Správa CHKO Třeboňsko, 17 pp., msc. (in Czech only).*

Ševčík J., 1997: [Ornithological news from Třeboňsko.] *Zpravodaj IBA, 1997: 2 (in Czech only).*

Ševčík J., Bureš J., 1996: [Building artificial istats in ponds in Třeboňsko PLA] *Zpravodaj IBA, červen 1996: 2 (in Czech only).*

Ševčík J., Janda J., 1989: [Inventory survey of the Velký and Malý Tisý ponds State Nature Reserve.] *Správa CHKO Třeboňsko, 72 pp., msc. (in Czech only).*

Šťastný K., 1985: [Birds and mammals of fishpond dams in Třeboň region from an ecological standpoint.] *Jihoč. muz., Č. Budějovice, 64 pp. (in Czech with a German summary).*

Šťastný K., Bejček V., Janda J., Hlásek J., Ševčík J., Dostálová L., 1987: [Water birds breeding on pond islands of Třeboň basin – comparison of years 1978/79 and 1985.] *Proc. of conf. Avifauna jizních Čech a její změny, Č. Budějovice 1986: 249–259 (in Czech with a German summary).*

Zasadil P., 1994: Bird communities of fishpond dikes in the Třeboň region: a comparison of periods 1970/71 and 1993. *Sylvia 30: 32–40 (in Czech with an English summary).*

009 – Nové Mlýny middle reservoir

Buček A., Pelikán J., (eds.), 1985: [Geoecology aspects of waterworks in southern Moravia.] *GÚ ČSAV a ÚVO ČSAV. Brno: 299 pp. (in Czech only).*

Chytil J., 1993: (Ramsar site candidate Wetlands of lower Dyje river and its importance for the protection of birds). *Zprávy MOS 51: 35–49 (in Czech with an English summary).*

Chytil J., 1996: [Nové Mlýny Middle reservoir]. *Zpravodaj IBA, listopad 1996: 4 (in Czech only).*

Chytil J, 1998: [Restriction of hunting on the Věstonice Reservoir.] *Ptačí svět V/4: 7(in Czech only).*

Chytil J. 1999: The present status of Mediterranean Gull *Larus melanocephalus* in the Czech Republic, with notes on Slovakia. *In: Meininger P., Hoogendoorn W., Flamant R., Raevel P. (eds.): Proc. of the 1st International Mediterranean Gull Meeting, Le Portel, Pas-de-Calais, France, 1998. EcoNum, Baillent: 39–40.*

Chytil J., Macháček P., 1997: [South-moravian Important Bird Areas.] *Zpravodaj IBA, 1997: 6 (in Czech only).*

Chytil J., Macháček P., 1998: [From south-moravian Important Bird Areas.] *Zpravodaj IBA, 1998: 5 (in Czech only).*

Chytil J., Macháček P., 1999: [Autumn/winter in south-moravian IBAs.] *Zpravodaj IBA, prosinec 1999: 2 (in Czech only).*

Chytil J., Macháček P., 1999: (The breeding of Yellow-legged Gull on the Middle reservoir of Nové Mlýny.) *Zpravodaj jihomor. pobočky ČSO, 14: 46–48 (in Czech with an English summary).*

Chytil J., Macháček P., 2000: (Nové Mlýny middle reservoir.) *Sylvia 36/1 – Aktuální problémy ochrany ptáků a jejich prostředí v ČR: 15–20 (in Czech with an English summary).*

Chytil J., Macháček P., 2000: (Development in breeding population size of gulls and terns in the southernmost Moravia.] *Sylvia 36: 113–126 (in Czech with an English summary).*

Čapek M., Kloubec B., 1990: The avifauna of the Nové Mlýny Waterworks in the period 1981–1985. *Acta Sc. Nat. Brno, 24/6: 1–51.*

Havlín J., 1986: Birds of the dams of the Nové Mlýny waterworks. *Folia zool. 35: 239–256.*

Heteša J., Marvan P., (eds.), 1984: (The biology of a newly filled reservoir.) *Studie ČSAV 3: 1–175 (in Czech with an English summary).*

Hubálek Z., Pellantová J., Hudec K, Halouzka J., Chytil J., Macháček P., Šebela M., Kubíček F., 1991: (Botulism of birds on Water Works Nové Mlýny, district Břeclav). *Vet. med., Praha 36/1: 57–63 (in Czech with an English summary).*

Hudec K., 1984: [Water Works Nové Mlýny and the fauna of the Podyjí region]. *Živa 32/4: 156–157 (in Czech only).*

Macháček P., 1988: [The influence of water regime management in South Moravia on waterfowl communities of Lednice fishponds reserve.) *PHd thesis, ÚSEB ČSAV Brno: 194 pp. (in Czech only).*

Macháček P., 1992: (The present situation and perspectives of the Middle reservoir of Nové Mlýny.) *In: Hora J. et al., 1992: Významná ptačí území v České a Slovenské republice. Proc. of sem. Čsl. sekce ICBP. Třeboň 1992. Čsl. sekce ICBP, Praha: 83–85 (in Czech with an English summary).*

Macháček P., Chytil J., 2000: (IBA Middle reservoir of nové Mlýny.) *In: Málková P., Jandová J. (eds.), 2000: Významná ptačí území na konci tisíciletí. Proc. of sem. IBA, Mikulov 1999. ČSO, Praha: 58–61 (in Czech and in English).*

Vyhnálek V., Chytil J., Macháček P., Horal D., 1999: [The restriction of geese and ducks hunting in the district of Břeclav.] *Crex 14: 88–98 (in Czech only).*

010 – Pálava

Chytil J., 1990: [Geese on trees?] *Veronica 4/4: 28 (in Czech only).*

Chytil J., 1992: (IBA Protected Landscape Area Pálava.) *In: Hora J. et al., 1992: Významná ptačí území v České a Slovenské republice. Sbor. ref. ze sem. Proc. of sem. Třeboň 1992. Čsl. sekce ICBP, Praha: 73–75 (in Czech only).*

Chytil J., 1996: [Pálava IBA.] *Zpravodaj IBA, listopad 1996: 5 (in Czech only).*

Chytil J., Macháček P., 1997: [South-moravian Important Bird Areas.] *Zpravodaj IBA, 1997: 6 (in Czech only).*

Chytil J., Macháček P., 1998: [From south-moravian Important Bird Areas.] *Zpravodaj IBA, 1998: 5 (in Czech only).*

Chytil J., Macháček P., 1999: [Autumn/winter in south-moravian IBAs.] *Zpravodaj IBA, prosinec 1999: 2 (in Czech only).*

Chytil J., Macháček P., 2000: IBA Pálava. *In: Málková P., Jandová J. (eds.), 2000: Významná ptačí území nakonci tisíciletí. Proc. of sem. IBA, Mikulov 1999. ČSO, Praha: 46 (in Czech and in English).*

Danihelka J., Chytil J., Peřinová V., Bagár M. 1996: [Biosphere reserve Pálava.] *In: Jeník J. et al., 1996: Biosférické rezervace České republiky. Příroda a lidé pod záštitou UNESCO. Empora, Praha: 89–112 (in Czech only).*

Gaisler J., Chytil J., Vlašín M., 1990: The bats of S-Moravian lowlands (Czechoslovakia) over thirty years. *Acta Sc. Nat. Brno 24/9: 1–50.*

Gaisler J., Zukal. J., Nesvatbová J., Chytil J., Obuch J., 1996: Species diversity and relative abundance of small mammals (*Insectivora, Chiroptera, Rodentia*) in the Pálava Biosphere Reserve of UNESCO. *Acta Soc. Zool. Bohem. 60: 13–23.*

Hudec K., Pellantová, J., 1985: Assessment of the avian community in part of the foot zone of Pavlovské vrchy Hills (Southern Moravia) comprised in a landscape improvement scheme. *Ekológia (ČSSR) 3/4: 345–363.*

Kolektiv, 1980: [Geography of Protected Landscape Area Pálava.] *Geograf, ústav ČSAV Brno: 166 pp. (in Czech only).*

Kux Z., 1978: [Qualitative and quantitative studies on avifauna of particular landscape types in southern Moravia.] *Čas. Mor. muz. 63: 183–212. (in Czech with a German summary).*

Raušer J., 1989: (Biogeography conditions of Děvín reserve and their protection.) *Geograf. ústav ČSAV Brno: 15 pp. (in Czech with an English summary).*

Šmarda J., 1975: (Plant communities of rocky steppes of Pálava hills, Moravia, Czechoslovakia.) *Čs. ochrana přírody 14: 5–57 (in Czech with an English summary).*

011 – Lednické rybníky ponds

Chytil J., 1995: (Mist-netting of birds on Nesyt fishpond in 1994.) *Zprávy ČSO, 40: 33–35 (in Czech with an English summary).*

Chytil J., 1996: [Lednice fishponds.] *Zpravodaj IBA, listopad 1996: 3 (in Czech only).*

Chytil J. 1996: (The occurence of Moustached Warbler in the Czech Republic.) *Sylvia 32: 66–70 (in Czech with an English summary).*

Chytil J., Antonínová V., 2000: (Mist-netting of birds on Nesyt fishpond in 1999). *Zprávy ČSO 50: 10–12 (in Czech with an English summary).*

Chytil J., Macháček P., 1997: [South-moravian Important Bird Areas.] *Zpravodaj IBA, 1997: 6 (in Czech only).*

Chytil J., Macháček P., 1998: [From south-moravian Important Bird Areas.] *Zpravodaj IBA, 1998: 5 (in Czech only).*

Chytil J., Macháček P., 1999: [Autumn/winter in south-moravian IBAs.] *Zpravodaj IBA, prosinec 1999: 2 (in Czech only).*

Chytil J., Pellantová J. 2000: (Mist-netting of birds on Nesyt fishpond in the period 1978–1984.) *Sylvia, 36: 106–112. (in Czech with an English summary).*

Gaisler J., Chytil J., Vlašín M., 1990: The bats of S-Moravian lowlands (Czechoslovakia) over thirty years. *Acta Sc. Nat. Brno 24/9: 1–50.*

Hachler E., 1971: [The bibliography of avifauna of Lednice fishponds]. *Čs. ochrana přírody 12: 227–242 (in Czech only).*

Hudec K., 1975: Density and breeding of birds in the reed swamps of Southern Moravia ponds. *Acta Sc. Nat. Brno 9/6: 1–40.*

Kux. Z., 1950: [Contribution on biology of Red-crested Pochard and Greylag Goose in the ornithological reserve in Lednice.] *Čas. Mor. muz. 35: 190–215 (in Czech with a German summary).*

Květ J. et al., 1973: Littoral of the Nesyt pond. *Studie ČSAV 15: 1–172.*

Macháček. P., 1988: [The influence of water regime management in South Moravia on waterfowl communities of Lednice fishponds reserve]. *Kand. dis. práce, ÚSEB ČSAV Brno, 194 pp. msc. (in Czech only).*

Macháček P., 1992: (The present situation and perspectives of IBA Lednice fishponds.) *In: Hora J. et al., 1992: "Významná ptačí území v České a Slovenské republice". Proc. of sem. Československé sekce ICBP. Třeboň, 24.–25. března 1992. Československá sekce ICBP, Praha: 78–80 (in Czech with an English summary).*

Macháček P., 1995: (IBA Lednice fishponds.) *In: Hora J. et al., 1995: Významná ptačí území v České republice. Proc. of sem., Kostelec n. Č. l. 1995. ČSO, Praha: 39–41 (in Czech with an English summary).*

Macháček P., Chytil J., 2000: (IBA Lednice fishponds.) *In: Málková P., Jandová J. (eds.), 2000: Významná ptačí území na konci tisíciletí. Proc. of sem. IBA, Mikulov 1999. ČSO, Praha: 56–57 (in Czech and in English summary).*

012 – Confluence of the Morava and Dyje rivers

Chytil J., 1992: (Current status of and prospects for conservation of the IBA Soutok – Floodplain of the Rivers Morava and Dyje confluence.) *In: Hora J. et al., 1992: Významná ptačí území v České a Slovenské republice. Proc. of sem. Čsl. sekce ICBP. Třeboň 1992. Čsl. sekce ICBP, Praha: 76–77 (in Czech with an English summary).*

Chytil J., 1993: (Ramsar site candidate: "Wetland of lower Dyje river" and its importance for the protection of birds.) *Zprávy MOS 51: 35–49 (in Czech with an English summary).*

Chytil J., 1996: [Confluence of Morava and Dyje rivers.] *Zpravodaj IBA, listopad 1996: 4 (in Czech only).*

Chytil J. 1999: (Does the phenomenon "Moravian gate flyway" exist?) *Sylvia 35: 31–35 (in Czech with an English summary).*

Chytil J., Macháček P., 1997: [South-moravian Important Bird Areas.] *Zpravodaj IBA, 1997: 6 (in Czech only).*

Chytil J., Macháček P., 1998: [From south-moravian Important Bird Areas.] *Zpravodaj IBA, 1998: 5 (in Czech only).*

Chytil J., Macháček P., 1999: [Autumn/winter in south-moravian IBAs.] *Zpravodaj IBA, prosinec 1999: 2 (in Czech only).*

Chytil J., Macháček P., 2000: IBA (Confluence of Morava and Dyje rivers.) *In: Málková P., Jandová J. (eds.), 2000: Významná ptačí území na konci tisíciletí. Proc. of sem. IBA, Mikulov 1999. ČSO, Praha: 47–48 (in Czech and in English).*

Čmelík P., Chytil J., Šimeček K. 1999: (The influence of large-scale floods on occurrence of waterfowl in the Morava river alluvium.) *Sylvia 35: 19–29 (in Czech with an English summary).*

Čmelík, P. Šimeček, K., 1998: (Water birds in the Morava river floodplain, South Moravia, after the flood in July 1997.) *Zpravodaj JMP ČSO 12: 6–25 (in Czech with an English summary).*

Horák P., 1998: (The successful nesting of Imperial Eagle, *Aquila heliaca*, in Moravia, Czech Republic.) *Zpravodaj JMP ČSO 12: 27–28 (in Czech with an English summary).*

Horák P., 1999: (The tree-nesting population of Greylag Goose, *Anser anser*, is extinct.) *Crex 14: 41–45 (in Czech with an English summary).*

Horák P., 1999: (The late records of Waxwing, *Bombycilla garrulus*, and its epigamic behaviour.) *Crex 14: 57–58 (in Czech with an English summary).*

Horák P., 2000: [Breeding density and population dynamics of raptors in the floodplain forest of Dolní Pomoraví in 1981–2000.] *In: Proc. of abstracts, Dravci a sovy 2000, Mikulov na Moravě, 2000.*

Horák P., 2000: (Development of Saker Falcon, *Falco cherrug*, population between 1976–1998 in Moravia, Czech Republic.) *Buteo 11: 57–66 (in Czech with an English summary).*

Horal D., 1995: [Corncrake *(Crex crex)* – return to floodplain?] *Zpravodaj JMP ČSO 5: 42–43 (in Czech only).*

Horal D., 1995: [Migration and roosting sites of Kites in the Břeclav region.] *Zpravodaj JMP ČSO 4: 21–24 (in Czech only).*

Horal D., 1997: [Košárské louky meadows near Lanžhot – locality of four crake species.] *Zpravodaj JMP ČSO 9: 16–19 (in Czech only).*

Krause F., 1996: [Return of the Wryneck *(Jynx torquilla)* to Břeclav region.] *Zpravodaj JMP ČSO 8: 30–31 (in Czech only).*

Lošťák B., 1982: [Green Pearl.] *Panorama. Praha, 296 pp. (in Czech only).*

Vačkař J., 1998: (Some facts about birds of Soutok game preserve, Břeclav district, South Moravia.) *Zpravodaj JMP ČSO 11: 5–9 (in Czech with an English summary).*

Vicherek J. et al., 2000: (Flora and vegetation at the Confluence of the Morava and Dyje rivers.) *Masarykova Univerzita, Brno, 362 pp. (in Czech with an English summary).*

Vrška T., 1997: (Cahnov virgin forest after 21 years, 1973–1994.) *Lesnictví – Forestry, Praha 43: 155–180 (in Czech with an English summary).*

Vrška T., 1997: (Ranšpurk virgin forest after 21 years, 1973–1994.) *Lesnictví – Forestry, Praha 44: 440–473 (in Czech with an English summary).*

Zuna-Kratky T., Kalivodová E., Kürthy A., Horal D., Horák P. (eds.), 2000: Die Vögel der March-Thaya-Auenim öster-reichisch-slowakisch-tchechischen Grenzraum. *Distelverein. Deutch-Wagram, 258 pp.*

013 – Beskydy mountains

Bartošová D., 1983: [Zoological inventory of the Mionší State Nature Reserve.] *KSSPPOP Ostrava: 43 pp., msc. (in Czech only).*

Bartošová D., 2000: (History and perspectives of Capercaillie, *Tetrao urogallus* L., in the Protected Landscape Area Beskydy Mts.) *In: Málková P. (ed.), 2000: Proc. of internat. conf. Tetřevovití – Tetraonidae na přelomu tisíciletí. Č. Budějovice 2000: 44–51.*

Čapek M., 1991: Bird species composition of mountain ecosystems damaged by air pollution. *Folia Zool. 40/2: 167–177.*

Čapek M., 1991: A further nesting of ural owl *Strix uralensis* in the Moravskoslezské Beskydy mountains (northern Moravia), Czechoslovakia. *Čas. Slez. Muz. Opava (A) 40: 89–90.*

Čapek M., Heroldová, M. and Zejda, J., 1998: Bird and small mammal communities in a clearing caused by air pollution. *Folia Zool. 47: 21–28.*

Hudec K., Kondělka D., Novotný L., 1966: [Birds of Silesia.] *Opava, 364 pp. (in Czech with a German summary).*

Kondělka D., 1984: [Breeding of the Ural Owl *(Strix uralensis)* in Moravskoslezské Beskydy Mts.] *Čas. Slez. Muz., Opava (A) 33: 192 (in Czech with German and Russian summaries).*

Pavelka J., 1983: (The knowledge of the distribution of the White-backed Woodpecker, *Dendrocopos leucotos*, Bechst. and Three-toed Woodpecker, *Picoides tridactylus* L., in the district of Vsetín.) *Sylvia 22: 61–68 (in Czech with an English summary).*

Pavelka J., 1987: (The bird communities in fir-beech primeval forest Razula in out breeding time.) *Zprav. Okres. vlastiv. muz. ve Vsetíně, 1987: 40–42 (in Czech with English and Russian summaries).*

Pavelka J., 1988: (The autumn and winter bird communities in carpathian fir-beech primeval forest.) *Čas. Slez. Muz., Opava 37: 147–159 (in Czech with English and Russian summaries).*

Pavelka J., 1989: (The bird communities in village of Velké Karlovice.) *Zprávy MOS 47: 75–91 (in Czech with an English summary).*

Pavelka J., 1992: (IBA Beskydy Protected landscape Area.) *In: Hora J. et al., 1992: Významná ptačí území v České a Slovenské republice. Sbor. ref. ze sem. Čsl. sekce ICBP. Třeboň 1992. Čsl. sekce ICBP, Praha: 91–98 (in Czech with an English summary).*

Pavelka J., 1995: [From IBA Beskydy Mts.] *Zpravodaj IBA, listopad 1995: 6 (in Czech only).*

Pavelka J., 1995: (IBA Beskydy mountains in 1993–1994.) *In: Hora et al., 1995: Významná ptačí území v České republice. Sbor. ref., Kostelec n. Č. l. 1995. ČSO, Praha: 60–61 (in Czech with an English summary).*

Pavelka J., 1996: [Beskydy Mts.]. *Zpravodaj IBA, listopad 1996: 5 (in Czech only).*

Pavelka J., 1997: [Beskydy Mts.]. *Zpravodaj IBA, 1997: 3 (in Czech only).*

Pavelka J., 2000: [IBA Beskydy Mts. in 2000.] *Zpravodaj IBA, prosinec 2000: 2 (in Czech only).*

Pavelka J., Maceček M., Pavelka K., 1991: (The breeding birds in virgin forest Razula in the years 1978–1982.) *Zprav. Okres. vlastiv. muz. ve Vsetíně, 1991: 39–42 (in Czech with an English summary).*

Pavelka J., Pavelka K., 1990: The bird communities in Abieto-Fagetum virgin forests (Western Carpathians). *In: Šťastný K., Bejček V. (eds.): Bird Census and Atlas Studies. Proc. XIth Int. Conf. on Bird Census and Atlas Work. Praha 1989: 291–293.*

Pavelka K., 1987: [Ornithocenoses of selected native forests of the Moravskoslezské Beskydy Mts.] *PHd Thesis, UAEE VŠZ Praha v Kostelci n. Č. l., 53 pp. + příl., msc. (in Czech only).*

Pavelka. K., 1990: Breeding bird communities in three types of primeval forest (Western Carpathians). *In: Šťastný K., Bejček V. (eds.): Bird Census and Atlas Studies. Proc. XIth Int. Conf. on Bird Census and Atlas Work, Praha 1989: 287–290.*

Polášek Z., Foral M., 1989: [Preliminary report of ornithological and herpetological research in the Mionší State Nature Reserve in the Moravskoslezské Beskydy Mountains.] *Acrocephalus, Ostrava 11: 33–35 (in Czech only).*

014 – Poodří

Hudec K., Kondělka D., Novotný L., 1966: [Birds of Silesia.] *Opava, 364 pp. (in Czech with a German summary).*

Hudeček J., 1990: [Golden-eye breeding in the "Moravian Gate".] *Vlastiv. sbor. okr. Nový Jičín 46: 68–71 (in Czech only).*

Kondělka D., 1998: (The Greylag Goose, *Anser anser,* bred in the Protected Landscape Area.) *Čas. Slez. Muz. Opava (A) 47: 96 (in Czech with an English abstract).*

Kondělka D., 2000: (The Cormorant, *Phalacrocorax carbo*, bred in the Moravian Gate.) *Čas. Slez. Muz. Opava(A) 49: 188 (in Czech with an English abstract).*

Košťál J., 1995: (Problems in nature conservation in the IBA Poodří.) *In: Hora et al., 1995: Významná ptačí území v České republice. Proc. of sem., Kostelec n. Č. l. 1995. ČSO, Praha: 55–59.*

Košťál J., 1997: [Exhibition Poodří – landscape and people.] *Zpravodaj IBA, 1997: 5 (in Czech only).*

Literák I., Honza M., Kondělka D., 1994: Postbreeding Migration of the Sedge Warbler *Acrocephalus schoenobaenus* in the Northeastern Part of the Czech Republic. *Ornis Fennica 71: 151–155.*

Literák I., Honza M., Pavelka K., 1995: Postbreeding Migration of the Reed Warbler *Acrocephalus scirpaceus* in the Northeastern Part of the Czech Republic. *Die Vogelwarte 38: 100–105.*

Pavelka J., 1988: [Breeding ornithocenosis of the Odra river alluvial forests.] *Zprávy MOS 46: 115–118 (in Czech only).*

Pavelka K., 1996: [Poodří IBA.] *Zpravodaj IBA, listopad 1996: 4 (in Czech only).*

Pavelka K., 1997: [Poodří IBA.] *Zpravodaj IBA, 1997: 5 (in Czech only).*

Pavelka K., 1998: [Poodří IBA.] *Zpravodaj IBA, 1998: 5 (in Czech only).*

Pavelka K., 2000: Comparison of breeding bird communities in the Bartošovické rybníky ponds (Poodří floodplain) in years 1982–86 and 1992–97. *Sylvia 36, Suppl: 59.*

Pavelka K., Foral M., Košťál J., 1995: Conservation and monitoring activities of the IBA Poodří Patron Group in 1992–1994.) *In: Hora et al., 1995: Významná ptačí území v České republice. Proc. of sem., Kostelec n. Č. l. 1995. ČSO, Praha: 45–54 (in Czech with an English summary).*

Pavelka K., Kašinský J., Foral M., 1992: (Influence of agriculture and fishery on avifauna of Poodří PLA.). *In: Hora J. et al., 1992: Významná ptačí území v České a Slovenské republice. Proc. of sem. Čsl. sekce ICBP. Třeboň 1992. Čsl. sekce ICBP, Praha: 86–90 (in Czech with an English summary).*

Pavelka K., Košťál J., 2000: Water and wetland birds on fishponds with different carp fishstocks in the Poodří floodplain, 1993–98. *Sylvia 36, Suppl.: 17.*

Pavelka K., Košťál J., Pospíšil J., 2000: (Avifauna of ponds and the Odra river in Protected Landscape Area and IBA Poodří in 1992–1998 and activities of patron group in 1995–1998.) *In: Málková P., Jandová J. (eds.), 2000: Významná ptačí území na konci tisíciletí. Proc. of sem. IBA, Mikulov 1999. ČSO, Praha: 65–91 (in Czech with an English summary).*

Pavelka K., Košťál J., Pospíšil J., 2000: [IBA Poodří – news in 2000.] *Zpravodaj IBA, srpen 2000: 3 (in Czech only).*

Petro R., Literák I., Honza M., 1997: Breeding biology and migration of the great reedwarbler *Acrocephalus arundinaceus* in the Czech Silesia. *Biológia, Bratislava 53/5: 685–694.*

Rast G., Obrdlík P., Niezňanski P., 2000: [Atlas of Odra floodplains.] *WWW Deutschland, 103 pp. + 61 maps (in Czech, German and Polish).*

Šindlar M., 1999: [Odra river – an important ecosystem of a lively meandering river when compared with the rest of the Czech Republic]. *Proc. of conf. POODŘÍ – Současné výsledky výzkumu v chráněné krajinné oblasti Poodří, Ostrava 1999: 19–22 (in Czech only).*

015 – Heřmanský stav pond – Stružka wetlands

Foral M., 1999: [Interesting ornithological observations.] *Zpravodaj Ostr. Muz. 4/3: 25–26 (in Czech only).*

Honza M., Literák I., Petro R., 1993: Postbreeding occurence of the Reed Bunting *(Emberiza schoeniclus)* in the upper reaches of the Odra River and its migration to the Paduan Lowland. *Ornis Hungarica 4: 49–55.*

Hurt R., 1960: [History of the fishpond cultivation in Moravia and Silesia. Vol. 1.] *Krajské nakl., Ostrava, 274 pp. (in Czech only).*

Juřík R., 1995: (Birdwatch 1994.) *Acrocephalus, Ostrava 16: 65–66 (in Czech with an English summary).*

Kondělka D., 1974: (Breeding of Bittern, *Botaurus stellaris,* in Silesia. *Zprávy MOS, 1974: 29–31 (in Czech with an English summary).*

Kondělka D., 1989: (White-spotted Bluethroat, *Luscinia svecica cyanecula,* breeds in Silesia.) *Čas. Slez. Muz. Opava (A) 38: 283–284 (in Czech with an English summary).*

Kondělka D., 1993: (The first case of the breeding of the Greylag goose, *Anser anser,* in Silesia.) *Čas. Slez. Muz. Opava (A) 42/1: 88–89 (in Czech with an English summary).*

Kondělka D., 1996: (The first proved breeding of the Mediterranen Gull, *Larus melanocephalus,)* in Silesia.) *Čas. Slez. Muz. Opava (A) 45: 86–88 (in Czech with an English summary).*

Kondělka, D., Hudeček, J., 1993: (Whimbrel, *Numenius phaeopus,* in Northern Moravia and Silesia.) *Čas. Slez. Muz. Opava (A). 42 (1): 83–86 (in Czech with an English summary).*

Koutecká V., Foral M., Lojkásek B., 1998: (Nature of the Karviná district.) *RZP OÚ Karviná, 96 pp. (in Czech with an English and German summary).*

Literák I., Honza M., Kondělka D., 1994: Postbreeding migration of the Sedge Warbler *Acrocephalus schoenobaenus* in the Czech Republic. *Ornis Fennica 71: 151–155.*

Literák I., Honza M., Pavelka K., 1995: Postbreeding Migration of the Reed Warbler *Acrocephalus scirpaceus* in the Northeastern Part of the Czech Republic. *Die Vogelwarte. 38/2: 100–105*

Literák I., Honza M., Stolarczyk J., 1993: The post-breeding occurence of the Penduline Tit *(Remiz pendulinus)* in the reedbeds of the upper Odra plateau. *Egretta 36/2: 57–66.*

Petro R., Literák I., Honza M.,1998: Breeding biology and migration of the great reed warbler *(Acrocephalus arundinaceus)* in the Czech Silesia. *Biológia, Bratislava 53/5: 685–694.*

Polášek Z., 1995: (World Birdwatch 1993, "Heřmanský" pond and Karviná ponds.) *Acrocephalus, Ostrava 16: 63–65 (in Czech with an English summary).*

Polášek Z., 1995: (Proposal of the Important Bird Area Heřmanský stav-Stružka.) *In: Hora J. et al., 1995: Významná ptačí území v České republice. Proc. of sem., Kostelec n. Č. l. 1995. ČSO, Praha: 76–79 (in Czech with an English summary).*

Polášek Z., Juřík R., Jakubec M., 1994: (The Bluethroat – a progressive bird species in the Czech Republic.) *Živa 42: 132–134 (in Czech with an English summary).*

016 – Jeseníky mountains

Baláž P., 1984: [Ornithological inventory in the Bílá Opava State Nature Reserve.] *KSSPPOP Ostrava, 9 pp., msc. (in Czech only)*

Baláž. P., 1987: [Ornithological inventory in the Vrchol Pradědu State Nature Reserve.]. *KSSPPOP Ostrava, 10 pp., msc. (in Czech only)*

Baláž P., 1995: (IBA programme and problems in nature conseravtion in the Jeseníky PLA.) *In: Hora J. et al., 1995: Významná ptačí území v České republice. Proc. of sem., Kostelec n. Č. l. 1995. ČSO, Praha: 62–63 (in Czech with an English summary).*

Bureš S., 1996: [Jeseníky Mts.] *Zpravodaj IBA, listopad 1996: 5 (in Czech only).*

Bureš S. et al., 2000: [Jeseníky.] *Sylvia 36/1 – Aktuální problémy ochrany ptáků a jejich prostředí v ČR: 31–34 (in Czech with an English summary).*

Chmelíček L., 1989: [Restoration of forests in the higher altitudes of the Hrubý Jeseník Mountains.] *Zprav. CHKOJ, KÚSPPOP Ostrava: 24–28 (in Czech only).*

Hajný L., 1991: [Monitoring endangered bird species in the Jeseníky PLA.] Jeseníky. *Správa CHKO Jeseníky, 20 pp., msc. (in Czech only).*

Hajný L., Baláž P., 1992: (Important protected and endangered bird species in the Jeseníky Protected Landscape Area.) *In: Hora J. et al., 1992: Významná ptačí území v České a Slovenské republice. Proc. of sem. Čsl. sekce ICBP. Třeboň 1992. Čsl. sekce ICBP, Praha: 99–105 (in Czech with an English summary).*

Hajný L., Baláž P., 1999: [About activities in the IBA Jeseníky Mts.] *Zpravodaj IBA, červenec 1999: 4 (in Czech only).*

Honza M., Čapek M., 1998: (Bird communities in the area of the Dlouhé Stráně Hydroelectric Power Station complex, Jeseníky Mountains, Czech Republic.) *Čas. Slez. Muz. Opava (A) 47: 205–212.*

Kavalec K,. 1989: [Forest and forestry in the Jeseníky PLA.] *Zprav. CHKOJ, KÚSPPOP Ostrava: 15–17 (in Czech only).*

Kočí K., 1989: (20 years of the Protected Landscape Area Jeseníky.) *Památky a příroda 14/8: 489–495 (in Czech with English, German and Russian summaries).*

Suchý O., 1990: [Eagle Owl *(Bubo bubo* L.*)* in the Jeseníky Mts. after ten years.] *Zprávy MOS 48: 7–32 (in Czech with a German summary).*

Weber H., 1985: [Breeding of Dotterel *(Eudromias morinellus* L.*)* in the Jeseníky Mountains.] *Prunella 11: 23–24 (in Czech only).*

Important Bird Areas in the Czech Republic
Editors: Petra Málková and David Lacina
Published by the Czech Society for Ornithology, Prague, 2002
Design and preparation for the press Vladimír Vyskočil - KORŠACH
144 pages, 1000 copies
Printed by PBtisk Příbram, Czech Republic

ISBN 80-902216-6-1